D0224837

WOMEN AND POPULAR MUSIC

From Janis Joplin to Tori Amos, *Women and Popular Music* explores the changing role of women musicians and the ways in which their songs resonate in popular culture. Through a series of artist case studies Sheila Whiteley examines the interaction between feminist debates and music culture over thirty years of pop history. Why did 1960s' pop culture marginalise female performers such as Dusty Springfield and Marianne Faithfull? And how have women artists like Annie Lennox responded to changing debates within feminism?

Opening with the 1960s, Sheila Whiteley examines the counter culture's reactionary attitudes to women through the lyrics of the Beatles and the Rolling Stones. She explores the ways in which artists like Janis Joplin and Joni Mitchell confronted issues of sexuality and freedom, redefining women's participation in the industry, and assesses the personal cost of their achievements. She considers how stars such as Annie Lennox, Madonna and k.d. lang have explored issues of gender stereotyping and sexuality, through pop videos like *Sweet Dreams (Are Made of This)* and *Justify My Love*, and looks at the enduring importance of the singer-songwriter through artists such as Tracy Chapman. She then assesses the contribution of figures like Tori Amos, P.J. Harvey and Courtney Love, and asks whether the Spice Girls are just a 'cartoon feminist pop group', or positive role models for teenage girls.

Sheila Whiteley is Professor of Popular Music at the University of Salford. She is the author of *The Space Between the Notes* (Routledge 1992) and editor of *Sexing the Groove* (Routledge 1997).

WOMEN AND POPULAR MUSIC

Sexuality, identity and subjectivity

Sheila Whiteley

UCD WOMEN'S CENTER

ROUTLEDGE

London and New York

First published 2000
by Routledge
11 New Fetter Lane, London EC4P 4EE

Simultaneously published in the USA and Canada
by Routledge
29 West 35th Street, New York, NY 10001

Routledge is an imprint of the Taylor & Francis Group

© 2000 Sheila Whiteley

Typeset in Garamond by Taylor & Francis Books Ltd
Printed and bound in Great Britain by St Edmundsbury Press, Bury St
Edmonds, Suffolk

All rights reserved. No part of this book may be reprinted or
reproduced or utilised in any form or by any electronic, mechanical, or
other means, now known or hereafter invented, including
photocopying and recording, or in any information storage or retrieval
system, without permission in writing from the publishers.

British Library Cataloguing in Publication Data
A catalogue record for this book is available from the British Library

Library of Congress Cataloging-in-Publication Data
Whiteley, Sheila, 1941–
Women and popular music : sexuality, identity and subjectivity /
Sheila Whiteley.
p.cm
Includes bibliographical references and index.
1. Women musicians. 2. Popular music–Social aspects. 3. Feminism and music
I. Title.

ML82 .W48 2000
781.64'082–dc21
99–058596

ISBN 0–415–21189–1 (hbk)
ISBN 0–415–21190–5 (pbk)

This book is lovingly dedicated to my grandchildren present – ALEX, LUISA and BELLA and forthcoming– in the hope that they will enjoy and contribute towards a future which acknowledges and celebrates diversity and difference;

To my daughters LUCINDA, BRYONY and ANNI who grow more beautiful every year and whose creativity and sparkle so enrich my life;

To my parents MAURICE and RUTH for their enduring love and guidance;

To my cat MILLI for sitting beside me and purring.

CONTENTS

CONTENTS

ACKNOWLEDGEMENTS

I should like to thank Laura Joplin for her thoughtful response to my manuscript on her sister Janis; Dr Edison Amos for permission to quote lyrics and music by Tori; Tom Verlaine for his e-mail on Patti Smith; Ed Evans, Derek Scott, Nicola King, Andy Callen and Salford University popular music students past and present for their helpful ideas and suggestions; Stan Hawkins, John Richardson, Jon Epstein, Thomas Swiss, Mary Routh and Sharon Lowenna for their friendship and intellectual support; Jamie White for sorting out problems; Graham Ratcliffe for being there at the right time; the editorial team at Routledge - in particular Rebecca Barden for her insight and thoughtful reading of my manuscript, Alistair Daniel, Shankari Sanmuganathan, Sarah Hall and Belinda Latchford for their support and commitment; Routledge readers for their constructive critique on my original book proposal; and Lisa Martin for a perceptive and memorable cover design.

I should also like to thank Terry Whittaker (Carlin Music), Ross Pelling (MCA Music Publishing), Jane Pickford (IMP), Michelle Hills (Music Sales Ltd) and Peter McLaurin (BMG) for their hard work in obtaining copyright and the following for permission to reproduce copyright material in the book :

One Night Stand, words and music by Neil Sedaka and Phil Cody © 1977 Neil Sedaka Music and Kirshner Songs Inc., USA and Warner/Chappell Music Ltd, London, W6 8BS. Reproduced by permission of IMP Ltd.

Kozmic Blues, words and music by Janis Joplin and Gabrielle Mekler © 19 Strong Arm Music and Wingate Music (administered by MCA Inc.).

Lyric reproduction on behalf of Strong Arm Music by kind permission of Carlin Music Corp., Iron Bridge House, 3 Bridge Approach, London NW1 8BD.

Mercedez Benz, words and music by Janis Joplin © 1970 Strong Arm Music.

Lyric reproduction on behalf of Strong Arm Music by kind permission of Carlin.

ACKNOWLEDGEMENTS

Gloria, words and music by Van Morrison © 1964 Carlin Music Corp. Lyric reproduction by kind permission of Carlin Music Corp., Iron Bridge House, 3 Bridge Approach, London NW1 8BD for the UK, USA and Canada.

Lyrics from *Ball and Chain*, (Thornton) used by kind permission of Crysteval Music/MCA Ltd. © 1968.

Lyrics from *Kozmic Blues* (Mekler/Joplin) used by kind permission of American Broadcasting Music Inc/MCA Ltd/Carlin Music, © 1969.

Big Big Love used by kind permission of Acuff-Rose and Music Sales Ltd.

Carcass, words by Sioux/Severin © 1979 Dreamhouse Music and Sparta Florida Music Group 75% Warner/Chappell Music Ltd, London W6 8BS. Reproduced by kind permission of IMP Ltd.

Metal Postcard, words by Sioux © 1978 Dreamhouse Music, Warner/Chappell Music Ltd, London W6 8BS. Reproduced by permission of IMP Ltd.

Nicotine Stain, words by Sioux © 1978 Dreamhouse Music, Warner/Chappell Music Ltd, London W6 8BS. Reproduced by permission of IMP Ltd.

Suburban Relapse, words by Sioux © 1978 Dreamhouse Music, Warner/Chappell Music Ltd, London W6 8BS. Reproduced by permission of IMP Ltd.

Sweet Dreams and *Who's That Girl*, words and music by Annie Lennox and Dave Stewart © BMG Music Publishing Ltd/DNA Ltd. All rights reserved. Used by permission.

Express Yourself & *Justify My Love* (Cicone/Kravitz/Chavez) used by kind permission of IMP and Warner/Chappell.

Me and a Gun, China, Crucify, Little Earthquakes, Icicle (Under the Pink) Professional Widow, Hey Jupiter (Boys for Pele) by kind permission of Sword and Stone Publishing.

While every effort has been made to contact owners of copyright material, we have not always been successful. In the event of a copyright query, please contact the publishers.

INTRODUCTION

It is now nearly thirty years since Joni Mitchell released her album *Blue* (1972). It describes one or two years in her life – what she learned, what she experienced. She is the theme and is placed at the centre of her story. The first track 'All I Want' shows her to be 'on the road', typically the male domain of rock, evocative of Jack Kerouac and the *gestalt* of Route 66. Mitchell is the lonely traveller, but she is one who is there by choice, aware that the counter culture of the 1960s had done little to extend its freedoms to women, especially in terms of musical equality. Moreover, she is trapped by that seemingly irreconcilable dilemma of wanting a man but, at the same time, needing to be free. Many of us shared – and continue to share – that very real problem, but Joni Mitchell knew how to sing about it. She also demonstrated that she was capable of earning a living through selling her creativity. In contrast, Janis Joplin, often overweight, generally insecure in an arguably male-dominated environment, died alone, having accidentally injected a lethal dose of pure heroin. Intelligent, witty and well read, she was – like many of us at the time – trying to come to terms with her identity.

It is a problem that has not disappeared, and as we move into a new millennium we still look to artists who can provide specific insights into subjective experience – whether this is about love or rape, sexual desire or sexual assault, childbirth, miscarriage or abortion – or simply having fun. It is this focus on identity and experience that informs my essays on women and popular music. In particular I am concerned with female performers who can be considered catalysts within their respective genres – Janis Joplin, Joni Mitchell, Patti Smith, Madonna, k.d. lang, Tracy Chapman, Tori Amos – and how and why they have moved the goalposts of what is arguably a male-dominated industry. Their contribution to popular music – not least in opening the doors to the next generation of women musicians – is equalled only by their personal struggle against the inherently sexist attitudes that underpin the 'material world' of the music industry. In this respect, there is a comparability with the broader struggle against sexism that characterises second-wave feminism in aspects like the emphasis on practicality and

1

pragmatism – equality in law, equal pay for equal work, control over body and image, and access to the production of knowledge, culture and so forth.

In the 1960s, the identification of women as an oppressed group united feminists around the need to establish theories of causation. Although there were disagreements as to the primary causes of oppression (the need for a docile workforce, inheritance laws, male control over fertility) gender conflict became established as the most basic form of human conflict, replacing class as the principal *raison d'être* for women's social subordination, their secondary position relative to men. By the 1970s a growing understanding of the diversity of both gender and sexism led to an identification of the separation of the domestic and the public sphere as the most significant boundary in society. With women bearing and raising children, their lives were largely bound to the domestic sphere. Conversely, men spent more time outside the home and were thus able to engage in activities which had the potential to generate political structures. Normalisation of gender roles thus resulted in a situation whereby women might possess power in the home, but where access to the public sphere was perceived as illegitimate and disruptive.[1]

Although such explanations of sexual oppression raise problems in their emphasis on cause and effect, the significance of gender-identity, which informed the writing of such social theorists as Nancy Chodorow[2] (and which rests on the premise that there is a deep sense of self which is perceived differently for women and men) should not be underestimated. However, because gender identity theories focused on sexuality, reproduction and mothering, and because written texts largely reflected the experiences of the heterosexual, white, middle class women who dominated second wave feminism, theories of sex-role socialisation raised problems. In particular, they constructed a universalistic social theory, which failed to take account of cultural difference and diversity. During the 1980s, critiques of the racist and ethnocentric assumptions of white middle-class feminism by, for example, bell hooks (*Feminist Theory: From Margin to Centre*, Boston: Small End Press, 1984) further undermined the certainties of 1970s' feminist theory. At the same time, a growing interest in psychoanalytic theory and issues of sexual difference and identity highlighted the need to reconsider the earlier certainties of the sex/gender distinctions which had characterised contemporary Western feminism. By the late 1980s, an increasing emphasis on sexual, racial, class and ethnic awareness brought with it the recognition that grand narratives obscure the very real differences between women and, indeed, the various forms that sexism can take.

The concept of 'post' (postmodernism, postfeminism) thus implies a process of change and for feminists this is characterised by a conceptual shift from 'equality' to 'difference', 'otherness' and 'plurality' where gender, race, ethnicity, sexual orientation, age and class are all recognised as relevant in the formation of social identity. Pragmatism, scepticism towards absolutes, and the recognition and acknowledgement of complexities are thus a positive aspect of postmodernism and central to contemporary feminism. However, while it is evident that feminism has always been an evolutionary movement, the collapse of consensus during the 1980s around such defining concepts as 'oppression', 'patriarchy', 'sexuality, identity and difference'[3] seemed initially to posit both a breakdown of critique in theoretical terms, and an anti-feminist feminism. Although, in retrospect, this can be interpreted as a redefinition of feminism which took account of the political impact of Black feminism as a political and intellectual movement, of issues surrounding sexual difference, and the intersection of feminism with postmodernism and postcolonialism (see, for example, Walby 1990, 1992, Barrett and Phillips 1992, Butler 1990, Harvey 1993), the questioning of feminist goals and achievements suggested initially a curious alliance with a more public, popular conception of feminists as 'women who want too much'. As Susan Faludi explains in her book *Backlash* (1992), 'the media declared that feminism was the flavour of the seventies and that 'post feminism' was the new story – complete with a younger generation who supposedly reviled the women's movement'.[4] In particular, there was an attack on the issue of equality itself:

> In the eighties, publications from the *New York Times* to *Vanity Fair* to *The Nation* have issued a steady stream of indictments against the Women's Movement, with such headlines as 'WHEN FEMINISM FAILED' or 'THE AWFUL TRUTH ABOUT WOMEN'S LIB.' They hold the campaign for women's equality responsible for nearly every woe besetting women, from depression to meagre savings accounts, from teenage suicides to eating disorders to bad complexions ... .[5]

However, as Faludi points out 'What has made women unhappy in the last decade is not their 'equality' – which they don't yet have – but the rising pressure to halt, and even reverse, women's quest for equality.'[6]

Within popular music, there is little doubt that inequality still persists despite the increasing presence of women in the corporate sphere and middle management. Over the past twenty years no more than five women have been appointed heads of any UK based record companies, major or otherwise, and the statistics in the United States are even less comforting. Artistes & Repertoire (A&R) also remains a male bastion and although Ethel Gabriel (Producer, A&R at RCA), Nancy Jeffries (Senior Vice-President of A&R, Elektra), Kate Hyman (independent A&R management consultancy) and Vivian Scott (VP of Black Music and A&R, Sony) are notable successes, the frustrations of working within a corporate world dominated by male protocol has resulted in many top executives moving sideways into the independent sector. Lisa Anderson (Managing Director of RCA UK between

3

1989 and 1991) cites the problems of dealing with power management: 'For all their protestations about encouraging you to be different, in a hierarchical structure the bosses want you to say what they're saying.'[7] More specifically she identifies the key problem as 'handling things practically rather than politically ... of not being seen as a strong manager i.e. blaming and sacking heads of departments for falling sales ... even if they're good at their jobs'.[8]

Role-play and its relationship to gendered identity (to include the traditional split between career/family) is still considered a stumbling block for British women managers. In particular, the promotion of a woman to head of a department is perceived by many top MDs as a political statement[9], (a point that is born out by *Vox* magazine's list of the music industry's 'Twenty Most Powerful People'. Like most annual lists, the top twenty culture is always prone to subjectivity. In particular, editors look for balance and new and interesting people to write about and, as such, they are more an indicator (rather than a true measure) of power in the industry. Even so, women seldom merit more than a quarter of the credits. In the States, the glass ceiling is less evident in activities such as marketing, press and publicity and women generally have a greater share of upper management positions in the music industry. Michele Anthony (Sony), Sylvie Rhone (East-West Records) and Polly Anthony (Sony 550) are all notable for reaching top corporate positions, but it is evident that there is still more opportunity to succeed in the independent sphere and in less mainstream genres, such as indie rock, soul and rap where Monica Lynch, for example, has launched such best-selling acts as Afrika Bambaata, De La Soul, Queen Latifah and Digital Underground on the Tommy Boy label. In Britain, a comparable situation exists with Regine Moylett (ex head of press with Island Records) establishing an all-women team and managing such headlining groups as Massive Attack. Gail Colson's management of Morrissey, Peter Gabriel, Jesus Jones and Alison Moyet is also noteworthy, establishing her as one of the most consistently successful artist managers of the late 1980s and early 1990s.

However, while the 1990s show some significant inroads by women into the music industry, production continues overall to be gendered in quite conventional ways, especially with regard to positions of power (producers, managers, executives, technicians). This tendency is particularly evident in the areas of engineering and DJ-ing where an increasing sophistication in technology has been accompanied by yet another history of marginalisation. On the July 1998 cover 'of the dance magazine *Ministry* ... under a picture of the topless model turned jungle muso DJ Rap, a headline screams out: "Screw the rest – here's the ultimate deck diva ... ".'[10] As Brian Logan observes, 'It's an ugly innuendo, which wouldn't accompany the image of a male. But, for all clubbing's subculture (which stresses equality on the dance floor) its attitude towards women is more Stone Age than New Age.'[11]

Mixmag (July 1998) was similarly sexist in its advertisement of 'the UK's first all-girl DJ club tour', stressing glamour rather than ability, and conveniently overlooking the fact that the club scene is now over ten years old and was never intended to be about good looks. The flyers, the adverts and, indeed, television's treatment of club culture, however, continued to suggest otherwise and the result is 'a male biased, testosterone-addled culture where the dice are loaded against females – and female success'.[12]

It is outside of the industry, at the level of consumption, however, that the final weak link emerges. As Lucy O'Brien observes, 'women don't buy music. They internalise and use music differently to men ... (And) although pop's biggest market is teenage girls, by the time they reach their twenties, their interest in music significantly declines'.[13] Indeed, according to HMV, 'rather than buy records, many women tape compilations for themselves or friends. It is a common form of cultural referencing and cross-referencing, a network of exchange, particularly among lesbians.'[14] The effect has been to create a separate and powerful arena for women as active makers of meaning, where the significance of the chosen music lies in its assertion of difference and subversion, so relating to a distinctive musical identity. At the same time, the effect of not buying records and CDs has resulted overall in women listening to a boyfriend or husband's record collection, in vicariously experiencing the power of music through their men. This, in turn, has also had a significant effect on the rating of women artists in music press polls and, more disturbingly, in the critical evaluation of top artists across the last thirty years of popular music history.

Over the period November/December 1998, for example, Rocklist (a US e-mail network of academics dedicated to the discussion of popular music to which I belong) debated the issue of whether or not *Jagged Little Pill* (1995, Alanis Morissette) should merit a place on their 101 Greatest Albums list. The problem centred around authenticity – 'I don't think she writes her own music ... '. In fact, she writes her own lyrics and collaborated with AOR artist Glen Ballard in composing the music for the album under discussion. 'I don't think she has ability as a singer' (subjective); 'I don't believe she speaks for the majority of the population' – with sales of 28 million, there is certainly an implication that she is communicating with a significant number, bringing what has been described as singer songwriter angst and post alternative rock arrangements to an expanding fan-base. The crucial point, however, is that for many Alanis Morissette is 'way too me-me-me', and this sense of music-as-personal-therapy couched within an angst-ridden vocabulary that insists that it's meaningful, authentic, is what riles.

Although it is conceded that the making of lists is a very male activity, the discussion of women artists – particularly why they are significant within the terrain of popular music – is important. Compared with such predecessors as Courtney Love, Björk, P.J. Harvey and Kim Gordon, Morissette does appear less aggressive, less visceral. There is a commercial edge to her albums which is already attracting what might be termed industrial cloning – and here Natalie Imbruglia comes to mind – and commercial still brings with it connotations of superficiality and artifice. Maybe, then, she is not sufficiently innovative to move alongside the top league of such critically acclaimed singer songwriters as Lauryn Hill (whose 1998 album, *The Miseducation of Lauryn Hill*, won critical acclaim for both her arrangements and production), or such male performers as the Verve, whose 1998 album *Urban Hymns* was, paradoxically, second only to the Spice Girls in terms of sales world wide. It is equally possible that, after the late 1980s surge of women performers, whether in mixed gender bands or as solo artists, and the 1992 emergence of such 'self-consciously' female bands as Hole, L7 and the Riot Grrrl movement, Morissette's laundry list approach to lyrics 'I'm broke but I'm happy, I'm poor but I'm kind, I'm short but I'm healthy', and lines laden with images suggesting a particular kind of lifestyle: 'It's a black fly in your Chardonnay' could only attract adverse comparison.[15]

Even so, the question arises as to why Alanis Morissette should be a big issue. Arguably, it is because any sense of innovation in her albums remains at the level of content and that for active consumers of popular music (and the Rocklist is certainly that) notions of autonomy, of seriousness, of expressive truth are important. In other words, 'the cult of the artist, of auteurism, of 'poetic' elevation and 'emotional depths', all rooted in the lineages of nineteenth-century Romanticism, remain deeply embedded in the views that many musicians express about their own aims',[16] not least those with a background in rock. This sense of originality and authenticity is equally significant when critically evaluating the relationship between rock and pop. As Simon Reynolds and Joy Press observe in their afterword to *Sex Revolts*, 'even the most striking and powerful of the new female artists are musical traditionalists, bringing new kinds of subject matter and subjectivity to masculine formats'.[17] Returning to the Rocklist, it is interesting to note which women have received the members' critical acclaim and to note some of the personal comments on the cited albums.

Tori Amos: Little Earthquakes

We might eventually decide that some of her more recent work is better, but when *Little Earthquakes* was first released it was so raw and so stark in its power. Amos is one of the greatest artists alive, and this CD is in many ways her signature effort.

Liz Phair: Exile in Guyville

If we do this list again in two years I'll almost certainly pick her new disc (*Whitechocolatespaceegg*), but for now we'll have to settle on

Exile. This record sets out to shatter every repression we have, be it musical, sexual, canonical (I love the way it mirrors *Exile on Main Street*) and succeeds more than it fails.

These comments were written by a female subscriber, Ceilli Saier Mckie, and her choice of artists/albums was strongly reflected in the final top 101 (with Liz Phair reaching 27th position). It is also interesting to note that other significant women artists included Joan Armatrading, Tracy Chapman, Joni Mitchell, Janis Joplin and Patti Smith whose album *Horses* produced the honest acknowledgement that 'I find her unlistenable, but she's just too influential and too important to omit.' It is a view that is shared by commentators and artists alike. Smith, as discussed in my chapter 'Daughters of Chaos' (pp. 95–118), attempted a radical feminisation of rock, but like Yoko Ono, the Raincoats and the Throwing Muses she remains, as Reynolds and Press put it, 'strangely isolated – [a] landmark on the rock landscape that no one visits, least of all women'.[18] Although this may be considered somewhat of a sweeping generalisation, it is fair to point out that it is often the idea of Patti Smith that is inspirational and that artists such as P.J. Harvey only listened to her after hearing innumerable comparisons between herself and Smith. In contrast, it would be difficult to trace a contemporary female singer songwriter who does not owe and acknowledge a debt to Joni Mitchell whose albums have consistently furthered musical style in her transition from folk to jazz/pop fusions.

The Rocklist is not unique in what seems to be an increasing preoccupation with reviewing the past. The *Guardian's Friday Review* (29 January 1999) was no exception and the banner headline 'Our great overlooked genius? The century's alternative top 100 albums' promised an increased presence for women performers. But no. The first named female artists were Laura Nyro (*New York Tendaberry*), Joni Mitchell (*Court and Spark*) and Dusty Springfield (*Dusty in Memphis*) at 19, 23 and 26 respectively. It is not insignificant that Mitchell should also rate 36 with *The Hissing of Summer Lawns*, or that Laura Nyro should re-enter at 60 with *Eli and the Thirteenth Confession*. Four more artists are also there – Aretha Franklin *Young Gifted and Black* ('Bubbling under at 46'), Blondie *Eat to the Beat* (73), P.J. Harvey *To Bring You My Love* (74) and Jane Siberry *When I Was A Boy* (joint 75 with Todd Rundgren's *Todd*). It is also interesting to note that the banned 'classics' (i.e. those that were excluded from consideration by the panel) included Björk (*Debut*), Blondie (*Parallel Lines*), Carole King (*Tapestry*), Madonna (*Like A Prayer, Like a Virgin*) Joni Mitchell (*Blue*), Alanis Morissette (*Jagged Little Pill*) and Patti Smith (*Horses*). Significantly, the voting panel included such eminent women writers and critics as Lucy O'Brien, Sylvie Simmons and Caroline Simmons as well as musicians Mary Lorson, Lucinda Williams and Ruby Turner.

It is not really surprising that the top places in the alternative charts were all held by men – with Nick Drake, Tom Waits, the Band, Gene Clark, Nick Drake (again) and the Beatles notching up the first seven. Nor is it so surprising that there were so few female artists, or that the albums achieving highest acclaim were from the 1960s and early 1970s. It is, however, depressingly sad. Over the last ten years women have had an increasing presence as performers. In Britain the Spice Girls are consistently in the charts and each week new all-singing, all-dancing girl groups emerge, following in the footsteps of All Saints and B*witched. Celine Dion, Mariah Carey and Whitney Houston retain a worldwide market and they are joined by women who front (predominantly) male bands – Cerys Matthews of Catatonia and Saffron of Republica, for example. Instrumentalists, although not so commercially successful, include such artists as Gillian Gilbert, keyboards, New Order, Angie Pollock, keyboards, Lightning Seeds and the new darlings of the media, Sharon and Caroline Corr of the Corrs (fiddle and drums respectively). Finally, I would mention the recent success of such established stars as Debbie Harry, Suzi Quatro, and Cher whose single 'Believe' was the top selling British single of 1998. In the new millennium, then, it can be said with a certain degree of confidence, that women generally have an increased presence, but that there is still a long way to go. Indeed, as is so often pointed out, the female artists who feature most prominently on Top 100 charts are primarily concerned with subjectivity, more interested in communicating and telling stories[19] than in taking on the more masculine obsession of sonic wizardry associated with, for example, the 1990s drum 'n' bass world of Goldie and Tricky or the innovatory approach of such rock bands as Radiohead, Rage against the Machine and Space Team Electra. However, as my previous discussion of women DJs observes, is this really so surprising?

Even so, I would argue that the 'telling of the tale' is as important in the 1990s as it was in the 1970s in its connection to the still-evolving relationships between women and society. As Reynolds and Press observe, female innovations in rock remain mostly at the level of lyrics, self-presentation, ideology and rhetoric,[20] but this similarity of approach should not prevent us from noticing the interesting divergences and differences that characterise such artists as, for example, Björk, P.J. Harvey and Tori Amos. Personal insights, life stories, retain a compelling power and Elaine Showalter's discussion of women's literature provides a useful analogy for women musicians and singer songwriters:

> ... each generation of women writers has found itself, in a sense, without a history, forced to rediscover the past anew, forging again and again the consciousness of their sex. Given this perpetual disruption ... that has alienated women writers from a sense of

collective identity, it does not seem possible to speak of a 'movement'.[21]

Showalter's identification of disruption, alienation and collective identity is certainly apposite to popular music. Unlike the male founding members of the rock dynasty, Presley, Berry, Hendrix, Cream, the Beatles, the Doors and so forth, female innovators have had few, if any, progeny.[22] Rather, those artists who are cited by new generations of women musicians tend to be regarded as having something special to express which stresses individuality rather than lineage, estrangement rather than belonging. At the same time they provide insights into musical genres – clues as to what the rock world of the 1960s was like, why women have been so significant to the singer songwriter tradition – and, in doing so, they frame the listener's experience of the wider political history of women. More specifically, the artists' investment (of identity and experience) in their music enables us to place ourselves in imaginative cultural narratives and, as such, they help both to construct and provide insights into that wider experience.

An overview of the book

Women and Popular Music has a case-study focus with each major chapter concentrating on just one or two women performers, situating them within a social and historical context, and in relation to popular music styles and genres. My analysis also takes account of the changing debates within feminism and the changing style of women artists, particularly in their challenge to the issues surrounding sexuality, identity and subjectivity. I make no apology for my choice of performers. They are familiar both because of their artistic and commercial success, their relevance to debates on feminism and sexuality, and their challenge and transformation of gender-related boundaries. As such, they should be familiar to all students with an interest in this field of research. However, it is acknowledged that such criteria leave out many creative women artists who may not have achieved commercial success and here I would refer readers to Lucy O'Brien (1995) *She Bop: The Definitive History of Women in Rock, Pop and Soul*, London: Penguin Books, to Gillian Gaar (1993) *She's a Rebel: The History of Women in Rock & Roll*, London: Blandford, to Mavis Bayton, (1999) *Frock Rock*, Oxford: Oxford University Press, and to Simon Reynolds and Joy Press (1995) *The Sex Revolts, Gender, Rebellion and Rock 'n' Roll*, London: Serpents Tail, who share a similar interest in popular music, gender and sexuality.

Chapter 1, 'Wonderful World, Beautiful People' discusses the 1960s' counter culture and examines the role of women within the framework of progressiveness and the stylistic ascendancy of rock. While the early 1960s had seen an explosion in pop with such girl groups as The Shirelles, The Shangri-Las, The Crystals and The Ronettes, and Motown artists Martha

Reeves and the Vandellas, the Marvelettes, and Diana Ross and the Supremes, there were few successful American solo singers – Aretha Franklin and Dionne Warwick being notable exceptions. In Britain, women singers generally occupied a 'second division' pop status when compared to the male beat groups. Sandie Shaw, Lulu, Dusty Springfield and Cilla Black were obvious exceptions, but as Marianne Faithfull observed, 'When I finally did run off with Mick (Jagger), I felt I should stop working, because he was such a great star ... I put my ambition on hold and did what was required, which was to be there and to give him everything I had.'[23] While this is but one example, it is contended that the traditional tug between domestic/public, passive/active that characterised gendered identity continued to create a conflict of interest for women performers, and this was exacerbated by the continuing emphasis on women as home-makers within the so-called progressive counter culture.

It is a salutary fact that the counter culture, despite its challenging stance against inequality and its recognition of music as part of its revolutionary strategy, was largely reactionary in its attitude towards women. In particular, discussions about 'sexual liberation' were framed in terms saturated with male assumptions, including the very male fantasy of 'dope, rock and roll and fucking in the streets'.[24] The extent to which this is attributable to the way in which the 1960s' canon is dominated by 'big books by big men about big movements'[25] is open to debate, but it is evident that the political emphasis on progressiveness, modernisation and youth which, in mid-1960s popular music, was reflected in the development of progressive rock, was not extended to women. In particular, the counter culture's emphasis on fraternal individualism resulted in a conservatism which promoted the traditional role of women as mother/nurturer. This was enshrined both in the songs of the period and in such significant role models as the Jefferson Airplane's 'housemother' Sally Mann whose cooking and cleaning earned the gratitude of the band but, significantly, no financial reward. 'Wonderful World, Beautiful People' examines women's roles within the prevalent discourses of the counter culture and the ways in which music, as a unifying bond, provided a commonsense framing of femininity which was oppressive and reactionary.

The relationship between musical characteristics and cultural identity is then given a specific focus in Chapter 2, 'Repressive Representations' which examines culturally dominant images of women in late 1960s' rock from a mainly British perspective. More specifically, I explore groups such as the Beatles, the Rolling Stones and Led Zeppelin, whose music provided specific representations of women which drew largely on mid-Victorian iconography. My analysis of 'meaning' in music in this chapter draws on theoretical perspectives taken from film studies, and the way in which meanings are 'circulated between representation, spectator and social formation'.[26] Questions are raised about the nature of voyeurism and debates surrounding the construction of femininities/masculinities, power and knowledge. In particular, I examine how femininities are constructed through representations in music.

Chapter 3, 'The Personal is Political' returns to the emergence of second-wave feminism (or, as it was termed at the time, the Women's Liberation Movement) and discusses the significance of power relations with particular reference to the emerging debates surrounding sexuality, gender, freedom and repression. My discussion of how women's sexuality is both constructed *and* rooted in lived experience is then related to ways in which art, music and popular culture provided a focus for challenging established representations of femininity, especially those concerned with body image. More specifically, the question is raised as to whether the call for sexual liberation – whether within the Women's Movement or the counter culture – provided any real improvement in the opportunities afforded to women performers and the extent to which they were obliged to be either a feminised rock chick or 'one of the boys' if they were to succeed.

Chapter 4, 'Try, Just a Little Bit Harder: Janis Joplin and the search for personal identity' provides my first case study on women performers. Although primarily concerned with a musicological analysis of her music and lyrics, I start with a discussion of her image. Joplin consistently criticised the press for being more interested in her body than her music and my analysis shows the ways in which she challenged traditional representations of femininity. In the 1990s she is recognised as the outstanding blues rock artist of her generation. Her cover version of, for example, Big Mama Thornton's celebrated classic 'Ball and Chain' reflects how she moved the aesthetics of blues sensibilities into the rock arena, situating herself at the centre of the narrative as a woman who was all too often confused and 'fucked around'. Her sense of frustration is also reflected in the problems presented by the developments in blues based rock. As her recordings with Big Brother and the Holding company show, the band were interested in exploring the competitive potential of rock – not least its emphasis on guitar virtuosity – and, as such, she had little choice but to lead with arrogance and become 'one of the boys'. However, as her ex-lover Country Joe revealed, this inherent sexism was largely responsible for her subsequent dependency on alcohol and heroin and, by extension, her untimely death at the age of 27. Songs discussed include 'Ball and Chain', 'Piece of My Heart', 'Little Girl Blue', 'Kozmic Blues'. 'One Night Stand', 'Tell Mama', 'Try, Just a Little Bit Harder' and 'Mercedes Benz'.

The progressive rock scene of the 1960s and 1970s remained hostile to women who were unable to breach its extreme fraternalism. The folk protest movement, however, proved more amenable and Chapter 5, 'The Times They Are A-Changin' ' provides a contextualisation for the 1970s' singer songwriters, which is given a specific focus in Chapter 6, 'The Lonely Road'. My second case study provides a personal analysis of Joni Mitchell's 1972 album, *Blue*, placing it in its historical context and examining the implications of the songs on female subjectivity. Although Mitchell has resisted the label 'feminist', my choice of a feminist framework for discussion is, I believe, valid. Both in her music and in her public persona, she has offered, and continues to offer, a model of female experience, and of coping with the realities of earning a place in the male-dominated music industry. As such, she has been of seminal importance both to subsequent singer songwriters and to her broader audience, particularly women. My choice of feminism as a framework for discussion is also defensible from the standpoint of her more recent songwriting, much of which openly engages with issues that have traditionally occupied feminists: 'Magdalene Laundries', for example, describes the illegal incarceration of Irish women who had been institutionalised for committing adultery, bearing illegitimate children or being sexually provocative. 'Sex Kills' expresses her anger at the brutality of rape. See also songs like 'Cherokee Louise', 'Not To Blame' and, from her latest album, 'Lead Balloon'. As John Richardson observes, it appears that she may have turned towards a more overtly feminist stance in her mature work, which encourages the listener to view the early songs from a somewhat different perspective.[27]

Joni Mitchell's legacy to popular music was to demonstrate that women could earn a living through composing and performing in a personal style which expressed individualism and a developing musical identity. Her move from the acoustic base of *Blue* into more rock influenced idioms had an established precedent in, for example, Bob Dylan and was greeted with critical acclaim. The more experimental world of jazz and world beat, however, created problems. Initially, the integration of jazz and rock met with an enthusiastic response and *Court and Spark* (1974) reached no. 2 in the charts. This was equally true for *Miles of Aisles*, a live double-album of her supportive tour with Tom Scott's LA Express. Mitchell's exploration of jazz continued in *The Hissing of Summer Lawns* (1975), *Hejira* (1976) and *Don Juan's Reckless Daughter* (1977), culminating in the 1979 release of *Mingus*. Recorded with top jazz musicians Charlie Mingus, Herbie Hancock, Wayne Shorter, Peter Erskine and Don Aliaz, the album was considered by critics to be too stylistically hybrid to have any real credibility. An expatriate from folk and rock/pop, she was equally rejected by jazz purists.

With hindsight, it is evident that Mitchell's ability to cross genre boundaries demonstrates a musicality which has proved an inspiration to women musicians who search for creative fulfilment rather than mainstream chart success. However the problems of attracting mainstream audiences persisted well beyond the 1970s for those artists who did not sit easily within generic conventions. Joan Armatrading, for example, encountered problems due to her distinctive but often erratic style. Born in St Kitts, but brought up in Birmingham, England, she is a self-taught musician whose early work was presented with the dubious accolade of 'original. She's not the next anybody.

She's just a brave black lady who won't accept compromise'.[28] *Joan Armatrading* (1976) was a mix of musical styles and although this gave the album a wide-based appeal, with 'Love and Affection' reaching the UK Top Ten, the fact that audiences still expected black musicians to perform within such established musical genres as blues, jazz, R&B, soul and Motown-styled pop created problems. For American audiences, the fact that her music was neither R&B nor pop created particular barriers and although she switched producers in an attempt to find a more commercial sound, and while later albums such as *Me, Myself and I* (1980) and *The Key* (1985) reached the American Top 40, sustained commercial success in the US continued to elude her.

The fact that Armatrading was taken seriously by the musical critics of the period was significant, however, in breaking down one more barrier between black music and white music.[29] Even so, the singer songwriter genre remained primarily associated with women who were white, educated and musically articulate – Joni Mitchell, Carole King, Carly Simon. As Lucy O'Brien so accurately observes, 'It seems as if each decade could only allow one token woman to "break rank" and play acoustic rather than dance music ... in the '50s and '60s it was folk/gospel singer Odetta, in the '70s it was Armatrading'[30] and in the 1980s Tracy Chapman.

The inroads made by Janis Joplin were equally difficult to sustain. Moe Tucker, the drummer for the seminal East Coast band Velvet Underground left the group in 1969 to have a baby. She then vanished. Later it was discovered that she had married and had five children. It was not until the early 1980s that she managed to get back into the music business, working around the children and releasing her first album *Playin' Possum* in 1982. As Tucker succinctly observed, 'Nappies, bath time, picking up kids from school ... it just ain't rock 'n' roll.'[31] Slide guitarist and singer Bonnie Raitt found it similarly difficult to achieve mainstream success, despite releasing a series of highly acclaimed albums throughout the 1970s. Her seriousness as a performer in country, rock and blues, allied to a drink problem, made her difficult to promote and Warner's finally dropped her in the mid-1980s. Her career was relaunched in 1989 with the album *Nick of Time*, which sold over three million copies and achieved three Grammy awards – including Best Female Rock Vocal Performer.

It is difficult not to attribute the problems encountered by Tucker and Raitt to the tightly knit male community of mainstream rock. It is equally evident that the emphasis on musicianship, progressiveness and art which had characterised progressive rock, created new problems as the commercial restraint of the three-minute single was abandoned for the longer, larger and more profitable long playing record. Roots bands, including Cream (1966–9) had increasingly moved towards extended compositions with curiously middle-heavy structures which allowed for extensive, and often self-indulgent improvisation. Led Zeppelin also restricted their output to

LPs and by 1972, a year in which no new material was released, they accounted for 18 per cent of Atlantic Records' business. The band's emphasis on driving bass, soaring male vocals and distorted guitar came to characterise the stranglehold of male dominance in heavy rock. Yes, Genesis, Rush *et al.* were all-male bands and attracted predominantly male audiences. Their output was typified by tracks of at least seven minutes duration, with highly structured virtuoso solos, variations and developmental passages.[32]

The emergence of heavy metal in the early 1970s presented yet another barrier to women. Dominated by powerhouse drums, bass and guitar-gods strutting in front of banks of Marshall amps, the genre was unequivocally male. Bands such as Deep Purple, Black Sabbath and Blue Oyster Cult fetishised metal as explicit male aggression. Most significantly, the lyrics were frequently misogynistic, often violently brutal.[33] It was apparent that women rockers continued to be judged more on appearance than performing ability. Bass player Suzi Quatro, for example, challenged convention by dressing in tight leather jeans and bikers' jackets. *New Musical Express* described her as *Penthouse* fodder 'all lip-smacking hard-on leather'. In the US only one of her singles reached the top 40 ('Stumblin' In', 1979) and her image as 'a cartoon parody of a male rocker was sealed by her characterisation of "Leather Tuscadero", the sister of an ex-girlfriend of the Fonz on TV series *Happy Days*'.[34]

The challenge to gender stereotypes by such performers as Quatro, Raitt and Tucker was, at best, a partial success. Too much expertise in a male-defined rock environment tends to mark the woman as an intruder. Supergroup superiority equalled male superiority and it was not until the late 1970s, when punk challenged the elitism of progressive rock, that a new space opened up for women performers. As Lucy O'Brien observes, it was 'to be both their inspiration and their nemesis'[35] but given the extreme fraternal structures of rock at the time, the need for a 'feminisation' of musical content was becoming increasingly urgent. The significance of Patti Smith as the precursor of punk style and as a woman who redefined women's role in rock is, for me, indisputable and yet, as my survey of academic texts reveals, she is largely ignored. As such, one of the aims of Chapter 7, 'Daughters of Chaos' is to raise her to the prominence she deserves. I also discuss Siouxsie Sioux, who is foregrounded as the first real role model offered to women within the context of British punk. Her eccentric persona and manner of performance, and her idiosyncratic use of language placed her in a unique position which arguably added a whole new dimension to punk as it was then understood.

My discussion of Patti Smith's music draws on writings by Julia Kristeva. As John Richardson observed,

> The choice of Julia Kristeva's model of 'semiotic' and 'symbolic' affective modalities, as argued in her essay 'Revolution in Poetic

Language', as a means of explaining the primary *modus operandi* of this music is a very insightful one. Much of the discourse of early punk rock music appears to conform to Antonin Artaud's notion of 'the poetic', which Kristeva uses as a basis for her own psychoanalytically grounded model. In Patti Smith's and Siouxsie Sioux's music both the destructive and the constructive aspects of the chora are clearly manifested. Phonetic-musical aspects of her discourse are picked up on and identified as subversive elements in relation to the Lacanian symbolic with all of its phallogocentric connotations.[36]

Songs analysed include 'Gloria', 'Redonda', 'Break It Up' (which I would like to dedicate to Professor Kjell Skyllstad whose shared enthusiasm for the erotic discourse at my seminar presentation at Oslo University earlier this year was so inspiring), and 'Land of 1,000 Dances' from Patti Smith's 1975 debut album *Horses*; and 'Carcass', 'Metal Postcard', 'Nicotine Stain' and 'Suburban Relapse' from Siouxsie Sioux's 1978 album, *Scream*.

My next three case studies (Annie Lennox, Madonna, k.d. lang) are, to an extent, comparable to a triptych in that they provide specific, yet complementary, insights into the challenges made to traditional representations of femininity. Together they span a decade, and their exploration of identity through masquerade and drag brought into question the 'naturalness' of gender roles and their relationship to clothing and body parts.[37] It is somewhat of a paradox that pop, and more specifically, MTV should provide the context for the 1980s' challenge to the feminised image. Clearly this was not the original aim of MTV which recognised the potential of pop promos as providing a new and vital selling platform for records. In return, they demanded a heightened and glossy sexuality from their stars but the opportunity for ironic commentary was there, and my essays on Annie Lennox and Madonna provide a critical evaluation of their role in challenging the performative dimension of femininity. More specifically, I return to the problems surrounding image and representation. Here, Luce Irigaray's contention that women simply constitute the fetish of representation provided a useful conceptual approach for my own analysis. In particular, her insistence that women should focus attention on representations of representations that remind her of her sex, her sex organs, her sexes[38] was especially useful in problematising Madonna's erotic performance in her videos *Express Yourself* and *Justify My Love*.

Chapter 8, 'Challenging the Feminine' opens with a discussion of Luce Irigaray's critique of Freud, her challenge to the phallomorphic logic of 'sameness', and her discussion of female desire. In particular, attention is drawn to her strategies for confronting patriarchal power through the development of a feminine language (*écriture feminine*) which corresponds to the complexities of feminine pleasure, feminine sensuality and feminine creativity. Her encouragement of autoeroticism, and her confrontational call to challenge phallocentric discourses by exaggerating traditional feminine stereotypes is then discussed with reference to popular music, before a more specific focus on Annie Lennox. As one of the first women to benefit from the exposure offered by MTV she demonstrated a coolly manipulative image that was, at the time, unique, particularly in her play on androgyneity, control and power. Two videos are examined: *Sweet Dreams (Are Made of This)* (1983) and *Who's That Girl* (1984).

It is, of course, impossible to discuss the impact of MTV and disco pop without reference to Madonna. It is equally difficult to examine the 1980s' discussions surrounding gender politics without encountering her controversial position as feminist, feminist icon or sensational opportunist. Madonna's play on contradictory subject positions, organised around the plurality of pleasure, is given a specific focus in my analysis of two videos, *Express Yourself* and *Justify My Love*. Both foreground explicit sexual images, references to sado masochism and pleasuring, dreams and fantasies, so framing the opposing views of Madonna as opportunist and feminist icon. In particular, it is argued that any analysis of her work as reflecting a feminist interrogation of sexual imagery and representation, depends on an acceptance (or rejection) of her intentions as *ironic*, as deliberately destabilising traditional representations of, for example, pornographic imagery by intentionally playing on the inflections of feminised imagery. More specifically, I return to the problems inherent in mimicking sexually suggestive representations of women. In particular, reference is drawn to Luce Irigaray's contention that in mimicking patriarchal definitions of femininity, women may be drawn back in, that they may, in fact, be regarded as inviting a sexual response.

While both Lennox and Madonna flirted with androgyneity as a way of combatting patriarchal power, k.d. lang's self-invention was embedded in her lesbian identity. Thus, while it is important to recognise that the 'reality' of any identity is questionable, that gender is performed, there are nevertheless instances where a certain *self*-hood shines through. As such, I would distinguish between the concept of 'performance-as-acting' (which is reflected in k.d. lang's acting out of the particular conventions of country music and which is concerned with over-playing stereotypes) and performance-as-gendered-role-play which relates specifically to her embodiment of androgyny and difference.[39] It is also argued that to be successful in challenging the underlying homophobia of country, lang depended upon a specific relationship to her audience, one which relied on an interpretation of her music through an understanding of lesbian seduction, pose, gesture and body language. In context, then, lesbian sensibilities inform what are essentially straight texts to create a 'space of possibility between the conventional and unconventional, fixed and fluid, queer and straight'.[40]

I begin with a discussion of the codes and conventions of country music and the ways in which gender is grounded in a stable identity, thus ensuring that sex, gender and desire are shown to be internally coherent. At the same time, it is argued that such performance codes provide an opportunity for irony and camp, for a humorous critique of the excessive femininity of such country divas as, for example, Dolly Parton. More specifically it is argued that k.d. lang's performance effects a parody of the gender identification that lies at the heart of country music. In contrast, her vocal delivery, her musical persona, effects a more knowing butch identity. As such, there is a conflict, a play on multiple, heterogeneous difference that invites lesbian identification and which is reflected in such k.d. lang classics as 'Three Days' and 'Big Big Love' from her 1989 album *Absolute Torch and Twang*. I then turn to the soul-searching of lang's album *Ingenue* before a final evaluation of 'coming out' for both a lesbian and mainstream audience.

My discussion of the 1980s ends with a tribute to Tracy Chapman whose socially conscious songs make her an icon for, and part of the self-defining presence of, contemporary black women.[41] I start with a brief resume of the 1980s' folk scene (Suzanne Vega, Michelle Shocked, Sinead O'Connor and Natalie Merchant, lead singer of 10,000 Maniacs) where a focus on anomie, social deprivation and sexual abuse provide a comparability with the experiences framed in Chapman's self-named debut album and with growing up poor, black, working class and female in Cleveland, Ohio.

My analysis of *Tracy Chapman* (1988) is contextualised by a discussion of the 1960s Civil Rights' movement, Malcolm X and Stokeley Carmichael's demand for Black Power, and the systematic repression of Black Radicalism. In particular, I consider the problems ensuing from the effects of over-population and unemployment in such major cities as New York, Chicago, Cleveland and Los Angeles and how these frame the social critique of such songs as 'Talkin' 'bout A Revolution', 'Fast Car' and 'Across the Lines' within a composition style that moves between reportage, personal commentary and the dramatic *a cappella* of 'Behind the Walls'. Chapman's musicality, her ability to complement lyrics with a reflective and resonant ear for instrumentation and arranging is also evidenced in the contrast between the rock ballad 'Baby, Can I Hold You', the up-tempo groove of Caribbean hi-life ('Mountain o' Things'), reggae ('She's Got her Ticket') and solo acoustic guitar of 'Deep in my Heart'.

Finally, I turn to the 1990s and consider two contrasting musical practices which characterise women's music during the period under discussion. The first is concerned with 'authenticity, truthfulness and community' and relates to the continuing significance of the singer songwriter.[42] In particular the question is raised as to whether the 1980s' questioning of identity and the exposing of femininity as a mask, a cultural manifestation, implied that feminism had won and that there were no longer any battles to be won. As my discussion of Tori Amos shows, there were (and still are) key issues to be addressed, particularly those concerning the negative aspect of sexual desire and its manifestation in rape and sexual abuse.

17

Chapter 12 discusses selected tracks from Tori Amos's debut album, *Little Earthquakes* (1991). The first, 'Me and a Gun' provides a personalised musical reflection on rape. The song, which is sung *a cappella*, provides an insight into the personal traumas involved in sexual abuse – not least those associated with guilt and introspection – in an unadorned and truthful exposition of events. The feeling of anomie and distress is explored further in 'China'. Here, Amos reflects on personal barriers, the walls that are constructed partly as self-defence, partly as a way of obstructing communication. This sense of struggle (with her background, her emotions, her sexuality, her image) pervades the album as a whole, but equally it is characterised by a developing musicality which continues through to *Under the Pink* and *Boys for Pele*. My discussion of authenticity, truthfulness and community ends with a brief discussion of Courtney Love, P.J. Harvey – two performers whose explorations of female subjectivity and angst suggest a traditional alignment with the rock concept of living on the edge – and Björk, whose album *Debut* provided an insight into ten years of her life.

My final case study, 'Artifice and the Imperatives of Commercial Success' examines the cultural phenomenon of the Spice Girls whose career has attracted a feminist critique comparable to that of Madonna in the 1980s. In particular, I was intrigued by the way in which their rallying cry of 'Girl Power' reached down into Britain's Infant Schools and the fact that little girls of five and six took possession of the words (albeit without any understanding of their feminist overtones) to such an extent that they have now assumed the ordinariness of commonsense – 'girls are best, girls rule'.

Girl groups have continued to play a major role in late 1990s' pop, but while the Spice Girls have enjoyed another successful tour (summer 1999), there is an increasing suspicion that many girl groups are presently encountering a failing career syndrome. Irish stars, the Corrs have currently lost their chart edge, and All Saints switched the site of a recent London concert from Wembley Arena to the smaller Shepherd's Bush Empire, allegedly due to poor ticket sales. England's unsuccessful entry for the Eurovision Song Contest also featured an all-girl mixed race group, Precious. Even so, each week sees a new group emerge with the inevitable conclusion that the music industry is dangerously low on viable commercial ideas. Again, the trend seems to be to 'go solo' (echoes here of the earlier example of Take That). The Spice Girls' Mel C's single with Bryan Adams and her 1999 album *Northern Star* suggest a realignment with rock and has attracted sceptical reviews – especially because of her recent live performance of the Sex Pistols 'Anarchy in the UK'. Former Spice Girl Geri Halliwell's debut album *Schizophonic* also received a mixed reception. Meanwhile, she has continued her work as a United Nations' ambassador, speaking out on issues surrounding reproductive health. As the least emotionally secure of the Spice Girls it is not insignificant that she has been befriended by 41 year old British comedienne Dawn French. Nor is she the first to discover the advantages of a friendship with an older woman. As Cayte Williams observed ('Someone to lean on', *The Independent on Sunday*, 23 May 1999), the 'generation gap friendship has become sexy – Kate Moss invited Anita Pallenberg for a long trip to India, Stella McCartney (27) has grown closer to Marianne Faithfull (51) and 'increasingly women in their twenties and thirties are searching out a life mentor – someone who gives advice like a mother but acts like a friend'.

For me, this is one of the great achievements of the last thirty years. While the French have long accepted the older woman as both *sympathique* and sensuous, the English and Americans have been slow to accept that age does not necessarily mean social redundancy. Women such as Anita Pallenberg and Marianne Faithfull know the problems associated with the rock 'n' roll lifestyle, with fame, fortune and failed relationships and, significantly, have survived. More importantly, artists such as Faithfull (*Vagabond Ways*, April 1999) continue to attract critical acclaim. Joni Mitchell released *Taming the Tiger* (September 1998) and is due to release another album in the near future, evidence of a woman who continues to produce strong and musically challenging ideas. Patti Smith has had a successful tour, Debbie Harry is back on the road on the heavily publicised Blondie reunion, and Cher is enjoying yet another hit single. This book is a tribute to their success and to the other performers discussed. We would not be where we are today without your courageous examples.

NOTES AND REFERENCES

1   This approach, as Fraser and Nicholson point out, 'seemed to allow for both diversity and ubiquity in the manifestation of sexism. A very general identification of women with the domestic and men with the extra-domestic could accommodate a great deal of cultural variation both in social structures and in gender roles. At the same time, it could make comprehensible the apparent ubiquity of the assumption of women's inferiority above and beyond such variation. This hypothesis was also compatible with the idea that the extent of women's oppression differed in different societies.' Nicholson, L.J. (ed.) (1990) *Feminism/Postmodernism*, London: Routledge, p. 28.
2   Chodorow, N. (1978) *The Reproduction of Mothering. Psychoanalysis and the Sociology of Gender*, Berkeley: University of California Press.
3   See Brooks, A. (1997) *Postfeminisms. Feminism, Cultural Theory and Cultural Forms*, London: Routledge, p. 5.
4   Faludi, S. (1992) *Backlash*, cited in Alice, L. (1995) 'What is Postfeminism? Or Having it Both Ways', in Alice, L. (ed.) *Feminism, Postmodernism, Postfeminism*, Conference proceedings, Massey University, New Zealand, p. 14.
5   *Ibid.*, p. 18.
6   *Ibid.*, p. 18.
7   Gaar, G.G. (1993) *She's A Rebel. The History of Women in Rock & Roll*, London: Blandford, p. 407.
8   *Ibid.*, p. 410.
9   *Ibid.*, p. 412.

10 Logan, B. (1998) 'Provocations. So You Want to be a DJ? Let's See Your Legs', *The Guardian*, Saturday 11 July, 'Arts', p. 4.
11 *Ibid.*, p. 4.
12 *Ibid.*, p. 4.
13 O'Brien, L. (1995) *She Bop. The Definitive History of Women in Rock, Pop and Soul*, London: Penguin Books, p. 435.
14 *Ibid.*, p. 437.
15 Thanks here to my friend Jon Epstein (originator of the Rocklist) for this pithy critique. It is interesting to note, within this context, that class remains a contentious issue within the discourses surrounding pop and rock.
16 Middleton, R. (1997) *Understanding Pop Music*, Milton Keynes: Open University MA module, p. 73.
17 Reynolds, S. and Press, J. (1995) *The Sex Revolts. Gender, Rebellion and Rock 'n' Roll*, London: Serpent's Tail, p. 387.
18 *Ibid.* p.387 Reynolds and Press are, to an extent, correct in this observation. I would also refer to my earlier discussion of DJs and the sad fact that whereas it is possible for males to be spotty and geeky, sex still sells and DJ culture is regrettably reaffirming the music industry's traditional attitudes towards women performers.
19 *Ibid.*p.387.
20 *Ibid.* p.387.
21 Showalter, E. (1991) *Sexual Anarchy. Gender and Culture at the Fin de Siècle*, London: Bloomsbury, p. 55.
22 See David Sanjek's discussion 'Can a Fujiyama Mama Be the Female Elvis? The Wild, Wild Women of Rockabilly', in Whiteley, S. (ed.) (1997) *Sexing the Groove. Popular music and gender*, London: Routledge, pp. 137–67.
23 O'Brien, *op. cit.*, p. 97.
24 Widgery, D. (1973) 'What Went Wrong?' in *OZ*, 48: 7–17.
25 Tischler, B.L. (1994) 'Perspectives on the Sixties', *NEAA Newsletter*, 1444–28, Brown University, US.
26 Kuhn, A. (1985) *The Power and the Image. Essays on Representation and Sexuality*, London: Routledge, p. 6.
27 From discussions with Dr. John Richardson (South Bank University, England).
28 Accompanying advertisement for *Joan Armatrading*, 1976.
29 O'Brien, *op. cit.*, p. 111–86.
30 *Ibid.*, p. 111.
31 *Ibid.*, p. 34.
32 *Virtuosity*, as Rob Walser suggests, is always associated with the male performer – from Paganini to heavy metal. It is also associated with *virility* (Latin root, *vir*)with the obvious connotations of sexual potency. See Walser, R. (1995) *Running with the Devil. Power, Gender and Madness in Heavy Metal Music*, Hanover/London: Wesleyan University Press.
33 Gender-identification conflict is identified by some researchers as the root of misogyny in heavy metal. Played primarily by and for young white males, it is interpreted as combating insecurity by guaranteeing a place within the male-dominated power structures of American culture where social, economic and physical power are prime determinants of achievement. Anything that threatens masculinity is thus presented as a threat – as deadly and dangerous. Intimacy with a woman is seen as threatening male independence (unlike male-bonding intimacy which focusses on goals) and, as such, mistreatment is interpreted as self-defence. (From discussions with my friend and colleague, Dr Jon Epstein.)
34 Gaar, *op. cit.*, p. 218.

35 O'Brien, *op. cit.*, p. 130.
36 From discussions with Dr John Richardson, whose feedback on the appropriateness of my theoretical model is quoted here.
37 Reynolds, S. and Press, J. (1995) *The Sex Revolts. Gender, Rebellion and Rock 'n' Roll*, London: Serpent's Tail, p. 296.
38 Irigaray, L. (1985) *The Sex Which Is Not One*, Ithaca, NY: Cornell University Press.
39 See Butler, J. (1990) 'Gender Trouble, Feminist Theory, and Psychoanalytic Discourse', in Nicholson, L.J. (ed.) *Feminism/Postmodernism*, London: Routledge, pp. 324–40.
40 Bruzzi, S. (1997) 'Mannish Girl. k.d. lang – from Cowpunk to Androgyny', in Whiteley, *op. cit.*, p. 194.
41 O'Brien, *op. cit.*, p. 270.
42 The emphasis on authenticity, truthfulness to personal experience and community is clearly not confined to folk or the singer songwriter tradition. It is an association that is related to rock (and, for example, such artists as Bruce Springsteen) as well as to the hip hop tradition and rap. Although drum 'n' bass is stylistically a hybrid form which is arguably a musical abstraction of the cultural, political and social expression of jungle, there are also distinctions between the south London scene and, for example, the Asian Dub Foundation and Bristol, where Goldie's Metalheadz label signals a different, but equally significant relationship to the local community and a strong emphasis on authenticity.

1

WONDERFUL WORLD, BEAUTIFUL PEOPLE

The 1960s' counter culture and its ideological relationship to women

Historical accounts of the 1960s' counter culture generally point to 'an intense internationalism, which was based on shared dreams, strategies, styles, moods and vocabularies'.[1] Its origins lay in the beats (beatnik) movement of the 1950s which had developed in the student area of the Left Bank of Paris. Influenced by French bohemian artists and intelligentsia, and centred around the existentialist values of Jean-Paul Sartre (which espoused the primacy of experiences, subjectivity and individuality in social and interpersonal life), the beats were popularised in America by such writers as Jack Kerouac and Allen Ginsberg. Initially, the movement was centred on Greenwich Village, New York. Characterised by a romantic anarchism, an interest in Eastern mysticism, poetry, jazz and drugs (most specifically marijuana), the movement spread across America in the early 1960s and exercised a particular influence on the values of the 1960s' counter culture.

The counter culture can be defined as a generic label for a somewhat loose grouping of young people, a generational unit, who challenged the traditional concepts of career, family, education and morality and whose lifestyle was loosely organised around the notion of personal freedom. Although it was particularly evident in North American anti-conformist lifestyles (not least that exemplified by the hippies of the Haight Ashbury district of San Francisco), it quickly assumed an international dimension. While it is recognised that there were divisions between the British underground, which tended towards cultural upheaval, and New Left politics (e.g. the US-based Students for a Democratic Society) which focused on political protest, these groupings were also perceived as broadly consistent in their challenge to the dominant culture. The opposition to the war in Vietnam, for example, is generally identified as the one great unifier of the counter culture in that it demonstrated a concern for the developing world and, in particular, the racial and economic exploitation of other races. While confrontation was particularly acute in the United States, where there was both an increasing rejection of parental values and a lack of commitment by draftee servicemen, European students identified the war as symptomatic of the corruptions of advanced capitalism. As such, the focal activity directed against war was associated with wider social and moral issues. In particular, there was a growing recognition that a political system which perpetuated inequality and a general lack of freedom was untenable, and its institutions (parliament, national assembly, universities, business, the media and leisure itself) corrupt and therefore in need of radical change.

The second half of the 1960s, in particular, produced an escalation in student protest and rebellion in most of the industrially developed countries, including Japan. These revolutionary phenomena possessed somewhat similar features which came to a head in the years 1968–9. The wave of protest swept from the United States across the Atlantic to Germany, France, Italy and Britain. In Russia, Czechoslovakia and Yugoslavia, students and intellectuals also demanded very precise freedoms to study and to discuss, without the formal constraints of communist doctrine. In comparison, the students of the capitalist countries, who were influenced by the ideas of Marx, Lenin, Guevara and Marcuse, aimed to bring about the destruction of capitalism to make a world free from war, poverty and exploitation. There were also local grievances such as impersonal teaching and overcrowding, pedantic academicism and bureaucratic administrations, but these were only the outward manifestations of a demand for deeper social and political changes.

The role of music in establishing a sense of 'nationhood'[2] is clearly not unique to the counter culture,[3] and while there was no single song which summed up its crucial values,[4] there was a shared belief that rock (and, in particular, progressive rock) could articulate its concerns. The hippy's preference for psychedelic rock, for example, reflected the drug orientation of the movement, while the US Civil Rights Movement and the anti-Vietnam marches identified more with folk rock. 'Give Peace a Chance' (John Lennon), for example, assumed the role of a contemporary pacifist anthem in the US during the late 1960s. Music, then, had an evangelical purpose which tied it to the values of the group, expressing its attitudes, providing a particular location for self-identity, and establishing common cultural and political bonds.

The counter culture's marginalisation of women in rock is therefore particularly disturbing. Apart from biting social and political commentaries from such performers as Joan Baez, Buffy St Marie and Peter, Paul and Mary, and the success of such frontline performers as Mama Cass (The Mamas and the Papas), Grace Slick (Jefferson Airplane) and Janis Joplin (albeit at a cost, with Joplin dying in 1970 and Cass Elliott in 1974), both the lifestyle and the musical ethos of the period undermined the role of women, positioning them as either romanticised fantasy figures, subservient earth mothers or easy lays. It is not too surprising, then, that Elliott's size could only be accommodated by the pop world by giving her a *Mama* Cass' image – large and lovely. It was something she constantly fought against, not least because co-singer Michelle Gilliam was not afforded the same prefix, being described by the press as the sexy sylph-like member of the group. Similar problems emerged in the UK. For many people, Dusty Springfield's image (with her beehive hairdo and heavily mascara'd eyes) defined the face of the 1960s, yet she struggled to establish herself as a strong soulful singer. In a musical environment that preferred their women performers to subscribe to the ethos of light, romantic, dollybird pop, Springfield's championing of Motown and R&B and her dislike of the confines of mainstream initially proved frustrating. Hoping to achieve international status she refused to compromise her image by performing cover versions or inferior material, and gradually achieved useful working relationships with such prestigious songwriters as Burt Bacharach and Carole King. Her backing singers – former American gospel soul singers Madelaine Bell, Doris Troy and P.P. Arnold – were equally important in establishing her powerful soul sound and during the 1960s she produced nine top ten hits including 'Son of a Preacher Man', 'I Only Want to Be with You' (the first song ever performed on *Top of the Pops*), 'You Don't Have to Say You Love Me', 'Twenty Four Hours from Tulsa' and 'Anyone Who Had a Heart'. Her identification with Motown also led to her being the first white soul singer to perform in Harlem, sharing the stage with the Supremes and the Temptations, and her classic soul album *Dusty in Memphis* (1968). Despite her success, however, the 1960s' preoccupation with image and youth became increasingly oppressive and by 1968 Dusty was refusing to be photographed from the left (her bad profile) and worrying about laughter lines round her mouth. The press had also become increasingly curious about her private life, alluding to affairs with both men and women. It was a problem that was to remain throughout her life, with recent obituaries (she died on 2 March 1999, six weeks before her 60th birthday) failing to acknowledge that her escape to Los Angeles in 1972 was largely due to British attitudes towards her bisexuality. Thus, while she achieved an iconic status among the gay community – openly supporting gay issues and giving a lengthy interview to *Gay News* in the early 1980s, recording the hit song 'What Have I Done to Deserve This' in 1987 and 'Nothing Has Been Proved', the theme song to the film *Scandal* – her sense of alienation remained.

Dusty Springfield was not unique in her insecurity, sharing with Janis Joplin a sense of isolation that resulted in bouts of heavy drinking, narcotic use and sexual promiscuity. More specifically, both artists died without understanding how good they really were. Marianne Faithfull also suffered the problems associated with star status. Having achieved a hit in 1964 with 'As Tears Go By', she abandoned her career to become Mick Jagger's girlfriend and subsequently became more famous for her sexual image and non-conformist reputation – a situation that was remedied in 1979 with the release of her punk-influenced album *Broken English*. Her example provides a particular insight into the problems confronting women singers in the 1960s. Far from being accorded the status and freedom of their male counterparts they were castigated for being different and increasingly projected into the roles ascribed them by the more powerful male groups of the day.

As Theodore Roszak points out, the struggle for liberation was seen mainly

> as the province of men who must prove themselves by 'laying their balls on the line.' Too often this suggests that the female of the species must content herself with keeping the home fires burning for her battle-scarred champion or joining the struggle as a camp follower. In either case, the community is saved *for* her, not *by* her as well.[5]

Musically, this is reflected by two broad divisions: the 'love' school being represented generally by such groups as the Beatles[6] and Donovan, and the 'sex' school by, for example, the Rolling Stones, the Doors and Jimi Hendrix. In both cases, the woman is positioned as subservient to the man. While it could be argued that the love/sex division can be attributed to the different stylistic backgrounds of the groups themselves, it is arguably the case that these distinctions can be correlated to the difference in motivating philosophies within the counter culture itself. The concept of communality, the negation of bourgeois materialism (including the redefinition of marriage and bonding) may have been fundamental to all branches of the counter culture, but there was a marked difference between the transcendent spirituality promised to the followers of the Maharishi Mahesh Yogi and the revolutionary liberation of Jerry Rubins and his symbolic call for patricide.

These seemingly opposing philosophies are reflected also in the ethos of rock itself.[7] If its function is to celebrate the present and provide insights into the politics of consciousness – 'love, loneliness, depersonalisation, the search for the truth of the person, the attempt to set up an alternative life style'[8] – then the urge to establish a community based on love, however repressive in its attitude towards women, might seem a logical development. If, however, chaos and uncertainty are recognised as legitimate and necessary to life, and if these concerns are hinged upon notions of repressed sexuality, the conjunction with sensuality and death also appears logical – as was evidenced in the cult established by satanist Charles Manson. The relationship between particular forms of music and adopted philosophies is significant, then, in establishing referential points for group identification. The Beatles could project the dilemmas of contemporary society, the paranoia, the social distress, and set up a framework of 'Love, Love, Love' as the way to reconstituting a sense of community. For others, the cult of the 'beautiful' was no less a sham than the romantic notions of love extolled in much of the pop music of the pre-rock era.

The confrontational style of such groups as the Rolling Stones, for example, equated with sexual freedom, promiscuity and hedonism, [simultaneously identifying, describing and characterising the macho style of performance which was to be coined 'cock rock'.[9] Adjectives such as 'brutal', menacing', 'erectile', 'tough', 'obscene' and 'outrageous' can equally be pinned to the Doors, MC5 and Alice Cooper. Here, communal freedom had its darker side, and although the Stones had only a limited commitment to the counter culture, the fact that other groups and performers also communicated an aggressive sexuality is significant when analysing the relationship between performer/audience and their interpretation of the musical text. I would reference here – as an extreme example – Charles Manson's identification with the Beatles' single, 'Helter Skelter'.

It is therefore important to determine how music communicates meaning. As Lawrence Grossberg points out, 'culture communicates only in particular contexts in which a range of texts, practices and languages are brought together'. This may include 'musical texts and practices, economic and race relations, images of performers and fans, social relations (for instance, of gender, of friendship), aesthetic conventions, styles of language, movement, appearance and dance, media practices, ideological commit-ments'.[10] My own research into the counter culture certainly suggests a relationship between hallucinogenic experience and music which made it an inspiration for group consciousness and practice.[11] Dick Hebdige[12] also indicates that subcultures evolve and choose cultural styles that can be made to resonate with central concerns and experiences, that there can be a certain homology between musical characteristics and lifestyle. However, a major problem emerges when critically evaluating the extent to which music may be said to have meaning.

As John Shepherd observes 'music is not an informationally closed mode of symbolism relevant only to emotive, vital, sentient experiences' or 'inherent psychological laws or "rightness"'.[13] Thus, while the lyrics and song title might suggest a preferred reading, the musical text allows for a mapping of individual experience and meaning that provides a sense of fluidity of engagement. As such, if there is any assigned significance to music, this significance is generally located within the commonly agreed meanings of the group or society from which the music originates and to which it is addressed.[14] Philip Tagg's seminal analyses of the *Kojak* signature tune (1979) and the Abba hit 'Fernando' (1981) are also significant in providing a socially grounded theory of musical semiotics which stresses the way in which meanings arise in the encounter between text–listener, or artist–audience. In particular, his technique of 'hypothetical substitution' and 'intersubjective comparison' allows for a methodological approach to the interpretation of musical meaning through an analysis of musemes (a minimal unit of signification e.g. a riff) and museme compounds. Hence, for any museme, Tagg examines a range of similar usages drawn from compa-rable, influential, source and adjacent genres and styles.[15] However, while this comparative approach provides useful insights into secondary signification, there are problems – as Richard Middleton points out – in an over-dependence on extramusical aspects of the message and, for example, the playing down of historical specificity which puts in question whether all music tends towards combinations of 'effects' rather than synthesised wholes.[16]

While it is accepted that any analysis of musical signification presents problems, there is little doubt that music communicates. What is significant here is what Middleton defines as 'the variability of pertinence ... i.e. *what* is pertinent (that is, in the text); and, *to what, for whom* and *in what way* is it pertinent (the contexts, needs and place of the listening subject).[17] While such an analysis depends upon a sensitivity to structural inter-relationships (rather than the over-simple, internally validating systems of classical semiology), Middleton's identification of the interplay of musical and cultural characteristics provides some useful insights into the values and lifestyles of the counter culture, its subjective experience and the musical forms it used to express and/or reinforce its focal concerns. In particular, the music brought people together, engendering participation rather than passivity, as illustrated by the significance of the outdoor rock festivals of the period: Woodstock (1969), Bath (1969) and the Isle of Wight (1970). However, rather than being seen as entertainment, music was considered to say things of cultural and political importance. As such, the question of which musicians had access to the record industry, to A&R, marketing and promotion, and to rock festival stages and such 'in' venues such as UFO (London) and the Avalon Ballroom and Fillmore (San Francisco) is significant in determining power structures within the musical world of the counter culture. In particular, the fact that some groups have more say, more opportunity to communicate, is crucial to musical politics, to artistic value, meaning, power and effect. More specifically some definitions of the world remain marginalised. Thus

> when Mick Jagger sang 'Hey, I think the time is right for revolu-tion' ['Street Fighting Man', 1968] the message was inseparable from its musical expression, within the conventions of a specific generic tradition, and this was in turn given its power by the insti-tutional, discursive and ideological contexts that placed its reception.[18]

In contrast, and as discussed previously, women performers were largely viewed as ineffectual, as entertainment.

The concept and reality of equality is equally fundamental to any consideration of the role of women within the counter culture. The period leading up to 1969 – the high point of the counter culture and the emergence of second-wave feminism – can be characterised by an emphasis on freedom, equality and progressiveness. In 1964, the British politician Harold Wilson had attempted to shift the traditional image of the Labour Party, and under the banner of 'The White Heat of Technology' there was a new emphasis on progressiveness, modernisation and youth. The rights of protest had been legitimised within certain limits and, allied to an expansion in the university system, had led to a student attack on pedantic teaching methods and, in particular, the lack of seminars. The building of new universities had also led to an increase in staffing and in new areas of study to include sociology, social psychology and, in the latter part of the 1960s, a renewed interest in Marxist thought on the superstructure – ideas, culture, ideology – and its place within the social formation.[19] As part of this extension of higher education there was an expansion in women's education, and while this was still limited in the ratio of male to female, there was nevertheless a greater opportunity for women to take part in formal higher education and in informal debates and meetings around, for example, Vietnam and the meaning of progressiveness.

Debates surrounding liberation and the way in which individuals link ideas in the political field with individual needs and then transfer individual needs into action was also reflected in the relationship of Britain to the Commonwealth. Rhodesia had been given political independence in 1965, so reopening the debate on the freedom of black Africans to decide their own future development. The acceptance of a planned economy, which had been discussed during the 1930s and 1940s, had particular implications for British society during the 1950s and 1960s, raising the key question of whether or not a planned economy can still allow for the freedom of the individual. In many ways, too, the people who had put up ideas during the war were coming to occupy important places within the British state bureaucracy. The Labour Party, in particular, saw the need to regenerate Britain both in terms of industrial relations and an alliance between intellectuals and the traditional working classes.

For women, the war had highlighted their problems within society, but these had certainly not been solved during the postwar period. More specifically, the emphasis on *progressiveness* – which in the mid-1960s had found its voice in the progressiveness of rock, the fusion of technology and the exploration of space – did not appear to include progress towards the independence of women.[20] As Betty Friedan wrote in 1963 'there was a strange discrepancy between the reality of our lives as women and the image to which were trying to conform, the image that I came to call the feminine mystique'.[21] In Britain, it was evident that if the counter culture could not provide space for the specific experiences of women, then there was no alternative but to call on the traditions of the past or look elsewhere.

The feminist publisher Virago Press offered one such space; Germaine Greer, a woman who had established a position within academic debate and within the media, another. What is evident, however, is that even the most progressive men within the counter culture reneged on the rights of women.

Jim Haines, for example, had links with *OZ* and AC/DC; he had lived with Jean Shrimpton and had been instrumental in organising the Arts Festival in Edinburgh. But, as he states in his autobiography *I'm Glad I Came*, he wanted a photo of Germaine Greer – in the nude. It would appear that little progress had been made since Stokeley Carmichael's infamous reply to the 1964 Student Nonviolent Coordinating Committee: 'the only position for women in SNCC is prone'.

Women, then, remained marginalised. With 'women's liberation' constructed by the media as 'bra-burning radicals'[22] and misrepresented by so-called progressive men, the question under review at the end of the 1960s was where the women's movement could find a place even within a progressive counter culture. The situation was further exacerbated by the confrontation between socialist and radical feminists, and the challenging stand taken by Shulamith Firestone which called for the 'removal of sex/gender differentiation by eliminating the family and replacing it with institutionalised child rearing, artificial reproduction, and bisexual sex relations'.[23]

The contradictions between the politics of the counter culture, which stressed personal freedom, and the reality of women's lives – not only in society at large but also within the counter culture itself – thus raised problems. In general, the British counter culture was characterised by a sense of negation and disassociation and while such political commentators as Theodore Roszak and Herbert Marcuse applauded the political progressiveness of the New Left, the movement generally embodied significant contradictions. Not least, the relative economic prosperity enjoyed in the 1960s enabled substantial numbers of voluntarily unemployed to live on subsistence incomes while expressing an overt hostility to the traditional concepts of education, work, family and morality. It is also evident, as discussed previously, that the espousal of 'freedom' coincided with sexual stereotyping, often overt sexism and yet more contradictions. In particular, the more permissive, promiscuous sexuality brought its own pressures – how to be emancipated and yet deal with the romanticised construct of the *young*, single woman.

In summary, the fact that music was recognised by the counter culture as an audible signifying badge of belonging is of critical importance to a consideration of the role of women. As an essential focus for communication it forged deliberate and explicit links in the fusion of the mental and physical dimensions of group consciousness. At the same time, it provided a 'commonsense' notion of the ideological framing of women which was both spontaneous and repressive.

NOTES AND REFERENCES

1 Neville, J. (1971) *Play Power*, London: Paladin, p. 14.

2 The Woodstock Festival (1969) came closest, perhaps, to establishing the concept of nationhood.

3 There are clear precedents in the use of nationalistic songs and anthems as well as in songs associated with particular sub-cultures. The Who ('My Generation', 1964), for example, drew on the Mod lifestyle for their musical images.

4 With the possible exception of 'We Shall Overcome'. Otherwise songs summed up particular moments, e.g. the 1967 Summer of Love and Scott McKenzie's 'Are You Going to San Francisco?'; the significance of drugs and Bob Dylan's 'Mr Tambourine Man'.

5 Roszak, T. (1970) *The Making of a Counter Culture. Reflections on the Technocratic Society and its Youthful Opposition*, New York: Faber and Faber, footnote to p. 65.

6 John Lennon lies somewhat outside this generalisation. On the one hand wrestling with his own neurosis (*Crippled Inside*, his second solo LP), and on the other attempting an openly confrontational position with the political establishment. This latter position comes through on the album *Sometime in New York*. Lennon was moving between the personal and the political, as instanced by the overlap between the financial support he gave to the editors of *OZ* at the obscenity trial in October 1970. In that sense he was more in line with late 1960s' thinking, involved with overt protest and personal introspection and often moving uneasily between the two.

7 As Grossberg points out, 'rock refers to an affective investment in, and empowerment by, the cultural forms, images and practices which circulate with the music for different groups of fans, each defining its own taste culture (or apparatus). Rock is defined, for particular audiences at different times and places differently, by the affective alliances of sounds, images, practices and experiences within which fans find certain forms of empowerment'. Grossberg, L., 'Cinema, Postmodernity and Authenticity', in Frith, S., Goodwin, A. and Grossberg, L. (1993) *Sound and Vision. The Music Video Reader*, London: Routledge, p. 200.

8 Roszak, *op.cit.*, p. 156.

9 Frith, S. and McRobbie, A. (1990) 'Rock and Sexuality', in Frith, S. and Goodwin, A., *On Record. Rock, Pop and the Written Word*, London: Routledge, p. 375.

10 Grossberg, L. (1992) 'The Affective Sensibility of Fandom', in Lewis, L., *The Adoring Audience: Fan Culture and Popular Media*, London: Routledge, p. 54.

11 Whiteley, S. (1992) *The Space between the Notes. Rock and the Counter Culture*, London: Routledge.

12 Hebdige, D. (1979) *Subculture. The Meaning of Style*, London: Methuen.

13 Shepherd, J. (1991) *Music as Social Text*, London: Polity Press, p. 83.

14 It is possible to suggest a homology between the experience of LSD and certain styles of music. This may include

- an overall emphasis on timbral colour (blurred, bright, tinkly, overlapping, associated with the intensification of colour and shape experienced when tripping)
- upward movement in pitch (and the comparison with an hallucinogenic high)
- characteristic use of harmonies (lurching, oscillating and the relationship to changing focus)
- sudden surges of rhythm (the association with an acid 'rush') and/or a feeling of floating around the beat (suggestive of a state of tripping where a fixed point takes on a new perspective)
- shifting textural relationships (foreground/background, collages and soundscapes that suggest a disorientation of more conventionalised musical

structures and that stimulate a sense of absorption with/within the sound itself. These techniques provide a musical analogy for the enhancement of awareness, the potentially new synthesis of ideas and thought relationships that can result from hallucinogens).

In the main, musical effects were made possible by an advancement in music technology (studio effects, echo units, controlled random feedback, fuzz box, wah wah pedal, etc.).

15 See Tagg, P. (1979) *Kojak – 50 Seconds of Television Music. Towards the Analysis of Affekt in Popular Music*, and Tagg, P. (1981) *Fernando the Flute – Analysis of Affekt in an Abba number*, Stencilled papers from Gothenberg University Department of Musicology, no.8106.

16 See Middleton, R. (1990) *Studying Popular Music*, Buckingham: Open University Press, pp. 232–6.

17 *Ibid.*, p. 240.

18 Middleton, R. (1997) *Understanding Pop Music*, Milton Keynes: Open University MA module, p. 72.

19 While Chapters 1 and 2 examine the importance of experience and music as expression, Althusser's discussion of ideology is considered relevant insofar as he argues that human beings are constructed by ideology and that our ways of thinking about the world, of representing ourselves, become so 'naturalised' that we take our conception of the world for granted. See Althusser, L. (1971) 'Ideology and Ideological State Apparatus', in *Lenin and Philosophy and Other Essays*, London: New Left Books.

As Annette Kuhn observes, 'If ideology effaces itself, the process by which this takes place could explain this taken-for-granted nature of social constructs of femininity.' Kuhn, A. (1985) *The Power and the Image. Essays on Representation and Sexuality*, London: Routledge, p. 6.

20 Space exploration also interested musicians at the time. See, for example, Pink Floyd 'Astronomy Domine' and 'Set the Controls for the Heart of the Sun'.

21 Friedan, B. (1963) 'The Feminist Mystique', in B. Ryan (ed.) *Feminism and the Women's Movement*, London: Routledge, pp. 77–89.

22 The feminist concern with representation and image had led to a demonstration against the Miss America competition (1968) on the grounds that it promoted an impossible ideal of womanhood and that all women (not only participants) were perceived as no more than a set of bodily attributes.

It is interesting to note that the term 'women's liberation' or 'women's lib.' (in operation at the time of the above protest) was gradually dropped in favour of 'feminists'. However, as Germaine Greer observes,

> What none of us noticed was that the ideal of liberation was fading out with the word. We were settling for equality. Liberation struggles are not about assimilation but about asserting difference, endowing that difference with dignity and prestige, and insisting on it as a condition of self-definition and self-determination.
>
> Greer, G. (1999) *the whole woman*, London: Doubleday, p. 1

23 Ryan, *op.cit.*, p.49.

2

REPRESSIVE
REPRESENTATIONS

Patriarchy, femininities and 1960s' rock

In many ways 1967 was a microcosm of the struggle of the decade it divided, in the interplay between action and reaction, liberalisation and repression. Britain had finally passed the Sexual Offences Act (1967) so decriminalising homosexuality. The Abortion Act was also passed in 1967 after a lengthy campaign ('The Right To Choose') for safe and freely available abortion and contraception. *The Times* (London) published an advertisement advocating the legalisation of marijuana to which the Beatles were signatories. Even so, it is difficult to resist the argument that any doctrine that leads to greater freedoms of self-expression and individualism among the governed, but which is not sanctioned by the governors, will inevitably be suppressed. Regional drug squads were formed in March 1967 and LSD and marijuana were made illegal. In August, the Rolling Stones were arrested for possessing marijuana. Pirate radio was suppressed and raids on the *International Times* (*IT*) and underground music clubs reflected an increasingly repressive reaction by the establishment. By 1968 the counter culture was characterised by hippy anarchy and such sensationalised events as exorcising the demons from the Pentagon, nude grope-ins and joint-rolling contests. America, like Britain, reacted with punitive measures and Abbie Hoffman and Jerry Rubin were tried for conspiracy, the former being sentenced to five years' imprisonment.

The Beatles' popularity throughout the 1960s is well documented. The frenzied adoration by young female fans, both in Britain and America during the peak of Beatlemania has been described by some feminists as 'the first and most dramatic uprising of *women's* sexual revolution' in that it signalled an abandonment of control and a protest against the sexual repressiveness of female teen culture.[1] Essentially, the Beatles were a mainstream band, but their ability to popularise even the most esoteric trends in British and American rock, and the extent to which their music achieved worldwide dissemination, suggests why they remain one of the most significant forces in the history of popular music. Because they were examined by sociologists and critics alike for their potential influence on the morals and attitudes of youth culture, and because their music and (especially) lyrics were subjected to extensive interpretative analysis, the lead up to the release of the *Sgt Pepper's* album, in June 1967, was accompanied by an unprecedented level of antici-pation. As writer and critic Derek Taylor observed, 'It was the most amazing thing I've ever heard. For a brief moment, the irreparably fragmented consciousness of the West was unified, at least in the minds of the young.'[2]

Although it could be argued that the Beatles were simply jumping on the American psychedelic bandwagon, the fact that they had become 'under-ground converts' was significant. Their changed image and the attendant emphasis on love and drugs was newsworthy and inevitably stimulated comment and imitation. The *Sgt Pepper's* album was in perfect harmony with the mood of the time in its LSD-influenced acid rock, raga rock and social commentary; and its huge popularity indicates that without the Beatles, the British counter cultural scene would have been far less significant. In partic-ular, it established an agenda for the British counter culture in terms both of cultural themes and of music. Drug use had caught up with the drug orien-tation of rock and '*Sgt Pepper's*' had finally bridged the gap right down to suburbia'.[3]

The third track on the album, 'Lucy in the Sky with Diamonds', was central to British psychedelic rock in that it suggested a musical metaphor for hallucinogenic experience.[4] Musically, the gentle beat works towards a slowing down of the listener's own pulse rate, while the gradual shifting harmonies in the chromatic descent in the bass line suggest a relaxation into a comfortable and languorous 'dream' state. The melody line of the verse is trancelike, the repetitive phrases revolving around the third degree of the scale. For the listener, the effect is both reflective and reassuring as the gentle melodic contours respond to the dactylic metre of the words. 'For No One', 'And I Love Her', and 'Yesterday' were also structured around rising and falling phrases and short melodies and, as such, 'Lucy' evokes a feeling of reassurance. The listener may be entering new territory, but the guide is reliable. The use of a familiar melodic contour, juxtaposed with the exotic timbres of the celesta sound in the opening organ melody, the filtered vocal delivery, the surrealistic lyrics, are evocative of a good trip. As such, the song elicits a sense of confidence. The Beatles have enjoyed hallucinogenic experi-ence, they know the effects of LSD and can musically guide the initiate through to a new and heightened sense of awareness. The foregrounding of the psychedelic imagery ('tangerine trees', 'marmalade skies') is thus strongly supported by the musical coding to evoke a spatial dimension[5] comparable to that of a hallucinogenic trip, where heightened awareness causes the ordinary to take on new colours and dimensions. With the imagery strongly supported by musical effects, the opening sequence to 'Lucy' promises a seductive route through to a changed state of conscious-ness. It seems to say 'Follow this through to its logical conclusion – take Acid – have an authentic experience and with our guidance you, too, can meet Lucy – in the sky with diamonds.'

At the same time, the song establishes a particular definition of romanticised femininity, the insubstantial and etherealised Lucy. The image of 'the girl with the sun in her eyes' both reflects and constructs the preferred face of the late 1960s – the 'kaleidoscope' eyes, the waiflike figure epitomised by the omnipresent Julie Driscoll/Twiggy genre. Already represented as a fantasy figure, the Lucy refrain, with its brief and hypnotically repetitive phrases, 'inserts an element of "earthy reality" into an otherwise dreamlike experience'.[6] 'Lucy in the Sky with Diamonds' may be interpreted as a celebration of LSD, but the exuberant refrain makes it equally a celebration of possession. Lucy may have a dreamlike quality, a certain elusiveness ('Look for the girl with the sun in her eyes, and she's gone') but the stereotypical and cliched musical structures (the repetitive I-IV-V7 harmonies), and the unison vocal chant in the chorus reinstate her within the dominant catechism of rock where women are both attainable and containable.

The projection of nonreality linked to psychedelic imagery is carried further in 'Julia' (1968). The song is autobiographical, describing the mother Lennon hardly knew, and Julia thus retains the elusive beauty of a woman inscribed within the framework of fantasy. Sung to a slowly moving and unusually narrow-ranged melody, the shifting harmonies in the supporting chords nevertheless create an underlying tension – 'Julia, morning moon, touch me.' The imagery is that of the imagined woman, 'hair of floating sky is shimmering, glimmering', drawing on the symbolic associations of the lunar goddess who stands at both ends of the silver cord of life, presiding over fertility, birth and death. Associated with the astrological sign of Pisces, with the Druidic, the Celtic Triple Goddess and the sea, she represents equally sexuality and matriarchal energies and, as such, relates to the image of the earth mother (a concept which is discussed on pp. 39–40 of this chapter). At the same time she is a symbol of the unattainable and, like Lucy, is denied the self that is human. Unlike Lennon's intense expression of love 'I Want You (She's So Heavy)', where heavy metal inscribes an earthy sexuality to Yoko Ono, Julie (like Lucy) is denied the self that is human. She is a symbol of beauty and is given no other value than to be beautiful.

By the late 1960s a particular inscription of women as fantasy figures begins to emerge. Donovan carries the myth further in 'Jennifer Juniper', a song in which the background combination of strings, woodwind, and cor-anglais provides a wistful and romanticised commentary on the idealised image of a woman who evokes memories of Godiva, riding 'a dappled mare ... lilacs in her hair ... hair of golden flax'. The verse suggests a certain element of fantasy, with the repetitive rhythm and melodic riffs supporting the structure of a 'series of images seen in sequence',[7] while the rhetorical 'Is she sleeping? (I don't think so)' suggests voyeurism, 'the seeing rather than the feeling of the woman'.[8] The pleasure of both narrator and listener 'depends on the object of the look being unable to see him: to this extent, it is a pleasure of power, and the look is a controlling one ... (Jennifer) can be looked at for as long as desired, because the circuit of pleasure will never be broken by a returned look.'[9] Isolated by a pause, there is time for reflection before the key question – 'What 'cha doin' Jennifer, my love?' – and the possibility that Jennifer longs for what she lacks. Donovan, aptly dubbed at the time as a sentimental hero, the Aloysha or Prince Myshkin of pop[10] has, it would seem, the qualities to fulfil her needs. She can be reinstated within the dominant catechism of romance – 'Would you love her? Yes, I would sir.'

The idealisation of the image is subtle in effect. Lucy, Julia, Jennifer play on the 'desire of the spectator in a particularly pristine way: beauty or sexuality is desirable to the extent that it is idealised and unattainable'.[11] There is a sense of deceptive fascination in this particular genre, in that the image of the woman is enhanced by illusion. She is etherealised and inscribed within a dreamlike and unreal world, detached from reality, defined by the male as a fantasy escape *from* reality. The significance of this representation can be seen in the ways in which the idealised image was displaced on to the style of the period. The long hair, the emphasis on eyes and the use of body make-up reaffirmed the 'made-up-ness' of the image of the woman herself, as one composed of surfaces, defined by appearance. Lucy, Julia, Jennifer hold out a vision of idealised male-defined perfection. They are 'made-up' in the immediate sense in that their images are constructed by the songs and written by male singer songwriters, but they also

> occupy a place dangerously close to another tradition of representations of women, from myth to fairytale to high art to pornography, in which they are stripped of will and autonomy. Woman is dehumanised by being represented as a kind of automaton, a 'living doll': The Sleeping Beauty, Coppelia ... 'She's a real doll'.[12]

While no reading of music can be completely objective or entirely unambiguous, there is nevertheless an initial prefacing of what has gone before which results in certain representations of women becoming so 'naturalised' that they assume a taken-for-granted quality. There is, therefore, a certain element of surprise when similar fantasy figures appear in an overtly sexist band like the Rolling Stones. 'Gomper', from *Their Satanic Majesties Request* album (1967) is deliberately psychedelic in musical language and, like the Beatles 'Within You Without You' (*Sgt Pepper's*) uses the sitar and quasi-Indian scoring. The lyrics, however, with their allusion to the 'lily maid' draw heavily (if subconsciously) on the familiar heroines of the nineteenth century.

> If inscribed by masculine pens (they) are petite and fragile, with lily fingers and taper waists; and they are supposed to subsist on air and moonlight ... wandlike, with a step so light that the flowers

35

scarcely nod beneath it ... a little too spiritual for this world and a little too material for the next, and who, therefore seems always hovering between the two, is the accepted type of female loveliness.[13]

Evoking images of Elaine and Ophelia, the imagined woman floats down in blissful languor on or towards the surface of a pond partly overgrown with lilies as, for example, in American painter Walter Shirlaw's *Dawn* (1886). In common with many late Victorian paintings, there is an implied sense of voyeurism. 'She tripped naked through the woods, roamed carelessly among the bushes, and grew like a white-breasted human waterlily among the flora of the sea'[14] – or, in the words of the Rolling Stones, 'She swims to the side, the sun sees her dried ... I stifle a cry.' Similar to Louis Eilshemius' well-known painting of a cluster of women afloat in *The Afternoon Wind* (1899), the eroticised and naked body invites the man to take charge. In 'Gomper', femininity and female sexuality are also the object of an obsessive voyeuristic gaze, the woman among the lilies, drying herself in the sun while the man watches, unseen and unheard.

'In Another Land', arguably the most creative track on *Their Satanic Majesties Request*, is equally autoerotic in its focus on the primordial dream woman, floating hand-in-hand with her dream lover in a surrealistic blue landscape. In common with other psychedelic rock songs of the period, electronic filtering and sound effects are used to provide a musical metaphor for the hallucinatory imagery of the verse, which contrasts with the wide awake chorus in R&B style. There is, then, a strong resemblance to the musical structures in 'Lucy'. At the same time, within the context of the Stones' more usual precise and calculated sexuality, the chorus eroticises the unattainable, situating the initial experience of the woman within a sexually charged dream ('and I awoke'). As such, it mobilises the fear women have of seeing themselves inscribed within a male fantasy of control. She is an imaginary lover and 'the hand' he held, that gave him his ultimate pleasure is, by inference, grasped around the penis. Eroticised, an object of fantasy, the enigmatic woman becomes one more example of what might be termed *wank rock*, 'Champagne Jam', 'Pictures of Lily', 'Touching Me, Touching You'.[15]

'Gomper' and 'In Another Land' are unusually subtle for the Rolling Stones, but with music providing an audible map of learning whereby the counter culture could explore human relationships, such representations are clearly disturbing. As Paul Willis writes, 'only specific kinds of music were chosen because they – and not others – were able to hold, develop and return those meanings and experiences which were important to the hippy culture'.[16] Although such theories tend towards reductionism, it is nevertheless certain that there were connections between the musical and social structures within the counter culture, not least because of music's status as its major communicative organ. As such, the lyrics and the sound were considered to provide insights into, for example, expanded consciousness and personal freedom. What is obvious, however, is that this commitment to personal freedom was not extended towards women who continued to be inscribed with a chauvinistic frame of reference. 'Parachute Woman' (the Rolling Stones, 1968), for example, has a strongly pulsating rhythm which supports the sensual triplets in the melody line, the musical structures aligning themselves with Jagger's explicit demand 'come blow me out'. The melodic contour, in its constant movement between D natural-E-D natural works as an obsessive up-down-up-down vocal riff which is tied unequivocally to Jagger's itchin' 'heavy throbber'. 'Fellatio, which in itself is a simple act of pleasure between mouth and penis ... (thus) takes on the aura of an obsession' as Jagger, 'the hero turns fellatio into an act of aggression, a "forced feeding", an "overspill" '.[17]

In hardcore, subtlety is stripped away. The identity of the woman resides in her sex, in her mouth, in her ability to give pleasure, rather than in her 'flowing hair' and 'kaleidoscope eyes'. Stones' songs 'Backstreet Girl', 'Heart of Stone', 'Under My Thumb', 'Stray Cat Blues', 'My Obsession', 'Brown Sugar' and, in the 1970s 'Negrite' and 'Coming Down Again' also conflate 'femininity with femaleness, femaleness with female sexuality and female sexuality with a particular part of the female anatomy'[18] and 'hardcore' rock, like pornography itself, places the feminine as the object of enquiry. The women, through Jagger's performance, thus speak to the males' desire for pleasurable looking/listening, as exemplified in the observation of the trader in 'Brown Sugar' and his nightly whipping of female slaves. Again, there are parallels with Annette Kuhn's analysis of the 'Peeping Tom who separates himself in the act of looking (listening to) the object which cannot look back at him (hear him)'.[19] By identifying with Jagger ('you should have heard me'), the spectator's fantasy is given full rein: 'in one sense there is no risk of disappointment', he is quite safe because the woman in the song 'will never in real life turn him down or make demands which he cannot satisfy. By the same token, of course, he can never really "possess" her.'[20] Desire, however is fuelled and fulfilled: 'in the final instance its object is unattainable and unthreatening'[21] but, at the same time, the dominating presence of Jagger allows for positive identification for his male audience as he, in turn, possesses the woman, both in the song, and metaphorically in live performance. 'You should have heard me, just around midnight.'

Parallel themes of sexual domination appear throughout rock history: 'I'm gonna make you sweat, gonna make you groove' ('Black Dog', Led Zeppelin); 'Dance girl, lemme see the booty boom' ('Love 2 The 9's', Prince); or, at its most horrific:

> She liked the way it felt inside her,
> Fucking her, harder, harder'
> ('Fucked with a Knife', Cannibal Corpse)

It is suggested that this emphasis on woman as 'other' can be attributed, at least in part, to the fear of what Barbara Creed calls 'the monstrous feminine',[22] the *femme castratice* of Freudian theory. Represented as, for example, vampire, witch, possessed body, the woman here is horrific, the castrator rather than the castrated. 'Dolly Dagger' (Jimi Hendrix), for example, aligns the woman with the vampire figure 'who sucks the blood of its victims in their sleep while they are alive' so exhausting 'the vitality of her male partner – or victim'.[23] As a creature of the night she is once again associated with the moon, to become the primal counterpart of 'Lucy', but this time predatory and possessed of 'a love so heavy, it's gonna make you stagger'. The phallic connotations of the surname 'Dagger' underpin the nature of the predatory woman, with the second verse pointing to the fear of male castration – 'She drinks her blood from a jagged edge.'

The *femme castratice* also emerges in 'Strange Brew' (Cream). Here, the repetitive vocal line and the continuous bass riff suggest an underlying fixation, of being taken over by the 'witch in electric blue'. In particular, the sense of the demonic woman is opened out by the emphasis on 'strange brew' aligned to the chaotic 'on a boat in the middle of a raging sea/she would make a scene'. There is also the suggestion of the woman as siren, one whose physical allure spelt death to man's transcendental soul. As Bram Dijkstra points out 'such a fantasy of seduction allowed him to combine the pleasures of indulgence with the innocent state of the unwilling victim' who, by analogy

> was none other than the girl next door, who, cold and collected and with disdainful eyes, remained in the swim of things, while her unfortunate suitor slipped helplessly below the water level of economic survival, his hands still vainly reaching out to his destroyer as he went down.'[24]

To an extent, it is not surprising that musicians such as Cream should take on the traditional blues representation of 'woman trouble'.[25] The psychological state called 'the blues', the 'blue devils' is often associated with physical loss, betrayal, rage and the tensions of pain. This view of woman as soulless, one who fascinates desire but who must be repelled for fear of self-destruction is one which resonates most strongly with the traditional church view of women as witches. 'Witch burners believed themselves to be victims of the women they accused; we discover in their own accounts that they felt they were in mortal danger.'[26] 'If you don't watch out, she'll stick to you. Strange brew, killing what's inside of you.'

The traditional church view that 'witchcraft comes from carnal lust, which is in women insatiable'[27] has a curious resonance with the underground's stress on easy eroticism. If the woman, by nature, is insatiable, then she should welcome the liberating attitude of 'unlimited fucking' as promised by the so-called revolution of 'free' sex. The sensationalised reports of groupies,[28] the reputed sex practices of such pop stars as the Rolling Stones and their girlfriends, and the frankness with which underground agony columns discussed complications concerned with anal intercourse, cunnilingus, fellatio and bestiality[29] provide some indication of the more controversial sexual activities of the counter culture. At the same time, there is the implication that sexual candour, sexual curiosity are the norm and although anecdotes about the sexual activities of pop stars were largely media-hype, veracity was/is largely irrelevant. Rather *beliefs* spur imitation – not truth or falsity'[30] or, as Kate Millett observed at the time 'Every woman knows what is expected of her, what it means to be an adequate woman.'[31] The easy sexuality described in pop music, the emphasis on uninhibited sexual anarchy as reported in the underground press, provided an idealised vision of sexual freedom which was difficult to ignore but which was nevertheless diametrically opposed to the commonsense wisdom inscribed in most women's consciousness that losing control equates with sexual danger.

While heavy rock and, later, the various branches of heavy metal all too often represent women as dehumanised and degraded, fulfilling simply their role to gratify the male sexually, wanting to be humiliated, suppressed and physically harmed and objectified, the role of woman as earth mother was central to counter cultural mythology. Here, the woman takes on the role of the provider, the forgiver, the healer. The image of the woman decked in flowers is common to 1960s' iconography. Such songs as 'Mother Nature's Son' (the Beatles, 1968) convey some sense of the conception of woman as the 'receptive, seed-sheltering womb of a sweltering earth'.[32] She is a symbol of nature, she is the earth, sexual but protective, always there for the masculine ego to inhabit when he wants to escape from the realities of life.[33]

It is, perhaps, hardly surprising that the counter culture, with its emphasis on hallucinogenic experience, should resurrect that nineteenth-century image of the earth mother. Earl Shimm, in 1867, had described her symbolic significance as representative of the 'Opium Dream'.

> Beneath stretches a field of poppies, lifting up their stems and their shapely seed-pods, chiselled like Indian capitals; from among them, her feet disentangling themselves from their cold stems, floats up the Vision, a dim figure in human shape, her filmed eyes lifted, her arms crossed in Oriental adoration, and all her faint, smoky figure ready to blend with the clouds and fumes that overweave the unsubstantial heavens.[34]

Although the poetic language is replaced by a more declamatory rock style, the sentiments re-emerge in the Rolling Stones' 'Sister Morphine' and 'Dead Flowers'.

The earth mother as madonna can also be traced to the nineteenth century. For Ruskin, 'the path of a good woman is strewn with flowers; but they rise behind her steps, not beneath them',[35] an expression of both male sentimentality and their perception of the soul-healing power of the virtuous woman. One hundred years later Paul McCartney expressed much the same thoughts: 'To lead a better life, I need my love to be there ... Changing my life with a wave of her hand'. 'Lady Madonna', less naively ecstatic, neverthe-less conveys some of the understanding necessary for the contemporary earth mother as her lover 'Friday night arrives without a suitcase, Sunday morning creeping like a nun'. 'Hey Jude' conveys the sense of the woman as comforter and support – 'let her into your heart ... then you can make it better'. It is, however, Led Zeppelin's 'Stairway to Heaven' that most encapsulates the image of the etherealised earth mother, 'a lady we all know'. With its pagan imagery of trees and brooks, pipers, shining white light and forests echoing to laughter, the song 'is a paradigm of Spenser's *Faerie Queen,* Robert Graves's *White Goddess* and every other Celtic heroine – the Lady of the Lake, Diana of the Fields Greene and Rhiannon the nightmare'.[36] At one level the song can be read as woman's quest for spiritual enlightenment, one who has the power to determine who can enter the heavenly kingdom: 'If the stars are all closed, with a word she can get what she came for', and who acknowledges that her 'stairway lies on the whispering wind'. At the same time, it is a fitting epitaph for the woman within the counter culture. There is a sense of nostalgia, the lyrics conjuring up images of green pastures, forests and castles, while the acoustic guitar introduction harks back to the Renaissance, curiously reminiscent of 'Greensleeves'. Led Zeppelin had aimed to produce 'a new kind of music, with slower and lighter touches, music with dynamics, light and shade, chiaroscuro',[37] to 'provide an alternative way of looking at things'.[38] Musically they succeed, and the song constructs a feeling of a musical journey in its alternation of delicate scoring and dramatic guitar solo. The representation of the 'Lady', as May Queen remains, however, firmly entrenched within 1960s' iconography. She is, to an extent, earthbound in her love of gold, but her sense of otherness, a figure who 'shines white light' places her once again ' in the sky', an etherealised earth mother. 'Ooh, it makes me wonder'.

There is little to suggest, then, that in terms of musical experience, the counter culture gave serious thought to the individuality or, indeed, the diversity of women. There is little commentary on commitments, women's sexual desires and experiences. The preoccupation with love and loneliness is seldom confronted, except as an outsider's commentary (the Beatles' 'She's Leaving Home', 'Eleanor Rigby', the Rolling Stones' 'Mother's Little Helper'), or introspection linked to a drug culture which provided the chemical, rather than the objective means, to self-examination. Conversely, there is much to support the argument that women were still viewed as objects defined by, and for, men. There was no real conceptual progress from the Rolling Stones' 'Let's Spend The Night Together' to the anonymous woman in 'Bitch'. In both songs the woman is valued, quite simply, for her ability to satisfy.

What is apparent in an analysis of the relationship between the counter culture and its associated music is that the inscriptions of women are male-given. A survey of contemporary chart successes reveals the presence of women artists such as Lulu, Cilla Black, Sandie Shaw and Mary Hopkins, but their hits over the years 1967–9 suggest more an emphasis on pop music and fashion than any positive inroad into a male-dominated music business. Indeed, what chance was there of a progressive woman's perspective when Clodagh Rodgers could sing 'I'm still a little pussy cat, come give me some milk' – lyrics that curiously resembled the sentiments expressed by the Stones 'If you want someone to cream on, baby, cream on me'. *Melody Maker*'s 1972 conference 'Women in Rock' highlighted the problem. 'Elkie Brooks, then singing with Vinegar Joe, admitted that she had actually been singing "for ever", but until I started putting myself across sexually, wearing slits up the side and little bikini tops, nobody wanted to know.' Mary Hopkins, the Welsh folk singer, was a Paul McCartney discovery. She was frequently described as the epitome of the passive feminine role – England's sweetheart.

It is a sobering thought that feminist music critics were not taken seriously by academic institutions until 1988 when the conferences at Dartmouth and Carlton Universities (Canada) emphasised a feminist critique. Women musicians fared slightly better. The University of Illinois celebrated the first women's music festival in 1974. But then, as argued in this chapter, the counter culture was itself male-dominated in its musical agenda. Women provided a fantasy escape, a focus for easy eroticism. The breaking down of old restraints ('free love') privileged a male sexuality and autoeroticism, confirming the traditional definitions of masculinity and femininity under the dubious banner of progressiveness. At its most oppressive, rock music in the late 1960s embodied the patriarchal imaginary of the madonna–whore binary. It was not an easy image to dispel.

NOTES AND REFERENCES

1 Ehrenreich, B., Hess, E. and Jacobs, G., 'Beatlemania: Girls Just Want to Have Fun', in Lewis, L. (1992) *The Adoring Audience. Fan Culture and Popular Media*, London: Routledge, p. 85.

2 Taylor, D. (1974) *As Time Goes By*, London: Abacus/Sphere, p. 45.

3 McCabe, P. and Schonfield, R.D. (1972) *Apple to the Core. The Unmaking of the Beatles*, London: Martin Brian & O'Keefe Ltd., p. 84.

4 While the Beatles denied that 'Lucy in the Sky with Diamonds' was about the effects of LSD, the psychedelic coding and the lyrics in the verses suggest otherwise.

5 'Tomorrow Never Knows' (*Revolver*, 1966) is generally considered the first Beatles' song to draw on hallucinogenic experience and this was followed up by the single 'Strawberry Fields Forever' (1967). The emphasis on spacey sounds

with the analogy to being 'spaced out', has led to a blurring of the distinctions between psychedelic/acid rock and space rock.

6 O'Grady, T. (1983) *The Beatles*, Boston: Twayne Publishers, p. 125.
7 Kuhn, A. (1985) *The Power and the Image. Essays on Representation and Sexuality*, London: Routledge, p. 12.
8 Griffin, S. (1981) *Pornography and Silence*, New York: Harper and Row, p. 122.
9 Kuhn, *op.cit.*, p. 12.
10 Cohn, N. (1972) *Awopbopaloobop Alopbamboom. Pop From The Beginning*, London: Paladin, p. 179.
11 Kuhn, *op.cit.*, p. 12.
12 *Ibid.*, p. 14.
13 Dijkstra, B. (1986) *Idols of Perversity. Fantasies of Feminine Evil in Fin-de-Siècle Culture*, New York: Oxford University Press, p. 29.
14 *Ibid.*, p. 29.
15 Songs about masturbation range from the implicit 'Five Finger Exercise' (Christ Child) 'Making Love on the Phone' (Suzanne Fellini) to 'You Can't Go Home with Your Hard-On' (Leonard Cohen). It was not until the early 1990s that female masturbation became a subject for discussion in such songs as 'Icicle' from Tori Amos; second album *Under the Pink* (see pp. 203–4).
16 Willis, P. (1978) *Profane Culture*, London: Routledge & Kegan Paul, p. 46.
17 Griffin, *op.cit.*, p. 61.
18 Kuhn, *op.cit.*, p. 40.
19 *Ibid.*, p. 41.
20 *Ibid.*, p. 42.
21 *Ibid.*, p. 42.
22 Creed, B. (1993) *The Monstrous-Feminine. Film, Feminism, Psychoanalysis*, London: Routledge.
23 Griffin, *op.cit.*, p. 122.
24 Dijkstra, *op.cit.*, p. 83.
25 Cream (Eric Clapton, ex-John Mayall's Bluesbreakers, Jack Bruce and Ginger Baker, ex-Graham Bond Organisation) was originally planned as a blues trio and all three musicians came from bands with reputations for virtuoso blues performances.
26 Naish, C. (1994) *Death Comes to the Maiden. Sex and Execution 1431–1933*, p. 23.
27 *Ibid.*, p. 26.
28 At their most sensational, groupies were identified with the emerging cult of the 'starfucker', 'the sexological phenomenon of the sixties ... young, plentiful ... everywhere pop stars are ... and becoming celebrities in their own right'. Neville, J. (1971) *Play Power*, London: Paladin, p. 70.

However, the dubious accolade of 'equi'sexual with ease', 'chicks up front', 'pussy power' and 'groupiedom' did little to further the status of women within the counter culture. Rather it continued to situate equality within the confines of penetrative sex and 'the universal tongue bath' – as Neville terms it.
29 Neville quotes some of the more perverse. *Ibid.*, pp. 133–4.
30 *Ibid.*, p. 69.
31 Millett, cited in Tong, R. (1992) *Feminist Thought. A Comprehensive Introduction*, London: Routledge, p. 97.
32 Dijkstra, *op.cit.*, p. 83.
33 *Ibid.*, p. 86.
34 *Ibid.*, p. 90.
35 *Ibid.*, p. 269.

36 *Davies, S.* (1973) *Hammer of the Gods*, New York: Ballantine Books, p. 101.
37 *Ibid.*, p. 101.
38 Moore, A. (1993) *Rock – The Primary Text*, London: Oxford University Press, p. 98.

3

THE PERSONAL IS POLITICAL
Women's liberation, sexuality, gender, freedom and repression

> What finally knackered the underground was its complete inability to deal with women's liberation ... . Men defined themselves as rebels against society in ways limited to their own sex.[1]

Although the feminist critique of oppression can be considered autonomous, the emerging women's movement of the late 1960s was characterised by an eclecticism which drew largely on the social and political theories generated by contemporary radical politics. In particular, the revisions of Marxism produced by the New Left, and a renewed interest in Freud, had led to an identification of personal alienation as central to the discourses surrounding sexual liberation and repression. The shift from a preoccupation with class consciousness to *consciousness* consciousness, was critical to the redefinition of alienation. Defined by Roszak as the 'deadening of man's sensitivity to man',[2] alienation was perceived less as a proprietary distinction that exists between different classes, and more as a deep-rooted and universal psychological condition. Ideological politics – the subordination of the person to party and doctrine – was replaced by a new personalism, an intensive examination of the self, and the construction of a cultural base which would involve new types of community, new family patterns, and new personal identities.

The emphasis on the primacy of consciousness in effecting social change was reflected in the debates surrounding such formally structured institutions as law, religion and marriage, and the challenge to the traditional bureaucratic patterns of power and authority inherent in university education, health, welfare and paid work. While Vietnam provided a specific example of unification among the dissenting young in their stand against war, the Russian invasion of Czechoslovakia, writings on the cultural revolution in China, and Black Power debates on confrontation politics, for example, stimulated a wider-ranging discussion on inequality. For women, the questioning of power and status, oppression and subordination, provided a specific platform for the discussion of 'power relations in personal life – in reproduction, sexual relationships, the household division of labour',[3] popular culture and the arts.

With many of the early women's groups emerging from universities, education, self-education, and political intervention remained high on the agenda. Small-group interaction and discussion groups focused attention on women's health, fertility control, sexuality and childcare, drawing on the experience of earlier feminist campaigns. Liberal feminists drew attention to the ways in which the conflation of sex and gender accounted for the systematic and discriminatory legal constraints which blocked women's entrance and/or success in the public world. Marxist feminists challenged historical and class-related issues surrounding the workplace, identifying the ways in which family structures were underpinned by capitalist ideology. Questions were raised as to why certain groups (ethnic minorities, the working classes, women) were marginalised in their access to the production and consumption of knowledge and culture, and why they were not represented within, for example, the hierarchies of science and the arts.

Although such issues as access to work and civil rights were integral to second wave feminism, it is evident that the principal trajectory between the counter culture and the women's movement lay in the debates surrounding freedom and repression. In particular, the examination of psychology, by such social theorists as Marcuse, had led to the conclusion that social formations are all based on domination and that repression is historically, not biologically given, so suggesting a comparability with the feminist rejection of biological determinism.[4] Indeed, given that Freud's theories on women's nature are those that most angered feminists, it is not surprising that early theorists emphasised the experiential and cultural influences that shape women's behaviour. Friedan, Firestone and Millett, for example, all focused on the biological determinism of Freud, the former identifying an overemphasis on sex as one of the forces that keep women out of the public worlds of politics, economics and culture. Firestone identified the nuclear family as a micropower structure, rewriting Marx and Engel's theory of the dialectics of materialism in terms of sex. Millett combined political theory, sociology, psychology and literature in her identification of the 'sexual politics' of male/female interaction.[5] While there was divergence over Freud's emphasis on sexuality,[6] there was, nevertheless, a general consensus that women's sexuality had been socially constructed, that the penis represented power, and that the woman must probe the depths of her psyche in order to free herself from oppressive patriarchal systems.

The identification of patriarchy as 'a system of structures and institutions created by men in order to sustain and recreate male power and female subordination',[7] and the coalescence between theory and practice was fundamental to the political perspectives of radical feminism. In particular, there was an identification of the need for collective action and responsibility, and an acknowledgement that women's experience, whether heterosexual or lesbian, was rooted in the cultural and social circumstances of their lives. However, the recognition of women's oppression as universal, crossing race, class and other delineating boundaries such as age and physical ability, carried with it the implication that perfect equality is impossible and that matriarchy and separatism might well be the only viable solutions. In particular, the identification of 'sisterhood' as a cohesive revolutionary force for developing self-identity in relation to other women, for 'putting women first', led to a defence of separatism 'engaging in women only groups; engaging in political and social action with other women .... working in an environment which is run by and for women ... living in an all-women environment without contact with men',[8] with the inference that lesbian feminism was the only viable route forward. The identification of 'separatism as an empowering base and the belief in establishing and transmitting traditions, histories and ideologies that are women centred'[9] was significant in its challenge to patriachal definitions of art and culture. Grass-root discussion and consciousness-raising groups identified a broad range of concerns, including sexual relationships, motherhood and body image. More specifically, the debates surrounding sex/gender provoked a specific challenge to established representations of women as cultural norms, in literature, film and advertising. Kate Millett, for example, singled out D.H. Lawrence, Henry Miller and Norman Mailer as directly contributing to women's oppression through their descriptions of relationships in which women are sexually humiliated and abused. Virago Press evidenced a general concern to rediscover and re-chart the cultural map by publishing nineteenth- and twentieth-century 'classics' by women authors, while journals such as *Spare Rib, Women's Voice, Women's Report* and the *Red Rag* provided much needed communication networks.[10]

While the early 1970s were characterised by a rich diversity of feminist critique, the debates surrounding sex/gender, image and representation, and the control of women's bodies by men, led to direct confrontation with such established 'rituals' as beauty contests. In 1968 feminists demonstrated against the Miss America Pageant in Atlantic City, crowning a live sheep Miss America. Greeted with incredulity by the general press, the underground newspapers retaliated, protesting against the 'degrading mindless-boob-girlie-symbol of beauty contests', and the way in which women are 'forced daily to compete for male approval, enslaved by ludicrous beauty standards we ourselves are conditioned to take seriously'.[11] The *International Times* published an article on 'Miss America as Military Death Mascot', as representing the

> unstained patriotic American womanhood our boys are fighting for.
> ... The highlight of Miss America's reign each year is a cheer-leader
> tour of American troops abroad – last year she went to Vietnam to

pep-talk our fathers, husbands, sons and boyfriends into dying and killing with a better spirit'.[12]

Conjuring up images of the American college football stadium, a sense of team-spirit and the traditional gendering of the male as active − a fighter underpinned by a sense of fair play − the article was one of many which focused the irony of misplaced patriotism. More specifically, it drew attention to the role of women in embodying and validating nationalistic values.[13]

More belligerent articles, by such notorieties as Valerie Solanas, founder of SCUM (the Society for Cutting Up Men), attacked males as 'walking dildoes, obsessed with screwing', suggesting that 'the male claim that females find fulfilment through motherhood and sexuality reflects what males think they'd find fulfilling if they were female'.[14] Susan Lydon in *Ramparts* celebrated the liberation of women from the Freudian orthodoxy that vaginal orgasm is superior to clitoral orgasm −

> vaginal women being feminine, well-adjusted, maternal while clitoral women are immature, neurotic, masculine ... The definition of feminine sexuality as normally vaginal, was part of keeping them down, of making them sexually as well as economically, socially and politically subservient.[15]

Although such articles generally evidence attack, they reflect, nevertheless, the general concern for the relationship between gender and sexuality and the prescribed roles of women within a patriarchal society: 'young, juicy, malleable, judged for teeth and fleece', and passive, 'brainwashed into believing that such attributes constitute her essential femininity'.[16]

While the Underground Press Syndicate[17] was noted for its wide-ranging articles, its promotion of LSD and cannabis, its investigation into the gains made by corporations from prolonging the war in Vietnam, its support for the burning of draft cards, the inclusion of articles which identified the effect of female biology on women's self-perception and status is significant. Clearly Solanas can be seen to represent a minority viewpoint, but the contestation of the 'natural order' as subordinating women to men was an integral part of the radical feminist critique. Thus while many radical feminists came to recognise that women's reproductive capacity and the nurturant psychology that flows from it is a potential source of liberating power for women, the publication of such articles within underground magazines, albeit on the 'Ladies Page', evidences a growing recognition that men's *control* over women as childbearers and childrearers is oppressive. It would be misleading to suggest, however, that debates surrounding sexuality and gender were any more than part of a more generalised foregrounding of discussions on outmoded morality and the urge towards sexual revolution. As such, while the contestation of the biological *status quo* within underground magazines is significant, in that it evidences a recognition that gendered roles are implicated in the distribution of social power and structures of dominance, such articles must be balanced against those appearing in, for example, the New York tabloid *Screw* which had proclaimed its determination to legitimise pornography.[18]

Sexual equality, then, oscillated uneasily between such extremes as a general concern to confront the laws surrounding homosexuality, the imposed morality surrounding traditional family structures, birth control and abortion, to a joyful endorsement of group sex. As Richard Neville commented at the time,

> There is a change in sexual style. A shift in the structure of human relationships .... The Beverley Sisters reflected their time with the hit 'Love and Marriage ... (go together like a horse and carriage)'. Seduction is obsolete ... the prospect of having to tempt, beguile or entice today's freewheeling girls to bed is, well .... imagine having to entice Janis Joplin.[19]

Neville's observation draws attention to the way in which the traditional notions of 'one love syndrome' and 'waiting for the right man/woman to come along' had been superseded by a more frank sexuality. The independence of sexuality, frequency of lovers and, more importantly, dominance in heterosexual relations leading to freedom of choice, was an important part of the challenge to romanticised constructs of femininity.[20] However, while chastity and purity were largely interpreted as outmoded patriarchal concepts, feminists stressed the importance of being in control of one's sexuality, of being a thinking woman. As such, Neville's interpretation of a genuine sexual revolution with limitless penetrative sex is disturbing.[21] The underground might well be praised for its rally cry 'Make Love Not War', but uninhibited sex equally resonated with such claims as 'In one afternoon I fucked fifteen girls.'[22]

While seduction is oppressive, in that it implies persuasion to comply, the accolade of 'freewheeling' is problematic, not least when tied to such riders as 'One way to a girl's mind is through her cunt.'[23] The fact that Neville singles out Janis Joplin as a 'freewheeling woman' also highlights her importance to the debates surrounding sexual equality. The question that arises, then, is the extent to which feminist debates of the period (on image and representation, gender and sexuality) provided an appropriate climate and agenda for such women performers as Joplin, and whether there was any real opportunity to challenge sexual stereotyping given the power of the madonna–whore binary.

NOTES AND REFERENCES

1 Widgery, D. (1973) 'What Went Wrong?', *OZ*, no. 48.
2 Roszak, T. (1970) *The Making of a Counter Culture. Reflections on the Technocratic Society and its Youthful Opposition*, London: Faber and Faber, p. 58.
3 Harris, K., 'New Alliances: Socialist-feminism in the Eighties', *Feminist Review* 31, p. 35.
4 Herbert Marcuse and R.D. Laing were both leading mentors of the counter culture. R.D. Laing *The Politics of Experience and the Bird of Paradise* (London: Penguin Books, 1967) was particularly important to the British counter culture. Marcuse's major works at the time were *Reason and Revolution. Hegel and the Rise of Social Theory* (Oxford: Oxford University Press, 1941); *Soviet Marxism. A Critical Analysis* (Routledge & Kegan Paul, 1958); *One Dimensional Man* (Boston: Beacon Press, 1964).
5 See Millett, K. (1970) *Sexual Politics*, London: Abacus.
6 Psychoanalytic feminists see Freud as either liberating or repressive. In the 1970s, Betty Friedan, Shulamith Firestone and Kate Millett maintained that women's social position and powerlessness had little to do with female biology *per se*, but rather the privileged socio-economic and cultural status it confers. Further, as Firestone points out, even though Freud helped women to confront sexuality openly, feminists should continue to criticise him for making procreative sex the be-all and end-all of women's existence.
7 See Grosz, E. (1990) 'Philosophy' in Gunew, S. *Feminist Knowledge: Critique and Construct*, London: Routledge, pp. 149–51.
8 *Ibid.*, pp. 293–4.
9 *Ibid.*, p. 295.
10 *Spare Rib* was launched by 'women who had mainly worked for the underground press and who wanted to put their skills to a cause with which they could identify; the bi-monthly *Women's Report* collated news and comment about other women; *Women's Voice* [was] produced by women in the International Socialist Party; and *Red Rag* [was] put out by an editorial collective of women within the Communist Party and unaligned to socialist-feminists'. Wander, M. (1986) *Carry on Understudies. Theatre and Sexual Politics*, London: Routledge, p. 14.
11 *Helix*, September 1968 in Neville, R. (1971) *Play Power*, London: Paladin, p. 71.
12 'Miss America as Military Death Mascot', *International Times*, 14–27 February, 1969.
13 'Ask not what your country can do for you; ask what you can do for your country' (John F. Kennedy). For women this involved 'keeping the home fires burning' and actively encouraging the male to fight and die for his country.
14 Neville, *op. cit.*, p. 72.
15 Lydon, S., *Ramparts*, in Neville, *op. cit.* p. 73.
16 *Helix, op. cit.*, p. 71.
17 In 1969, ninety-nine publications were officially listed as members of the Underground Press Syndicate (UPS). Seven were published in New York, thirteen in California and eleven in London. Most of the newspapers were subscribers to Liberation News Service (LNS), the Reuters of the underground. Based in New York, it mailed twice-weekly bulletins of news, poetry, gossip, essays, interviews, photographs and cartoons to over 300 papers, and the estimated total readership of member publications was 5 million. Many of the big-city underground papers circulated internationally. *East Village Voice, East Village Other, Los Angeles Free Press, Kaleidoscope, Other Scenes* and *Fusion* were distributed, albeit haphazardly, throughout England and Europe. *OZ* and *IT*

were exported from London to the US and Amsterdam, Stockholm, Munich and other European centres. *IT* – formerly *International Times* until Lord Thomson's *Times* instigated breach of copyright proceedings – was the British underground's first and only regular newspaper. See Neville, *op. cit.*, for a more detailed discussion.

18 Although the underground generally had come out against pornography, Neville, among others, regarded *Screw* as satirical and amusing. Feminists did not agree.

19 Neville*, op. cit.*, p. 59. The counter culture shared, with feminists, a concern to question and transform the traditional institutions which reproduce dominant cultural–ideological relations – the family, education, media, marriage and the sexual division of labour. In particular, the move towards establishing a cultural base for New Left politics involved setting up new types of community, new family patterns, new personal identities, as exemplified in, for example, the extended family structure of the Grateful Dead.

20 The codes of romance which underpinned, for example, teenage magazines directed at the pubescent girl, were generally directed towards moving her 'safely' from family of origin to family of destiny. Sexual experience extended no further than the kiss, and the chosen partner was approved by both families. The young male is depicted as 'clean living' and caring, favourable attributes for the future husband and father. This coding persisted in teeny-bopper chart songs which contrasted with the more sexual songs associated with the rock genre.

21 It is a somewhat sobering thought to reflect that Neville, hailed at the time as 'totally involved in what he is doing' (*IT*), and whose book *Play Power* was considered to be the 'best work yet on what in pleasanter days used to be called the Lover Generation' (*Rolling Stone)* and which 'should be read in every school, office, army hut or other institution' (John Peel) should interpret a genuine sexual revolution with limitless penetrative sex. Quotes from the back cover of *Play Power, op. cit.*

22 Reply by a member of the Cohn-Bendit movement, when asked what he remembered most about his days behind the barricades. *Ibid*, p. 62.

23 *Ibid.*, p. 74.

4

TRY, JUST A LITTLE BIT HARDER

Janis Joplin and the search for personal identity

As discussed previously, both the counter culture and progressive rock were largely dominated by men who were reactionary in their attitude towards women. Inscribed as de-sexualised earth mothers, fantasy figures and easy lays, there was little real opportunity to either take control or enjoy the prestige afforded to male artists. Indeed, while the more challenging stance of progressive rock offered a new arena for experimentation,[1] the opportunities for women performers remained largely conventional in that they were not encouraged to compose or to become instrumentalists. Further, the emphasis on image remained. Front-line performers were expected to *look* feminine and in retrospect it is obvious that attitudes towards women artists had not undergone any significant change. To achieve success, it seemed that women had to take men on at their own game, and within the arena of rock this involved drink, drugs and sexual promiscuity.

As such, it is not insignificant that so many articles on Janis Joplin should focus in on her image. 'An orgasmic smile on her pimply, puffy face, she clutched and beat the air with her fists, kicked, shook her ass, scratched her frizzy hair, mouthed the microphone with a whispered groan, wailed and shouted, then danced away, clattering her plastic bracelets.'[2] Although it is not proposed to provide a linguistic analysis of the above text, it is nevertheless interesting to focus briefly on the choice of adjectives and how they potentially relate to a background of expectancies, what could have been said, but was not. There is, for example, an immediate attitudinal lexis: 'pimply, puffy, frizzy, plastic' which situates Joplin as conventionally unattractive in terms of traditional representations of feminine beauty. Returning briefly to my earlier discussion of Miss America, it is apparent that what is valued is how she looks. She has to be young, a tanned landscape of thighs and mammary glands. Within rock culture, women were equally valued for their looks, as evidenced by the 'goddess' cult of, for example, Marianne Faithfull and Anita Pallenberg,[3] models such as Twiggy and Jean Shrimpton and the particular inscriptions of women within the songs themselves, as suggested previously. While it is recognised that styles and images are subject to change[4] it is nevertheless suggested that an

51

understanding of the feminine within musical discourse relies on an interrogation of the ways in which representations are made within a social system, how they contribute towards commonsense ways of knowing, believing and experiencing.

As musicians, women have traditionally been viewed as singers, positioned in front of a band, the focus of audience attention not simply for what they sing, but for how they look. The preferred face, then, is certainly not pimply and puffy and, as a front-line singer, Joplin immediately confounds traditional audience expectations. The 'meaning' of female singer is turned on its head. Her hair is frizzy, her bracelets plastic. There is also a suggestion of neurosis. Joplin is the 'irrational woman', exposing her anxieties: 'she clutched and beat the air with her fists, kicked, scratched her frizzy hair'. When contextualised by the phrase 'an orgasmic smile on her pimply, puffy face' there are connotations of a certain crazed sexuality, an abandonment that situates her as 'other' to the norm of white female singers.

The relationship between overt sexuality and hysteria had long been established within patriarchal discourse. As Luce Irigaray points out, 'what we know about woman, including her sexual desire, has been told us from a male point of view. The only woman we know is the "masculine" feminine, the phallic woman, woman as man sees her'.[5] Traditionally, the phallic woman is submissive. Soft, gentle, non-violent and moral, she is controllable, pure, and, as such, 'the cornerstone of a healthy society'.[6] As an ideological construct, the juxtaposition of purity with a healthy society is powerful. As wife, the woman is characterised by stability, constancy and fidelity, loving rather than sexual. As mother, she is gentle and patient, her morality ensuring a virtuous continuity in the transition from embryo to child to adult. As such, the sexually active woman can only be juxtaposed as aberrant, as deviating from the established norm. Unlike her Madonna-like counterpart, she is a woman of flesh and blood, earthy rather than spiritual. Uncontrollable, degenerate, inclined to dissipation either through autoeroticism or through an 'unhealthy' sexual appetite, she is clearly not fitted to a role as wife and mother.

The binary relationships between pure/impure, active/passive, earthy/spiritual are deeply embedded in religious dichotomies. It is equally apparent that they are constructed within the terrain of representations, through art and literature, where images 'can be taken as referring to something else, something "real" ... something which was not made but is'.[7] Woman as mother, as nurturer, carer, is represented as fragile and pure through an association with both the Virgin, 'Holy Motherhood', and as flower. As Djikstra writes 'she was, in the eyes of painters, the bluebell, the rose, the *fleur de lys* made flesh', calming, refreshing, innocent, she was 'the Eternal Feminine on its best behaviour'.[8] A lack of purity, earthiness, can thus be represented through an association with the obverse. Here, representations of women are characterised by a lack of fragility. They display an 'indiscriminate abundance, a vast expanse of mottled and distended skin'.[9] Conversely, they are the seductress, the exotic head-huntress, the Salome, the Judith, 'a plumply enflowered vamp with sharp, hungry teeth and a malicious glint in her eyes'.[10]

The opposition between pure/impure, controllable/uncontrollable is also present in the fundamental binary, active/passive. The passive woman is the 'natural' woman, controllable; the active woman is uncontrollable and, as such, lies outside the dominant symbolic order. Within the field of representations 'uncontrollable' and 'un-natural' are frequently drawn into association through the image of the orgiastic dancer. Writing in 1912, Havelock Ellis cited dancers as having a special connection to hysteria and the sexual organs: 'One reason why women love dancing is because it enables them to give harmonious and legitimate emotional expression to this neuromuscular irritability which might otherwise escape in more explosive forms.'[11] The association of Joplin as dancer, shaking 'her ass', with Joplin as singer who 'mouthed the microphone with a whispered groan, wailed and shouted' is thus strangely resonant with late-Victorian representations of the Bacchantes whose 'wild dances, and insane cries and jubilation'[12] aligned them with nymphomaniacs, women with uncontrollable sexual desires, decadent, savage and wild – a description which resonates with popular representations of Joplin herself.

The 'meaning' of woman as controllable/uncontrollable, pure/impure, as constructed in and through representations, is persistent. As Threadgold observes, 'meanings are made, but they are also reified, 'used', 'consumed' .... (they) contribute to the social production of consciousness and of self-consciousness ... of knowing and believing and experiencing'.[13] Woman as flower, as fragile, as desirable, continues to be embedded and valorised within patriarchal societies.[14] As a cultural construction it underpins the social significance of desired feminine behaviour and desirable bodily attributes. As the review indicates, Joplin was the obverse.

As a teenager, Joplin had been stigmatised as different. Interested in poetry, music, art and reading, she was the 'weirdo', the misfit in a conforming 1950s' Texan society. Graduating from high school in 1960, she initially attended Lamar College before moving on to the University of Texas. As a female, peer group acceptance depends largely upon conformity to the accepted norm. Intelligence is tolerated, overt cleverness is perceived as aberrant, but fatness, spottiness, situates the woman as undesirable. Excluded by the prom-queen codes of femininity which dominated university life, and nominated by a contemporary 'the ugliest man on the campus' (a title she did not win) it is not surprising that Joplin's self-perception as attractive was based on the uneasy equation of frequency of lovers as an affirmation of love.

Joplin's outspoken attitude towards sex was widely publicised, but if her favourite, and most quoted metaphors, 'singing as fucking' and 'fucking as liberation' conformed to the ideology of rock, there was, at best, a limited congruence. With the counter culture defining freedom for women almost exclusively in terms of sexual freedom, the concept of sexual liberation had become charged with significance. At one level it signified a symbolic journey, from chastity to freedom of choice, a valorisation of female hedonism, the active female rather than the passive recipient. However, as sexual freedom continued to be defined by the male as availability, a woman who wholeheartedly embraced the dictum of unlimited fucking remained, essentially, submissive. As such, the blurring of the boundaries between being 'loved' and being 'fucked', being 'wanted' and being 'available' provoked a confusing instability. One night stands may uproot the common preconceptions of romance, but for the woman, they also evoke a sense of compromise. 'To love somebody' merges into 'to love anybody' and in doing so, reaffirms the blues dictum of 'Women is Losers'. The extent to which Joplin consciously understood the limitations of sexual rebellion is uncertain, but within the overall framework of her musical output, from her idiosyncratic covers of blues to the posthumous *Pearl* album, there is a fragile imbalance, a sense of sexual magnetism hinged to a self-tormenting insecurity.

Joplin's vulnerability, her need for affection, is particularly apparent in the 1967 recording of 'Ball and Chain', when she was lead singer with Big Brother and the Holding Company. Written by Big Mama Thornton, the lyrics initially suggest the archetypal wailing blues of the abandoned woman:

> Oh, oh baby, why you wanna do these ol' mean things to me
> Because you know I love you and I'm so sick and tired of livin' in misery

With Joplin, the sense of suffering persists, but there is an individuality of expression which suggests a personal experience of the immediacy of rejection. The bittersweet moan of the opening lines projects a claustrophobic intimacy, a sense of entrapment within the environment, which is enhanced by the imprisoning regularity of the vocal delivery: 'sittin' by my window, just lookin' out at the rain'. The structural simplicity implicit in blues is initially used to underpin the monotony of the situation. It suggests a conforming resignation in its repetitive rhythmic structure which draws the listener into the 'bluesness' of the situation. Blues is falling like rain.

The final couplet then moves towards an enactment of masochistic ecstasy 'love's got a hold on me, feels like a ball and chain' which focuses in on the meaning of blues itself, the suffering that comes from allowing the negative to dominate. At this point, the sense of resignation that characterises blues sensibility is swept aside, and Joplin turns introspection into anguish through primordial blue-note wails, 'tell me, honey, why has everything gone wrong, all gone wrong?'

Structurally, the song moves between an intimacy of delivery, breathy and close to the microphone, and an angst-ridden, power-driven scream. The reflective nature of the first and third verses is underpinned by the melodic contouring of the vocal which hovers around the interval of a blue third,[15] providing a musical metaphor for the questioning uncertainty implicit in love. The second and fourth verses move from the reflective to the intimacy of pain itself. The phrases are sharp and jagged, driven by a piercing insistence on vocal highs 'I want to know why' and exposed syllables 'b-b-b-b-baby', 'oh-woh-woh-woh-woh ... it ain't fair baby' before returning to a reprise of the first verse. This time, Joplin half-speaks the words, before moving into the final rawness of self-realisation 'this cannot b-b-b-be in vain, oh no. Tell me once in a while, why's love like a ball and a chain?'

To describe the end of 'Ball and Chain' as cathartic would be, perhaps, an over-statement. Rather, Joplin's singing, with its whispered intimacies ('I know you're gonna miss me baby') and anguished cries ('it's gonna last'), conveys an intensity which is both uninhibited and vulnerable. There is a turbulent self-awareness of the punishing nature of a love which both enables and torments, and which moves the traditional aesthetics of blues sensibilities into the underlying dilemmas of the 1960s' woman. Reason and emotion, defiance and resignation are replaced by a despairing protest of 'Why me?' which places Joplin at the centre of her own personal dilemma as woman, confused and 'fucked around'.

As Steven C. Smith wrote in 1992,

> Bluesness is neither purely passive, pure suffering, nor active, pure doing .... What the doers of blues do is hold themselves in a certain configuration in which the very forces that threaten them come to trace lines in their identity; the raggedness of oppressed existence becomes their own bold signature.[16]

Aptly titled 'Blues and our mind-body problem', Smith characterises blues as 'knowing the score', as 'adopting the spunky irony that best fits the situation'.[17] The focus on a 'mind-body problem' and 'knowing the score' seems particularly apposite to Joplin where an uncompromising commitment to sexual excess was tempered by insecurities and a consummate need to be loved.

As early as 1965, Joplin had identified her 'Trouble in Mind ' as man-centred. Partly self-deprecating, partly self-tormenting, it could appear, initially, that her choice of material was largely determined by an early love of such singers as Odetta and Bessie Smith. However, while it would be fair to state that 'bluesness' comes from want, desire, absence and frustration, the traditional interpretation of women as victims, moaning for lost love, is an over-generalisation. Clearly there are blues which express vulnerability, 'Empty Bed Blues' , 'You've Got to Give Me Some' (Bessie Smith), 'Lover Man, (Oh Where Can You Be?)' (Billie Holliday), where the woman's expression of sexuality resides in being wanted. But, as Rosetta Reitz points out,

> I discovered a lot of independent songs from the '20s with titles like 'Ain't Much Good in the Best of Men Nowadays', 'Movin' on Out of Here' or 'You Can't Sleep in my Bed' .... the question arose as to why was I finding blues songs saying 'I bake the best jelly roll in town', or 'I got the sweetest cabbage'? This is not a victim speaking .... My biggest coup was a test-pressing of Ida Cox's called 'One Hour Mama' .... She's saying I may need one hour or maybe four before I'm through, using the most beautiful metaphors she gives specific instructions about her requirements.[18]

Bessie Smith could be equally assertive, and her sexually explicit lyrics range from the search for her 'jelly roll' in 'Kitchen Man', a world-weary vulnerability in 'T'aint Nobody's Business if I Do', to a frustrated expression of longing in 'He's Got Me Goin' '.

It would thus appear that Joplin's choice of material reflected her own sense of inadequacy rather than a straightforward homage to blues queens. 'Tell Mama what you want ... I'll do what you choose', 'you didn't want a place in my life ... you left me here to face it all alone', 'Misery'. However, as Ellen Willis points out, 'Blues represented another external structure, one with its own contradictory tradition of sexual affirmation and sexist conservatism.'[19] As a broad generalisation, this is borne out by the countless songs which equate 'bluesness' with woman trouble, with desire, jealousy, guilt, and with a lyric explicitness, whether lascivious or complaining. Such lyrics equate largely with a knowingness about sex, about violence, about deprivation, and while it would be an over-generalisation to state that blues, as a genre, is unequivocally phallocentric, the language of blues is nevertheless significant. Passion and pain are acknowledged, but the sense of detachment or, as Smith puts it, 'spunky irony', constructs a pre-eminently masculine subjectivity whereby pain is 'ridden' – the devil got my woman – and where the female is either constrained or effectively silenced by 'moving on', 'hellhound on my trail'.

While the sense of being 'devilled by circumstances' is clearly not confined to the male, it is apparent that the language of blues both constructs and constrains.

> Because male dominance and female submission are the norm in something as fundamental as sexuality .... each and every element of the female gender stereotype is sexually charged ... a man takes a woman's sexuality, as it is mediated through her body, and through

his action proclaims that women's sexuality is for men – for what men want and need.[20]

For the male blues singer there is an underlying confidence ('The Red Rooster') and while this may be undermined by the physical pain of betrayal ('My First Wife Left Me'), the sense of being down ('Baby Please Don't Go', 'Moanin' for my Baby') is nevertheless counterbalanced by the reality of bouncing back ('Got my Mojo Working') and the certainty of sexual dominance ('Crawling King Snake').[21] Bluesness is 'knowing the score' and retaliating, 'most often in a violent way (and in the devil's company in, for example, 'Me and the Devil Blues').[22]

Male blues generally equate woman trouble with 'devil woman' (as referred to in my earlier discussion of Cream, pp. 38). The woman who defines her own sexuality, who refuses to conform, poses a challenge, and within the language of blues the solution is either to displace the problem on to a mythical other, to leave, or to situate the woman as 'doomed and unhappy'. Blues, then, constructs woman as 'other' and, while Joplin's vocals project a desperation tempered by lust and power, she would nevertheless appear to remain imprisoned within the confines of blues sensibility, 'like a ball and chain'.

Although the declamatory style of blues was a key ingredient in Joplin's vocal style, it is nevertheless evident from the recordings made with Big Brother and the Holding Company that the band were not always instrumentally supportive, and often appeared more interested in exploring the expressive potential of their own 'progressive' guitar-led rock. Whereas acoustic blues had relied largely on an intimacy of delivery, where the emotional weight of the lyric content is matched by the nuance of, for example, blue-note swerves, pulling/bending, and such formalised tensions as roughness of vocal and instrumental timbre, rock is power-driven, rhythmically emphatic and built around techniques of arousal and climax. Unlike acoustic blues, where the guitar provides a sonic intensification of the singer's loneliness and sense of alienation, and where call and response are an integral part of the projection of pain, rock is both complex and competitive. Above all it is guitar-led, riff-driven and heavily amplified. The singer competes rather than leads, 'the band throws down the gauntlet in beats and squealing riffs, the singer accepts the challenge and raises the stakes with each wild phrase'.[23] As such, Joplin was confronted by the problems inherent in a musical style which took on the blues tradition of sexual affirmation and sexist conservatism, but which harnessed it to a performance style which valued hardness, virtuosity and control. Her solution was both confrontational and conforming: lead with arrogance, project toughness and be 'one of the boys'.

'Piece of My Heart', released on the album *Cheap Thrills*, is considered one of Joplin's trademark songs. From the taunting 'Come on' with which the song opens, through the anguish of pain 'you never hear me when I cry at night' to the assertive 'I'm gonna show you, baby, that a woman can be tough', Joplin demonstrates her power as a rock singer. Her delivery is essentially rhythmic, tight and pushy. The song is again characterised by two contrasting moods: a pensive reflection on what she gave and how she was treated, and the strident 'take, 'break', 'have' of the chorus. It is interesting to note how the verse section suggests, once again, a sense of containment within the rhythmic structure. Joplin sings on the beat, following the essential melodic contouring of the lyrics. The words equally lack any sense of vocal elaboration and, underpinned by alternating major harmonies, the accompaniment is both functional and minimal

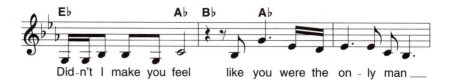

The move to C minor, and the vocal syncopation, thus suggests an underlying uncertainty which is juxtaposed by the major harmonies of 'it's never enough' and the resolute 'I'm gonna show you that a woman can be tough.'

The move into the chorus initially implies a deep-rooted sense of equivocation, with the word 'go' supported by Fminor7, and 'on' by Bb7, before the

powerfully assertive 'Take it !' From this point on there is little doubt that Joplin initiates the action. Supported by a male backing group (who act both as symbolic 'mental' props in their unaccompanied 'break it', 'have a', and a chorusing of assent in 'you know you've got it if it makes you feel good') the rhythm-driven vocal stays resolutely in an optimistic major. Any subservient connotations in the 'Take another little piece of my heart now, baby' are subverted by a tonal innuendo which constructs a feeling of ironic distancing. Joplin is not simply giving, as the words 'you know you've got it' might imply, but rather goading her lover into accepting her power as an active sensual force 'if it makes you feel good'. By singing this last phrase unaccompanied, there is equally a sense of confident detachment which reflects back on the 'didn't I make you feel like you were the only man' of the first verse. The 'didn't *I*' centres Joplin as the knowing lover, secure in her ability to deliver pleasure, while the 'like you were the only man' is undercut by uncertainty 'there have been/are/will be others.'

Within the structure of the song, the male ego is partially restored by the instrumental break, but even this is dominated by the challenging crescendo of Joplin's 'come on, come on, come on, come on !' As such, it was perhaps inevitable that she should be considered 'ballsy' by her male contemporaries. To an extent it was an accolade in a genre that valued male autonomy. At the same time, as her ex-lover Country Joe pointed out,

> sexism killed her. Everybody wanted this sexy chick who sang really sexy and had a lot of energy ... and people kept saying one of the things about her was that she was just 'one of the guys' .... that's a real sexist bullshit trip, 'cause that was fuckin' her head around ... she was one of the women. She was a strong, groovy woman.[24]

To an extent, the 'one of the guys' has a resonance with 'the ugliest male on the campus' and, although Joplin's status as female celebrity brought with it an opportunity to challenge the established conventions of beauty, and to take a countless stream of lovers, the accolade of strength was less apparent. Her split with Big Brother in 1968 may have evidenced a growing confidence to pursue her own career, but her subsequent addiction to heroin suggests a continuing sense of insecurity, 'What's gonna happen to me when I'm not number 1 any more?'[25]

Drugs were an integral part of the hippy scene and marijuana and LSD in particular were seen as enabling an exploration of the imagination and self-expression.[26] Heroin remained underground, but nevertheless it was perceived as the most conducive enabling drug for the performer.

> Heroin removes the need and replaces it with contentment. It takes the pain and turns it into pleasure ... It is enoughness in the extreme .... there is absolutely nothing you need or desire. It is a

59

spiritual encounter with yourself in a detached, euphoric, composed, contented state. It is completeness and warmth and serenity, security and ultimate peace.[27]

Both heroin and cocaine had been associated with the jazz scene since the 1920s and it is a well-known fact that such musicians as Billie Holliday, Charlie Parker and Bessie Smith relied on it to provide the sense of security and relaxation that is important to a well-rounded performance. In the 1960s Jim Morrison, Iggy Pop, Keith Richard, among many others, cited heroin as an enhancing drug which led to a relaxed state of mind while effecting a sense of control, two important factors in performance. The positive effects of heroin can include a feeling of invincibility, a lack of anxiety and stress. Possible side-effects are drowsiness and a slight slurring of speech. On the negative side, muscular spasms can, for example, affect the throat muscles, resulting in anxiety and leading to a constriction of tone. Withdrawal symptoms include aches, tremors, sweating and chills. Above all, the addict's constant need for heroin causes instability and, occasionally, violence. A continuing supply is vital.

Although Joplin's addiction to heroin is well-documented, there is no information on the type or quality of heroin used, dosage or tolerance level, or the extent to which this affected her performance. At the same time it is considered that such positive effects as an enhanced confidence level, serenity and security would have had the potential to affect her vocal expression. As Sugarman writes,

My whole brain slowed down and I was relaxed, calm and certain ... totally relaxed ... the insecurities I'd experienced had completely vanished .... Time, which had always been so unbearable to endure, simply melted away.[28]

The words are curiously apposite to Joplin's recording of 'Little Girl Blue' which evokes both a sense of timelessness, a relaxed delivery and a new delicate and compassionate insight into 'bluesness'.

Preceded by an arpeggiated solo guitar and bass, the opening lines of the verse are characterised by a sense of reflection. The tempo is slow and well suited to Joplin's lyrical interpretation. Her vocal style is relaxed, laidback, yet the phrasing comes across as confident and strong. She continually stretches the rhythmic confines of the piece by singing ahead and behind the beat, giving the song a deceptively lazy feel, 'what else is there to do?' The confidence in phrasing is equally evident in the contrast between words that simply follow the underlying melodic line, and which imply a directness of expression,

it's time, somebody told you

'cause you gotta know
that ....

words which suggest an overspill of impacted emotion as they fight to be contained within the bar structure:

all you're ever gonna count, or gonna lean or, or gonna feel ...

and words which reflect back on one of Joplin's metaphors of' bluesness

it's like those raindrops
that are fallin' down, honey,
all around you

The effect is both to distance Joplin, as she advises and instructs, and to draw her into the continuing presence of the blues as the song resonates with the sentiments earlier expressed in 'Ball and Chain', 'sittin' by my window, and I was lookin' out at the rain'. This time there is no uninhibited outburst. Rather, Joplin uses stresses and accents to disturb the rhythmic flow and to create variation and interest. In verse one, 'Sit there, counting ....' is broken by a reflective 'mmmm'; in verse two, the same words are anticipated by a melisma on 'Oh'. In the final verse, it is the 'there' that is opened out through an elaboration of pitch. This sense of rhythmic invention is projected with a sense of confidence and ease and is matched by a more controlled vibrato, which is reserved primarily for long, sustained notes at the ends of phrases, such as the word 'blue' with which the verses end.[29] The careful orchestration in the introduction to the second verse (where strings add an underlying warmth to the sparseness of the solo guitar line) and which continues into the second and third verses, is also indicative of Joplin's ability to control and shape musical effect. In this instance, they enhance the sense of compassion and empathy inherent in the lyrics,

My unhappy, my unlucky and my little, oooh, girl blue
I know you're unhappy
ooooooooh,
Oh honey, oh baby I know just how you feel

I would suggest that 'Little Girl Blue' evidences a new maturity in Joplin's exploration of the blues. There are few of the moaning, howling eruptions that characterised the performance of 'Ball and Chain' or 'Piece of my Heart'. Rather the song has an underlying sense of compassion and warmth, and an empathy with the 'bluesness' of being a woman. As such, while the delivery suggests that there is a certain homology with the sense of relaxation and control associated with heroin, it is equally possible that it taps into Joplin's alter-ego, that the' little girl blue' is an expression of her

61

bisexuality. The song asks for, rather than demands, attention. The 'I need you, I can't live without you, you can treat me bad and I'll still come running' has gone, to be replaced by a sense of 'I will show you who I am', through a delivery which has both strength and beauty. It is a musical expression of 'have courage, you are not alone', to 'try, just a little bit harder'.

The sense of knowingness is also present in the self-penned 'Kozmic Blues'. Here, Joplin acknowledges time, 'livin' and lovin', and a lack of certainty 'I can't help you no more than I did when just a girl'. Again, there is a sense of growing maturity, which is reflected both in the lyrics and in her growing knowledge and experience of blues. In particular, Joplin demonstrates an acute sense of appropriate stylistic characterisation, one which constructs a mood of melancholy introspection – the slow tempo, minor feel, and the bass chromatic descent of the piano introduction.[30] This time, she pays particular attention to word-painting:.'Time ... keeps movin' on' and 'Friends .... they turn away' are reflective and seem shrouded with an underlying sense of cynicism which resonated with the reality of Joplin's life. 'On stage I make love to 25,000 people, then I go home alone ... the more she gave, the less she got, and that honey, it ain't fair.'[31] Her tone, which sounds initially older, more tired, complements the 'I never found why', and the stop-time effect of 'I keep pushin' so hard an' babe, I keep try'n to make it right to another lonely day', words which drive against the restrictions of the underlying rhythmic structure to provide a musical underpinning for the sense of frustration expressed by the lyrics.

The chorus then moves to another Joplin trademark, the sense of equivo-cation which is underpinned by alternating major/minor harmonies. The sense of determination which characterises 'But it don't make no' is immedi-ately undercut by the minor mood of 'difference babe' which, in turn, moves back to the major for the resilient 'and I know that I can always try'. Any sense of buoyancy is, however, short-lived, and the chorus ends with a graphic musical metaphor for Joplin's continuing sense of insecurity. The 'I better use it till the day I die' is anticipated by a D major chord which moves downwards to A minor, with the 'day I die' highlighted and isolated both by the move from the major 6/8 to the minor 3/8, and a moving and controlled melisma over the word 'die' itself as it slowly subsides into the introspective piano outro.

Although the Kozmic Blues Band can be considered a transitional group, there is little doubt that Joplin's self-awareness as a performer evidenced, overall, a growing maturity. Her final sessions, which appear on the posthu-mous *Pearl* album equally indicate new directions coupled with a sense of taking stock. The preoccupation with time, the emphasis on 'live for today' is there in 'Get It while You Can'; 'Half Moon' injects acid rock into an otherwise standard roadhouse blues; 'Cry Baby', while revisiting the theme of 'You Gotta a Woman Waitin' for You', demonstrates a controlled seduc-tiveness in its extended melismas and blue note swerves.

It is, however, songs such as 'One Night Stand' which suggest most clearly the sense of new direction. Accompanied by the Paul Butterfield Blues Band, there is both a feeling of development from the sensual expressiveness of 'Little Girl Blue', and a move to a more sophisticated jazz idiom. Joplin's phrasing is relaxed and confident and her seemingly effortless delivery of such wordy lyrics as 'don't you know you're nothing more than a one night stand' has a tonal clarity reminiscent of Billie Holliday. In particular, her rhythmic and melodic ideas project a sense of precision and confidence. The timing of such phrases as 'When I'm on the road and playing in a town without a name' is effected with apparent ease. The emphasis is on the rhythm, and there is a carefully balanced interplay between the vocal line and the brass response. What most distinguishes the song, however, is the extent to which Joplin's voice is integrated with the rest of the sound. The fact that the musicians are working alongside her provides both a stimulating context and a sense of balance. The band neither backs, nor competes. Rather there is a sense of relaxed dialogue between the vocal and the rhythm section and, consequently, Joplin's performance comes across as coherent and controlled.

Whereas the smoothness in production of 'One Night Stand' suggests a studio performance, 'Tell Mama', with its raunchy delivery and upbeat tempo, comes across as the encore number to a successful gig. Loud and raucous, the full-throated 'tell mama baby' cuts through the guitar solo, suggesting that Joplin is fully in control, a point that is supported by her extended improvisation, partly narrated, partly sung, which implies a confident and conspiratorial exchange with the audience. 'If you're a woman I can only assume that you know what you're looking for ... I know what you're looking for, and I figured it out when I was 14 years old .... I tell you what you need man, you need a sweet-loving mama, babe, a sweet-talking baby, someone to listen to you, someone to use you, walk, talk, want you, need you .....' Culminating in 'anything I can do, do for you', the overall impression is of a red-hot, if slightly self-indulgent, blues mama.

This sense of characterisation is also present in 'Try, Just a Little Bit Harder'. Recorded live with the Full Tilt Boogie Band, Calgary, during the Canadian Festival Express, the song is presaged by the anecdotal story of the younger woman who scored first by getting up early. 'That chick hit the streets at noon ... every time you're looking for a little piece of action, and you ain't getting any ... you'd better try harder man.' Funky and upbeat, John Till's power-driven guitar complements the hurtling vocal solo of 'if it's a dream .... I don't want .... nobody to wake me' and the assertive 'Try, oh yeah' of the chorus. Stylistically reminiscent of the Rolling Stones' stomping classic 'Sympathy for the Devil', the male chorusing on 'Try, Just a Little Bit Harder' effects a sense of sexual urgency which complements Joplin's 'come on', 'push on', 'work', 'a little bit more', 'push on' as she moves against the stridently rhythmic piano accompaniment with a panting 'try, try, try'. As the tempo speeds up, stabbing piano chords move the song to the climactic 'Try, oh yeah ... woooh, oh yeah'. The song comes across as a showbiz performance, not least in the final 'Mind, don't you forget!', to provide a particular insight into the intensity and excitement of Joplin's concerts. In particular, the simulated sex of the final chorus reflects her own attitude 'my music's supposed to make you want to fuck',[32] a point which was picked up on by promoters in Houston who banned Joplin for 'her attitude in general', and which had resulted in her arrest some two years earlier for using 'vulgar and indecent language' at a concert.

Pearl, then, evidences both continuities and new directions and while the album overall reflects Joplin's prowess as a blues rock singer, it is interesting to note that the song which opens and closes the album harks back to her early days as a folk singer in Texas, where she once shared the stage with the country blues musician Mance Lipscomb. Recorded soon after Joplin had heard Kris Kristofferson's original, the two versions of 'Me and Bobby McGee' provide a particular insight into Joplin's crafting of a song.

Self-accompanied on acoustic guitar, the first version has an underlying hesitancy, doubts about her ability as a guitarist which are expressed both before and after the song. 'Not that I play that great .... it's too loud .... can't play that good' and which continue to inform the vocal delivery of the lyrics themselves. Gentle, direct and occasionally underpinned by blues inflections, there is an omnipresent feel of self-doubt. Musing and nuanced, the song again picks up on need, on being wanted, being loved and being alone again. Although the lyrics have a tendency towards sentimentality, Joplin's low-keyed vocal has a directness which cuts through the nostalgia, moving the folk associations of the politics of freedom into a personal confrontation with the reality of love between two people: 'feelin' good was good enough for me ... good enough for me and Bobby McGee'.

There are, however, moments when the songs slips into a feel of 'first take', not least in the outro and the repetitive 'la la la ... Bobby McGee'. The final version, is however, more positive, more assertive. There is a wholesale reworking of the song, a tremendous example of Joplin's musical creativity. The weaknesses have been ironed out and there is an overall sense of refinement and direction. To an extent this is provided by the backing band which forces Joplin's vocals to the front, overcoming the hesitancy of the guitar self-accompaniment of the first version. The tempo is more upbeat, and this time the 'la la la ... Bobby McGee' is given a sense of exaltation as it crescendos to an ecstatic 'I'm calling my lover, I'm calling my man .... hey, hey, hey Bobby McGee' before the powerful stride piano outro, overlaid by organ and percussion underpins the final 'Hey Hey Hey Bobby McGee, yeah'.

The placing of 'Bobby McGee' on the posthumous *Pearl* album was clearly an artistic decision. The final version was recorded on 25 September 1970. 'Half Moon' and 'Happy Trails', the birthday message to John

Lennon, were recorded on the 26th, 'Mercedes Benz' on 1 October, three days before her death. Recorded in one take, the song is preceded by a throaty chuckle and a brief discussion with producer Paul Rothchild, 'What did I say? No, this song ... Are you ready? Is the tape moving? I can do this song in one take ... don't count on me .... What? Well, I'll do the best I can.'

The presaging 'I'd like to sing a song of great social and political import. It goes like this' suggests, initially, a humorous dig at the somewhat inflated seriousness associated with many of the protest songs of the 1960s. The first two verses equally imply a humorous self-anecdote on her roving lifestyle, the need for a car, the colour TV to see her through the lonely nights in anonymous hotel rooms. At the same time, Joplin's vocal delivery expresses an underlying rawness, and it is not difficult to understand why the song was considered too heavy to close the album. The last verse, in particular, is too close to the reality of her death:

> Oh lord, won't you buy me a night on the town
> I'm counting on you lord
> Please don't let me down.
> Prove that you love me, and buy the next round
> Oh lord, wont you buy me a night on the town?

After an evening of drinking and bar-hopping with her band, Joplin returned to the Landmark Hotel, Los Angeles, where she died a few hours later from an overdose of heroin. The 'Everyone together now ....' thus takes on an ironic undertow as Joplin moves into a reprise of the first verse. There is no 'everyone'. She sings on alone and ends, as she starts with a spoken 'that's it' and another deep-throated chuckle.

Integration versus self-identity

Death always raises the question of retrospection, 'what was it about his/her life that was special'. For the famous, it equally exposes the problems, the weaknesses. Joplin was no exception, 'a flawed personality crippled by a drug habit',[33] 'throughout her life, Joplin fought insecurities about her sexual magnetism; she always hungered for proof that she could be loved'.[34] Even such accolades as 'She offered women an alternative and showed how far it was possible to go', are tempered by a sting in the tail 'which made her death even more poignant because she blew it.'[35]

For the custodians of public morality, it is evident that Joplin's death provided another opportunity to castigate the 1960s for its indulgence, its experimentation with drugs, and its hedonism. It is equally evident that her death highlighted the problems associated with the utopian philosophy of personal freedom which underpinned the counter culture's stand against the dominant ideology. While it would be reasonable to suggest that Joplin's personal edict of 'get it while you can' resulted in an excessive self-indulgence, not least in her drinking, drug addiction, temperamental outbursts and sexual escapades, it is equally apparent that these character traits were exacerbated by being a successful woman in an all-male rock environment where success hinged on being able to keep up and be 'one of the boys'. Within the context of a psychedelically charged environment, where colour associations spilled over into a performing arena which valued larger-than-life personalities, Joplin's dilemma as performer devolved around two conflicting polarities, integration versus self-identity.

In retrospect, it would appear that she was confronted with the personal and, probably, subconscious choice of reversing the codes associated with masculine/feminine, attempting to neutralise their effects, or demonstrating that the underlying ideologies surrounding the construction of sexualities and gendering can be independent of phallocentricism.[36] Her fronting of what can be considered an essentially male rock persona – rebellious and hard-living – suggested one viable route. It is obvious, however, that masculinity and femininity are valued quite differently in their sexed context. In a society which extols competitiveness, and where the 'fight' is seen as the ultimate demarcator of hardness and as a means whereby the best is selected from the rest, 'toughness' becomes a male accolade, a synonym for strength.

For the woman, however, such behavioural traits exude both a sense of the unnatural and the deviant. Joplin's aggressiveness marked her as uncontrollable, unnaturally active, and earthy and, as such, lying outside the dominant symbolic order. Thus, while her performing career suggests both a challenge and a compliance with the masculine codes of power, dominance, hierarchy and competition inherent in rock, it is suggested that her physicality, her fist fight with a Hell's Angel over a bottle of bourbon, the constant play on 'who's got the biggest balls', was interpreted, at the time, as either imitative or confrontational. At best, it represented a woman competing in a man's world, 'accepting the carrot, not avoiding the stick',[37] outdoing everyone in an attempt to prove herself. More often it was seen as 'mannish' behaviour, with the inevitable consequence that Joplin's wildness and assertiveness marked her as degenerate, rather than equal.

It is equally apparent that the constant emphasis on Joplin as 'one of the guys' reverberated uneasily with her underlying vulnerability, one of the character traits most commonly identified as accounting for her need for reassurance and her emotional outbursts. The image of a liberated rock goddess, who could sing with conviction 'I'm gonna show you that a woman can be tough' was constantly undermined by petulant outbursts at lost lovers and a public loss of control. There was also a lack of congruence between such masculine codes of conduct as hard-drinking-tough-talking and her love of flamboyant, sensual clothes, her long hair. Clearly, clothes are important to the portrayal of identity, and Joplin's exotic dress codes, the 'sleazofreak' costumes, the tattoos on her wrist and over her heart, suggest a guise which served both as a visual analogy for the traditional blues mama associations of brothel and bar, and an exotic masking of the reality of her pock-marked skin and intermittent weight problems. As Ellen Willis perceptively points out, 'women needed images simply to survive. A woman typically proceeded from the assumption that men would not allow her to be her "real" self'.[38]

Although it is difficult to come to any definitive conclusions as to Joplin's 'real self', it is nevertheless significant that she never openly acknowledged her bisexuality. While it is hypothetical to suggest that this might have reconciled the uncomfortable duality of her hard-drinking-tough-talking butch persona and the more vulnerable expression of her femme-sexuality ('It ain't fair ... this can't be ... I just wanted to hold you .... All I ever wanted to do was to love you'), it is evident that this was a matter of choice. There were precedents for blues singers to express their bisexuality, not least in the cross-race, cross-gender parties in Harlem during the 1920s.

> Ma Rainey, Bessie Smith, Alberta Hunter, Jackie 'Moms' Mabley, Josephine Baker, Ethel Waters, and above all, Gladys Bentley, cele-brated lesbian sex .... Many of the blues songs she and others sang mocked male sexual anxieties and revelled in female subjectivity:
> Went out last night with a crowd of my friends.
> They must've been women, 'cause I don't like men[39]

Joplin, however, appeared to be too bound by the conventions of her small-town upbringing to expose herself to the problems surrounding lesbian relationships. In the States, lesbian and gay male territories had been estab-lished in New York, Chicago, San Francisco and Los Angeles, but even so, sex laws generally remained harsh. As Gayle S. Rubin points out,

> A single act of consensual but illicit sex, such as placing one's lips upon the genitalia of an enthusiastic partner, is punished in many states with more severity than rape, battery, or murder. Each such genital kiss, each lewd caress, is a separate crime.[40]

While it is recognised that 'Sex law is not a perfect reflection of the prevailing moral evaluations of sexual conduct',[41] it is suggested that for a woman attempting to establish herself within the rock world, albeit one which outwardly embraced a freedom of sexuality, a public acknowledge-ment of bisexuality, would have attracted too much attention, not simply from the media, but equally from the state judiciary. Joplin was well aware that 'Interviewers don't talk about my singing as much as about my lifestyle'[42] and while it is possible that she could have taken her fans with her, and have said something about the real implications of feminine liberation, it is probable that the risk was too high. Even so, the implications of her bisexuality within her performances is interesting in that she attracted a strong following from both male and female fans alike. As Kaplan and Rogers point out, research indicates that

> sexual attraction is stronger to individuals who show a mix of male and female physical characteristics and of masculine and feminine behavioural traits .... In other words, a male may respond to a female not only because some of her physical and behavioural attributes are 'feminine', but because some of them are distinctly 'masculine'.[43]

If this is the case, and if sexual attraction is most powerful when there is a mix of masculinity/femininity, then it is arguably the case that Joplin used this complexity to her advantage. Her songs assumed a heterosexual mode of address, male fans idolised her but, as Ellen Willis acknowledges,

> something I always noticed and liked about Janis: unlike many other female performers, she never made me feel as if I were crashing an orgy that consisted of her and the men in the audience. When she got it on at a concert, she got it on with everybody.[44]

Whereas the problems associated with integration appear to be of their time, the sense of self-identity and difference spills over into the contemporary discourses surrounding feminine performance. To return briefly to Smith's discussion of blues as 'neither purely passive, pure suffering, nor active, pure doing ... that the very forces that threaten ... come to trace lines in their identity',[45] it is evident that Joplin's vocals projected both a sense of the extreme in her juxtaposition of lust and uncertainty. Her inventive vocal style suggests confrontation in the often vitriolic delivery, seduction, catharsis and humour, often expressed through the wry chuckle with which a song begins or ends. Her songs address the problems, the sexual needs and desires of women by drawing on the past, the strong blues singers such as Bessie Smith and Odetta, and by resiting established songs within the discourses of the 1960s. If the subject matter is rejection, then the reality of the 1960s suggested a viable alternative, go and find someone else, rather than accepting fate with resignation – 'get up early and catch a bit of the action'. The expression of love thus moves beyond the sentimental, the romantic, or indeed, the underlying discourse of blues itself. The woman is shown as an active sensual force, not a passive object of affection, as establishing her own agenda, albeit within the existing framework of an often male inscription of desire.

Joplin's performance style provides, above all, a particular trajectory into excess, raw emotion and, most significantly, a sense of power that was unique at the time. The fact that her sexuality comes across as contradictory is equally important. It suggests a grappling with the problems inherent in bisexuality, with the problems of image and representation and a revolt against conventional femininity, which was to find its real voice in the 1980s' generation of female rock artists. Above all, Joplin's short career, and a death that ironically established her as a rock icon, situates her less as a victim, or as someone who 'blew it', and more as a performer who raises a number of key issues: whether a woman has to have 'balls' to succeed in the brotherhood of rock; the extent to which image and personality are important in achieving musical success; whether the feminine subjective is musically different from the masculine subjective; and, in particular, the importance for women musicians to compose, perform and indeed, produce their own songs.

NOTES AND REFERENCES

1 Like the counter culture itself, rock musicians had opened up a range of divergent alternatives (blues, country, folk, Indian, raga) and romantic images of self-discovery (through their relationship to the metaphysical and hallucinogenic drugs) from which to compose their songs. It seems extraordinary that this diversity of experience was not seen as relevant to women musicians who were confronted with the very real problem of coming to terms with, rather than challenging, the male domain of rock culture which, since its inception in the 1950s, had remained resolutely fraternal in its structure and performance codes.

2 Pavletich, A. (1980) *Sirens of Song. The Popular Female Vocalist in America*, New York: Da Capo, p. 129. Joplin was outspoken about journalists who continually discussed her image rather than her singing. It is ironic that the quote is from a woman writer. She also identifies Joplin as one of the first female performers whose nipples could be seen through her transparent blouse – 'an irresistible draw for front line crowds'. Observations such as these are not opened out to discussion or critical debate. Rather they situate Joplin as a sexual object: the audience watch rather than listen.

3 Within rock culture there are four types of women: the goddess, who is generally the 'property' of lead band members, chosen for her looks; the boiler, the groupie who actively courts the one-night stand; the dodgy boiler (overly promiscuous and thus a potential carrier of disease); and the dog. This classification of women locks into the hierarchical structuring implicit within the rock 'entourage', from the band to the roadies, etc.

4 Clearly, such idealised representations change. Punk, for example, projects a representation of the female which ironically undercuts notions of romanticised femininity through the wearing of polythene bin-liners, safety pins etc. (See Chapter 7, 'Daughters of Chaos', pp. 95–118).

5 Cited in Tong, R. (1989) *Feminist Thought. A Comprehensive Introduction*, London: Routledge, p. 226. For a more detailed discussion of Luce Irigaray, see Chapters 8 and 9.

6 My discussion here draws particularly on the patriarchal discourse embedded in mid/late Victorian society and which continues to inform debates surrounding phallocentricity and representations of idealised femininity.

7 Threadgold, T. and Cranny-Francis, A. (eds) (1990) *Feminine and Masculine Representation*, London: Allen & Unwin, p. 2.

8 Djikstra, B. (1986) *Idols of Perversity. Fantasies of Feminine Evil in Fin-de-Siècle Culture*, London: Oxford University Press, p. 16.

9 *Ibid.*, p. 213. Djikstra identifies artists at the turn of the century who aligned the masculinised woman, the savage, the Amazonian, with the naked brawler, the feminist. Max Beckmann's 'Battle of the Amazons' is discussed as reinforcing the prevailing notion that women who strove to take on masculine traits were both degenerate and grotesque.

10 *Ibid.*, p. 376. The operatic stage was one of the major sites for depicting the head-huntress, warning the male of women's potential for cruelty. While Judith and Salome were particularly popular, other 'un-natural women' included Elektra (Strauss), Lulu (Berg) and Turandot (Puccini).

11 Ellis, H., *The Task of Social Hygiene*, cited in *Ibid.*, p. 244. Although dancing women were generally associated with sex-crazed women, the turn of the century evidenced such performers as Isadora Duncan. While she saw herself as a creative artist, such performers were nevertheless associated with hysterical eroticism.

12 It is interesting to note that Ada Pavletich draws on this comparison. 'To introduce her songs, she invented punch raps that allowed the audience a closer acquaintance with the person of Janis, 'the bachante, the eater of men' (*op. cit.*, p. 129). It is not clear whether this is meant as an accolade, but such comparisons, given their patriarchal connotations, reflect once again the emphasis on image and the overt sexism that caused so many problems in Joplin's career.

13 Threadgold and Cranny-Francis, *op. cit.*, p. 34. Bette Midler's film *The Rose* was supposedly based on the masochistic, hedonistic aspects of Joplin's life as constructed by the media. The choice of title is interesting in that it evokes the sexual imagery of the 'sick' rose (Blake), defiled by the 'invisible worm that flies in the night' rather than the associations of the rose with the Virgin (*Rosa Munda*).

14 Returning from a conference in Sydney in July, 1999 I was struck by the way in which the air hostesses on the Singapore Airline were all so similar in body size. Famously representing 'the face of Singapore' they had been chosen for their slenderness and femininity. Nothing really changes.

15 The indeterminate nature of the blues third is a defining characteristic of blues. It is unstable, neither major nor minor and thus suggests a sense of 'off-balance', of pleasure qualified by pain.

16 Smith, S.G., 'Blues and our mind-body problem', in Brady, B. and Horn, D. (eds) (1992) *Popular Music*, Vol. 11, No.1, Cambridge University Press, January, p. 50.

17 *Ibid.*, p. 48.

18 O'Brien, L. (1955) *She Bop. The Definitive History of Women in Rock, Pop and Soul*, London: Penguin Books, pp. 13–14.

19 Willis, E., 'Don't Turn Your Back on Love', Introduction to *Janis* triple CD, Sony Music Entertainment Inc., 1993, p. 24.

20 Tong, *op. cit.*, p. 111.

21 Willie Dixon, 'Little Red Rooster', 'My First Wife Left Me'; Lightnin' Hopkins 'Baby Please Don't Go'; Howlin' Wolf, 'Moanin' for My Baby'; Muddy Waters, 'Got My Mojo Working'; John Lee Hooker, 'Crawling King Snake'.
22 Smith, *op. cit.*, p. 43.
23 Powers, A., 'Janis Without Tears', in *Janis, op. cit.*, p. 33.
24 In Gaar, *op. cit.*, p. 107.
25 Discussion with Grossman after leaving Big Brother and the Holding Company. *Ibid.*, p. 106.
26 For a detailed discussion of the relationship between drugs and the counter culture see Whiteley, S. (1992) *The Space between the Notes*, London: Routledge and Whiteley, S., 'Altered Sounds', in Melechi, A. (1997) *Psychedelia Britannica. Hallucinogenic Drugs in Britain*, London: Turnaround, pp. 120–42.
27 Sugarman, D. (1991) *Wonderland Avenue*, London: Sphere Books, pp. 271–3.
28 *Ibid.*, p. 273.
29 And which is similar to a jazz terminal vibrato.
30 The time signature is itself unusual, 6/8 rather than the more usual 12/8, 4/4 and the harmonic structure of the final bar of the introduction implies equally a sense of equivocation: Dmaj7 added 6? Dm9 first inversion? Dm with internal pedal E?.
31 Willis, *op. cit.*, p. 24.
32 Gaar, *op. cit.*, p. 106.
33 Pavletich, *op. cit.*, p. 127.
34 Powers, *op. cit.*, p. 31.
35 Pavletich, *op. cit.*, p. 126.
36 Threadgold, *op. cit.*, p. 10.
37 Pavletich, *op. cit.*, p. 126.
38 Willis, *op. cit.*, p. 23.
39 Vicinus, M., 'They Wonder to Which Sex I Belong', in Abelove, H., Barale, M.A. and Helperin, D.A., (eds) (1994) *The Lesbian and Gay Studies Reader*, London: Routledge, p. 444.
40 Rubin, G.S., 'Thinking Sex', *Ibid.*, p. 19.
41 *Ibid.*, p. 19.
42 Gaar, *op. cit.*, p. 106.
43 Threadgold, *op. cit.*, p. 230.
44 Willis, *op. cit.*, p. 24.
45 Smith, *op. cit.*, p. 50.

5

THE TIMES THEY ARE A-CHANGIN'

Folk and the singer songwriter

As Aida Pavletich observes,

> each genre of popular music has a different ideal of womanhood
> which is part of the mystique of this girl singer who is wife, lover,
> mother. She is the fallen angel of country, the glamorous femme
> fatale of pop, the sassy fox of R&B, the sister of folk. She's tramp,
> bitch and goddess, funky mama, sweetheart, the woman left lonely,
> the hapless victim of her man.[1]

As a quick caricature, Pavletich's identification of genre representation has a
certain truthfulness. At the same time, it raises the question as to why image
and style should forge a particular genre representation and the extent to
which the image is driven by generic conventions. With regard to 1960s'
rock, for example, both the music and its culture were resolutely fraternalistic
and, as Janis Joplin's example so poignantly reveals, women were either
excluded from the inner circle or were drawn into being 'one of the boys'.
Folk, and more particularly, the folk protest movement of the 1960s,
however, provided a more viable space, not least for women with sweet voices.

The 1960s' alliance between political protest and folk had a clear prece-
dence in the 1930s when folk singers identified themselves with the union
movement and became a medium for the expression of radical views. Woody
Guthrie's 'Dust Bowl Ballads' (1940), for example, describe the forced
migration of families from their parched farmlands in Oklahoma to the
poverty of California. His influence on Bob Dylan and his own son, Arlo
(who was to star in the draft-dodging classic *Alice's Restaurant*) is well documented, and their protest against exploitation and alienation provides a
sense of continuity in the alliance between political activism and folk, albeit
that they were no longer confined to class or left-wing politics. Rather they
communicated a personalised reflection on issues of contemporary concern,
such as the war in Vietnam, the Civil Rights movement, and the threat of
nuclear war, and by the mid-1960s folk resonated more with the student
peace movement than with the underprivileged rural poor.

While the counter culture's emphasis on freedom of expression/freedom to experiment resulted in folk singers trying out their own compositions in public, they also looked to the past for inspiration, with their greatest influence coming from the white rural music of Woody Guthrie and the Carter Family, and the hollers of such country blues singers as Robert Johnson, Leadbelly and Skip James. As such, the audience for folk became accustomed to voices which lacked polish, and where off-key singing, drawls, twangs, falsettos and an untrained personalised delivery signalled authenticity. Bob Dylan's vocals, for example, are characterised by a whining, nasal delivery and an abrasive intensity which complemented his ability to express human and intellectual injustices. Leonard Cohen was equally valued for the poetic candour of his lyrics, but as Aida Pavletich points out, for women, aspirations remained high:'Style still counted as much as content.'[2] Joan Baez, for example, personified the anti-commercial roots of folk with her long hair, casual clothes, the simplicity of her playing and the reedy clarity of her vocal style. In particular, her whoop to a high note confirmed her status as pure, untrained, unsophisticated and, by implication, non-commercial.

Not surprisingly – as Charlotte Greig points out in her discussion of 'Female Identity and The Woman Singersongwriter' – the 1960s' folk revival attempted to rediscover the true radicalism of traditional folk music, with artists such as Anne Briggs reviving 'Gathering Rushes in the Month of May', a song which tells of the conception of a baby and the confrontation between father and daughter. Peggy Seeger, a songwriter from the Revivalist Movement, also wrote a number of songs on motherhood, including 'Nine Month Blues' 'a song commissioned by the National Abortion Committee in 1975 ... which describes the various inadequate methods of contraception that lead to unwanted pregnancy'.[3] The continuing history of women as providers and mothers is but one thread in the rich tapestry of folk. The traditional handing-down of ballads and songs which focus on both the everyday and the extraordinary dimensions of women's life experiences range from the starkly autobiographical to the humorous and poetic. More specifically, there is a characteristic sense of self-expression and attention to detail which is reflected in the lyrics and the nuancing of the vocal gesture itself.

Folk's relationship to jazz is also significant. During the 1950s the New Orleans jazz revivalists had formed an alliance with folk in their shared commitment to the Campaign for Nuclear Disarmament and active fundraising. Folk singers Ewan MacColl and Jeannie Robertson, for example, had shared the bill with Ken Colyer at a Royal Festival Hall concert in aid of the *Daily Worker*. In terms of musical development, the concert was significant. It was the first occasion when a jazz clarinet had been introduced into a folk song context, and Colyer's accompaniment to MacColl's 'Another Man Gone' created a precedent for the later use of electric guitar solos in folk groups, so influencing a line of development through to such electric folk bands as Fairport Convention and Steeleye Span.

Paradoxically, the 1950s' jazz/pop fusions were also to prove influential. Here, a glamorous image was matched by an idiosyncratic vocal style which ranged from the cool, intelligent vocals of Lena Horne, the sensual tension and effortless phrasing of Peggy Lee, the glossy tone of Dinah Washington, to the sharp, humorous exotica of Eartha Kitt with her arrogant, purring sophistication. It was a stylistic marriage that was subsequently to inform the musical vocabulary of singer songwriter Joni Mitchell ('Don Juan's Reckless Daughter', *Mingus*). Maria Muldaur also demonstrated an affinity with jazz in her vocal delivery and while her early loyalties lay in country folk and jug bands, her flowing, rangy style provided a sophisticated approach to melodic interpretation which was to influence the next generation of singer songwriters.

In the early 1960s, however, the folk revival was largely characterised by dissociation and protest. Vocal tone retained a narrative edge and singing was accompanied by the traditional country instruments of acoustic guitar, auto-harp and banjo. Its audiences were drawn from the escalating folk clubs which opened up in major cities across the US, Canada and Europe, university campuses and New York's Greenwich Village. Peter, Paul and Mary, for example, had a huge following among university students, and their performance of traditional ballads and cover versions of the Weavers' 'If I Had a Hammer', Guthrie's 'This Land is your Land' and 'Go Tell It on the Mountain' and Dylan's 'Blowing in the Wind' popularised socially conscious songs while demonstrating that it was possible to reconcile the political with commercial success. Although this alienated the group from folk purists, the broad-based acceptance of folk impacted on other musical styles, most specifically in Dylan's fusion of folk/rock. His adoption of an electric guitar and a more bluesy amplified rhythm section was seen at the time as a radical departure from the stylistic simplicity that had earlier characterised acoustic folk. In retrospect, it demonstrated a readiness to engage with a more diverse audience while remaining within the broad contours of tradition. In particular, by abandoning traditional instrumentation and expanding the subject matter of folk, artists such as Dylan and Baez created a repertoire of contemporary folk songs where politics were explored through a more personal, introspective style of delivery.[4]

Although folk protest remained firmly grounded in the 1960s, resonating with the counter culture's stand against war, personal alienation and exploitation, the move from acoustic folk was significant in that the bending of musical boundaries led to a more broad-based acceptance of stylistic diversity. Joan Baez, for example, provided an unflinching example of commitment to social and political issues not only in her songs, but equally in founding the Institute for the Study of Non-Violence in Carmel, California and joining Amnesty International. Buffy St Marie demonstrated an ability to project a diversity of images, to write unconventional love lyrics and songs which confronted social and political issues, nationalism and its impact on the American Indian. In particular, she provided an example for the composer, that different issues necessitate different stylistic approaches, so confronting the sense of entrenchment that characterised both country and folk purists at the time. Judy Collins, initially trained as a concert pianist, brought a classical refinement to folk with her particular style of singing, while expanding the repertory of folk crossover by popularising songs by Jacques Brel, Leonard Cohen and Stephen Sondheim.

It was this growing emphasis on individualism and self-expression that was to influence women singer songwriters most. In particular, there was an awareness that songs which focused on personal relationships could provide a microcosmic insight into the politics of love and hate which had earlier characterised folk protest. To an extent this was inevitable. The activist rage which had underpinned folk protest had been equally associated with the politics of the counter culture and the search for the truth of the person, the 'elusive, often erratic human something which underlies social systems and ideologies, and which ... serves as the ultimate point of moral reference'.[5] This sense of introspection, which was to find a particular expression in the drug culture of the late 1960s, moved folk rock from a concern with social injustice, anti-war, anti-exploitation, towards an investigation into the biographical, rather than the ideological, context of truth. While this privileged such concerns as love, loneliness and depersonalisation, so providing a particular trajectory for the contemplative solo albums of the 1970s, the association of rock with mysticism and drugs was to prove problematic. Psychedelic experience, in particular, had been considered both a radical rejection of the dominant culture and a means of tapping into creativity – as evidenced by the spatial dimensions inherent in acid rock and the surrealistic lyrics of such folk rock songs as Dylan's 'Mr Tambourine Man'. Drug culture, however, brought its casualties and by 1970 the deaths of Jimi Hendrix and Janis Joplin provoked vitriolic criticisms of the counter culture and a panic reaction to the adverse effects of drugs generally. At the same time, the killing of four students at Kent State University, Ohio, evidenced the gulf between those who wanted to change America and its policies in Vietnam, and the conservative majority who believed in law and order above anything else. Demonstrations were abandoned, and the wave of introspection which had followed Woodstock (1969) and which had highlighted the problems associated with the utopian philosophy of personal freedom, demonstrated how the movement generally was attracting hucksters who fed on the drug culture, as well as the more violent and anarchic elements of the radical underground.

It could be argued that the freeing of rock/folk rock from its social implications, whether drugs or the wider concerns of war and alienation, had left music relatively 'thin' in terms of content. However, it is apparent that the de-escalation in group consciousness (as evidenced by the break-up of such influential groups as the Beatles and Cream), and the general shift from activist rage to a more introspective examination of the self provided a specific space for women singer songwriters. In particular, they were to provide specific insights for the post-1960s woman through, for example, the evaluation of relationships ('Who was that man I married on the Vietnam march? 'How come I've ended up in suburbia just like my mother? Why don't we talk any more?'[6] and 'How can I exist as a one-parent family?') which resonated both with the downside of post-1960s' activism and the grassroots debates circulating within the women's movement.

By the early 1970s women had asserted themselves as a powerful voice in social, cultural and political debates, not least in the anti-war and Civil Rights movements. At the same time, it was apparent that feminism (as it had begun to be called) was failing to confront the realities of women who not only loved, but liked men and who were equally concerned with sexual equality and sexual politics. As Betty Friedan wrote in 1981, neither separatism – as urged by radical feminists – nor a retreat back into the private sphere of the home could necessarily achieve personal fulfilment. 'In the first stage, our aim was full participation (of the women's movement), power and voice in the mainstream. But we were diverted from our dream. And in our reaction against the feminine mystique, which defined women solely in terms of their relations to men as wives, mothers and homemakers, we sometimes seemed to fall into a *feminist* mystique which denied that core of women's personhood that is fulfilled through love, nurture, home.'[7]

Friedan's shift in emphasis suggests a recognition of the whole person, that reason, mind, emotion and body are necessary both to survival and to the richness of human experience. In particular, it implies a reflective rather than a revolutionary critique. It is tempting to suggest that this resonated with the maturing of the first stage of feminism, and Friedan was certainly aware of the frustrations of the suburban housewife who was dissatisfied with the constraints of being 'simply a wife and mother'. At the same time, it should be recognised that her initial solution – combine marriage and motherhood with a career – failed to address the problems that home and family are a joint responsibility, and that it encouraged women to *become* like men, rather than treating women and men as equal but different.

It is also apparent that women were mainly making progress in the area of sexuality, and that this progress was often more apparent than real. 'Taken to extremes, sexual liberation becomes a disguised form of sexual oppression. In the past, women were condemned for being whores; today women are condemned for being virgins.'[8] For the married woman, the problems inherent in sexual freedom resulted in an underlying frustration – how to act as a liberated woman within the constraints of a monogamous relationship – and which led to an escalating divorce rate and suburban wife-swapping parties.

The 1970s, then, were a time for growing older, for reflection, and for coming to terms with the isolation of the thirty-plus individual. To an extent this was mirrored by the maturing of popular music generally. This was reflected in the growing importance of albums which provided extended listening and a specific focus on lyrics which, since the Beatles' *Sgt Pepper's* album, were now printed on the inside sleeve. While this is not to suggest that there was no longer a young audience for pop, nor that singles disappeared from the market, it is evident that the simple categorisation of youth culture had expanded and that there was a growing market for adult oriented rock/pop. It is also evident that the trend towards a more harmonious and thoughtful mode of expression, while moving beyond a simple allegiance to style, forged a new and positive alliance between pop, jazz and folk. It was a fusion that was to be particularly relevant to the music of Joni Mitchell.

NOTES AND REFERENCES

1   Pavletich, A. (1980) *Sirens of Song. The Popular Female Vocalist in America*, New York: Da Capo, p. 14.
2   *Ibid.*, p. 209.
3   Greig, C., 'Female Identity and the Woman Songwriter', in Whiteley, S. (ed.) (1997) *Sexing the Groove. Popular Music and Gender*, London: Routledge, pp. 168–77.
4   Dylan's rock-based song 'Subterranean Homesick Blues', for example, revives the old acoustic 'barrel-house' style heard in much of Leadbelly and Guthrie's playing. The song is a social commentary on individual freedom within America and its nervous, clipped lines and internal rhyme are reminiscent of William Burroughs's 'cut-up' technique of writing. Dylan's observations of human relationships and the communicative processes that exist between them are explored within the context of paranoia and the erosion of civil rights.
5   Roszak, T. (1970) *The Making of a Counter Culture. Reflections on the Technocratic Society and its Youthful Opposition*, New York: Faber and Faber, p. 62.
6   Pavletich, *op. cit.*, p. 181.
7   Friedan, B., in Tong, R. (1989) *Feminist Thought. A Comprehensive Guide*, London: Routledge, p. 24.
8   *Ibid.*, p. 176.

6

THE LONELY ROAD

Joni Mitchell, *Blue* and female subjectivity

By the late 1960s, folk singers Joan Baez, Buffy St Marie and Judy Collins had established solo careers, and in 1971 Carole King emerged as a performer on her highly successful album *Tapestry*. Its promotional single 'It's Too Late/I Feel the Earth Move' topped the charts, while 'You've Got a Friend' became a no. 1 hit for James Taylor, who also played on the album. It won four Grammy awards and remained in the charts for four years. Janis Ian ('Society's Child') and Carly Simon ('You're So Vain') were also enjoying success as solo artists, while Laura Nyro's 1969 album *New York Tendaberry* provided a brilliant example of jazz/rock fusions. It seemed, then, that the early 1970s was a propitious time for women to break into the solo market. Yet, as Joni Mitchell's album *Blue* reveals, being independent, creatively single minded and original continued to raise problems, not least those of grappling with a career while, at the same time, maintaining relationships.

Being a long, blond-haired guitar player was a positive asset during the latter years of the 1960s but it was her particular musicality and personal insights that made Mitchell significant in forging a new world of possibilities for women. Not least, she offered a model of female experience in coping with the realities of working in a male-dominated music industry. For many, however, it is her grasp of the idiom of the day, her playful references to astrology, magic, travel, of being on 'the lonely road', of confronting the problems of giving birth to a child and giving her up to adoption, of exploring relationships while pursuing her own creative pathway that give her a special relevance. These tensions are most prominent in the songs from her early albums, *Clouds* and *Blue*, recorded when Mitchell was evidently searching for her own identity. Indeed, *Blue*, more than any other album, offers a window into her subjective universe, marking the start of a recognition of the problems associated with the feminine mystique and, more especially, the effect when this realisation hit home. As Mary Routh observes,

> This geographic memory is a hallmark of her imagery, and is firmly based in her desire to travel ... *Blue* is the description of a year or

two in her life, and she is telling us what she learned and what she experienced. She is the theme, and for the first time, she sets out to make her life her art.[1]

In contrast to her earlier work, where she sings narrative songs about made-up people, *Blue* places her firmly at the centre of her story.

It was obvious from her first albums, *Songs to a Seagull*, *Clouds* and *Ladies of the Canyon* that Mitchell (born Roberta Joan Anderson, 7 November 1943) had an ability to draw on her personal experience and then translate this into a musical idiom. Her marriage to Chuck Mitchell is traced in 'I Had a King' from her debut album, and her subsequent affairs underpin the thematic content of her albums, in particular opening out the concept of freedom and the problems inherent in *not* becoming too involved with lovers. Of equal importance, she exemplifies the singer songwriter who got there by her own efforts, and whose albums demonstrate an increasing level of artistic and technical control.

Joni Mitchell's musical career started in Calgary, where she trained as a commercial artist and sang traditional folk songs in local coffee bars. By 1964, after attending the Mariposa Folk Festival in Ontario, she started writing her own songs and performing in local clubs and coffee-houses in Toronto. In June 1965 she married Chuck Mitchell and moved to Detroit. The marriage lasted only two years and Mitchell then moved to New York, before settling in Laurel Canyon, outside Los Angeles, in 1968. At this point in time, she was already achieving success as a songwriter. Judy Collins recorded 'Both Sides Now' and 'Michael from the Mountains' for her album *Wildflowers* (1967), taking the former to no. 8 in the singles chart in 1968. Tom Rush recorded 'The Circle Game' and, in the UK Fairport Convention covered 'Eastern Rain'; Crosby, Stills, Nash and Young had a hit with 'Woodstock' in 1970 and shortly after it became a hit for Matthews' Southern Comfort in both America and the UK. Stephen Stills had also played bass on Mitchell's debut album *Songs to a Seagull*, and since they were handled by the same management, she became part of the same social circle, moving out to California and acquiring a certain notoriety for her various romantic attachments. These included an affair with Graham Nash which is reflected in the songs 'Willy' (which describes his rejection of her) and 'Our House'. 'Other lovers are characterised by transience. They play on street corners, they are husbands, they are generally to be pitied. She chooses men who will not stop her from her prime purpose which is to explore the planet and life. 'Life is our cause,' she says on *Blue*. And that is the key to what she says about men.'[2]

Clouds (1967), her second album was essentially folk-based with little supporting instrumentation. Produced by Mitchell herself, it included her own version of 'Both Sides Now', and was her first record to reach the Top 40, winning a Grammy for Best Folk Performance. The song's central metaphor of 'clouds' resonates with a youthful optimism tinged with reality. Focusing the 'ups' by a childlike evocation of pleasure:

> Rows and flows of angel hair
> And ice-cream castles in the air

and the 'downs' through a more cynical realism:

> But now they only block the sun
> They rain and snow on ev'ry one

the imagery of the first four lines is not dissimilar to the cotton-candy of Jimi Hendrix's 'Spanish Castle Magic'. But here the comparison with psychedelia ends. There is little sense of the hallucinogenic. Rather, the lyrics overall read like a thoughtful evaluation of relationships, a coming to terms with life rather than an escape from reality. The vocal delivery is distinctive and clear, with the highs and lows of the melody reflecting the imagery of the lyrics.

Verses two and three again focus in on the transitory, as the fairytale rapture of first love gives way to a realisation that things change and that feelings often need to be hidden. The realisation that experience does not necessarily bring a clarity of vision is opened out by the chorus. Here, Mitchell makes use of melodic contouring and word-painting to focus the imagery:

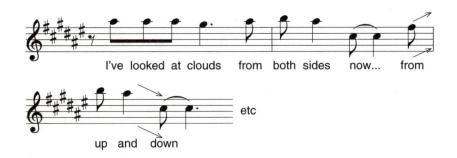

and reflective tied notes which are coloured by the shifting instrumental harmonies to effect a musical metaphor for the transitory nature of clouds, love and life itself.

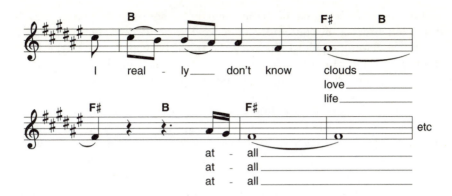

Above all, the song comes across as a personal statement of self-doubt – 'I really don't know' – and, as such, has a sense of candour and honesty which resonates with the introspection of the late 1960s. Within the broader arena of rock the questioning of 'Who am I?', the solipsistic 'I', 'Me', had informed such songs as 'Nowhere Man', 'Fixing a Hole' (the Beatles), 'Be Yourself' (Graham Nash), 'Dare to be Different' (Donovan), 'I've Got a Name' (Jim Croce) and 'Who Am I?' (Country Joe and the Fish). With Mitchell, the quest for self-identity – its many struggles, frustrations, confusions and confidences – is expressed through a richness of imagery where optimism and pessimism are informed by personal reflection. This, in turn, is enhanced by a sensually rhythmic use of language. Rhyme is used extensively, both to emphasise romantic clichés – 'Moons and Junes', 'Dreams and Schemes', and to draw more complex emotions into association:

> Tears and fears and feeling proud
> To say 'I love you' right out loud.

The exploration of positive and negative subjectivities, the juxtaposition of the poetic with the prosaic, is compounded by the sense of personal reflection/resignation in the chorus. Mitchell again makes use of clichés ('win and lose', 'give and take') but any sense of weighing-up, of coming to a conclusion, is compromised by her continuing emphasis on illusion which, as she points out, is what people both refuse to acknowledge in their continuing espousal of the romantic discourse of love and which, paradoxically, is what they ultimately buy: 'I also knew how fickle people could be. I knew they were buying an illusion and I thought, "Maybe they should know a little bit more about who I am." '[3]

'Both Sides Now' thus implies a truthfulness, a connection between the 'who I present and who I am' in its exploration of the personal in everyday life. The pacing of the song, the plateaux, the focus on change itself allied to the gentle ebb and flow of the supporting harmonies are far removed from either the 'timelessness' of hallucinogenic songs of the period, or the thrusting urgency of contemporary rock. The vocal delivery, in particular, aligns the feminine 'who I am' with the transitive experiences of the lyrics. Mitchell's wide ranging melody (octave plus perfect fourth), the clarity of her top register, the resonant lows and the overall flexibility in intonation are the most obvious points of reference. More specifically, her vocal style provides a metaphor for the highs and lows, the personalised experience of love and life as narrated in the lyrics. This alignment between lyric content and a deeply personalised vocal delivery suggests a self-involvement which is, at one and the same time, extraordinary and – at least for some listeners – disturbing in its range of power and register. In particular, the lyric's constant emphasis on *I* involves 'motion, perception, reflection, separation/connection, materiality, process, relationality'[4] and her aural impact is one of truthfulness to experience. It is about self-recognition, but she remains bombarded by contradictions which are picked up in her next solo album, *Blue.*

Blue was released in 1971 and sold over a million copies. It is an intriguing album, providing once again a personalised insight into relation-ships,[5] this time through a sensitive use of colour imagery. In particular, the musical and literary associations of blue/blues/bluesness provides a colour wash for her compositional canvas, a spectrum which draws into association such images as the sea, Little Green's blue eyes, her tattoo, and the blue TV screen light in 'A Case of You'. The significance of colour is also evident in the accompaniment to the songs. 'My Old Man', 'Blue', 'River' and 'Richard' are brought into association through reflective piano accompani-ments. The largely arpeggiated flow works like a musing counterpoint to the vocal line, providing a feeling of musical space which complements the introspection of the lyrics. In contrast, the guitar accompanied songs, 'All I Want', 'Little Green', 'Carey', 'California', 'This Flight Tonight' have analo-gies with the artist's sketch pad

> Oh, I am a lonely painter
> And I live in a box of paints

accessing the immediacy of personal thoughts through alternative tunings, complex extended chords, pedals and common notes that contribute to the effect of the connotations in the music.[6]

'All I Want', the first track on the album, begins quite simply by setting the scene 'I am on a lonely road and I am travelling, travelling, travelling.' Melodically, the phrase is narrow ranged, the iterative structure underpin-ning the anomie, the boredom, and the pressures of being on the road. The 'looking for something, what can it be?', then, provides a certain ironic twist. Mitchell knows what she wants ('applause, applause, life is our cause') – but the road is typically male territory – and the personal cost of pursuing a creative career creates emotional pressures. In particular, there is a tension between freedom and dependency which comes across in the spontaneous outburst 'Oh, I hate you some ... ' where the pitch rises on hate, following the natural inflection of the voice, before the more reflective 'love ... you some'. Here 'love' is mused over, given time and coloured by a minor tonality which draws it into association with the 'travelling' of the first phrase to create an underlying bluesness, a realisation that the cost of dependency is Self, and the recognition that relationships only work when 'I forget about ... me'.

In a song which is concerned primarily with self-reflection and coming to terms with the 'all I want' (from life and relationships), it is unlikely that the omnipresent *I* can be so easily dismissed. After a momentary pause, the *me* triggers a stream-of-consciousness needs which are again tempered by a mood of instability. The 'I want to be strong' for example, is compromised by the Bb minor on 'strong' to create a feeling of self-doubt, an underling insecurity. Travelling the lonely road takes strength, but as the song progresses Mitchell stakes out her needs – 'I want to laugh along, I want to belong to the living. Alive, alive, I want to get up and jive', etc. and while the contemplative 'I want to belong', 'I want to renew you again and again' suggests a certain *cri-de-coeur*, this is undercut by the challenging 'Do you want to dance with me ... do you want to take a chance ... ' where, once again, internal rhyme draws thoughts and ideas into association.

Musically, the song works because Mitchell's careful use of harmonic colour and melodic contouring act as word-painting for her emotional outbursts. The reflective 'Do you see how you hurt me, baby' is under-pinned by blunt, major tonalities. In contrast, the 'hurt you' is given time, both in the move to minims and the use of added colour in the Ab9 chord. The final phrase 'then we both get' draws pain into a shared experience by the avoidance of gendered coding (the defining major/minor third and its traditional associations with male/female) before an effective use of contemplative silence and the move to the climactic high on 'so'. The falling vocal contour on 'blue' then effects a musical metaphor of instability which is enhanced by the shifting harmonies in the guitar accompaniment, with the final Abm7 providing a pivotal bluesness before the lonely road of the final verse.

It is clearly no coincidence that the final word of the song 'free' should be supported by the same restless harmonies as 'blue'. The first song of a concept album is instrumental in establishing thematic content and from the onset Mitchell prioritises her ambition, aware that the 'road' will be problematic, but equally certain that it provides 'the key to set me free'.

Whereas the acoustic guitar is analogous to the sketch-pad and implies movement, (6) Mitchell's songs which are piano-accompanied are rooted in a bluesness where freedom and personal flight no longer appear a viable option. 'My Old Man' provides an insight into the 'I want's of the opening song. No longer an enigmatic presence, he is constituted by action – a singer, a walker, a dancer. In contrast, Mitchell is homebound and her happiness is dependent upon his presence, and while there is a certain optimism in the 'we don't need no piece of paper from the city hall' (with the implication that the bonds of marriage are no longer relevant in a freewheeling post-1960s' culture), the musical coding implies *bravado*. Mitchell's characteristic use of the equivocal sus4 chord implies an underlying instability and her personal experience of blues, bluesness, is then opened out through the tension between major/minor tonalities, a darkening chromaticism, and edgy vocal leaps:

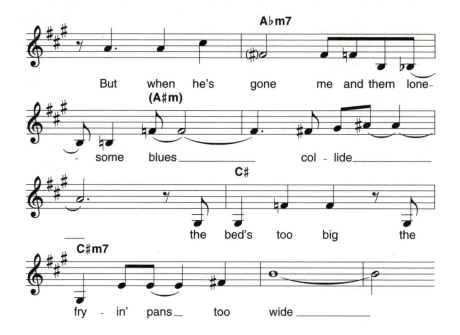

before the harmonic progression back to the tonic, A major. Even here, there is a sense of fragile insecurity, for although her lover returns ('then he comes home'), the displacement of accents, the vocal leaps and the E7sus on 'home' paint a feeling of wistfulness. This is equally implied in the fade out at the end of the song where the alternating major/minor tonalities resonate with the omnipresent bluesness of dependency.

The tensions inherent in dependency/freedom are developed further in the third song, 'Little Green', a lullaby to Mitchell's only child who was surrendered to adoption.

> Choose her a name she will answer to
> Call her Green and the winters cannot fade her ...

It is interesting to contrast this mother-to-daughter song with 'Eli's Song', a father-to-son song by country artist Jack Williams and sung by John Denver. Traditionally, theories have been posited that feminine modes of self-expression are characterised by an intuitive, figurative, more 'felt' lexicon than masculine modes which may be more coldly rational and concrete.[7] This is illustrated by the statement of fact in 'Eli's Song' ('Born in the month of June') and Mitchell's allusion to the astrological 'Age of Aquarius' in 'Little Green' ('Born with the moon in cancer') which is rich in iconography, with the moon linking the child to the sexuality of the mother, fertility and birth, Maiden and Mother. The child is, by analogy, the young goddess, the new moon, surrounded by the vibrant colours of spring – 'Just a little green like the colour when the spring is born' – and the endless cycle of life itself – 'There'll be icicles and birthday clothes'.

While 'Little Green' is primarily a poetic and highly personalised song about Mitchell's relationship to her child, it equally provides a particular insight into the problems surrounding the single mother. As Mifflin writes: 'To be pregnant and unmarried in 1964 was like you killed somebody ... Joni allowed her daughter to be given up for adoption and then relocated to a one bedroom billet in Manhattan's Chelsea district.'[8] As such, the under-lying poignancy of 'stay, baby' ('My Old Man'), with its restless harmonic instability locks into the starkness of 'He went to California ... He sends you a letter and she's lost to you' to create an articulate musical expression of loss.

At the same time, the song constructs a mood of underlying resilience ('You're sad and you're sorry but you're not ashamed') which, in its avoid-ance of the personalised 'I' implies a certain emotional distancing. 'Little Green' is situated within a qualitative experience of time – conception, birth, beginnings, endings. She may wish her child 'a happy ending', but the song nevertheless closes with the reflective 'sometimes there'll be sorrow'. There is, then, no easy solution, rather a continuing engagement with the ups and downs of life, the tensions between stability and freedom – a theme which is also present in the next track 'Carey' where the iconog-raphy surrounding the moon (and its relationship to the feminine) is replaced by the star.

Mitchell's use of imagery is closely linked to her mapping of personal identity. Traditionally the star is aligned with hope and faith, often in the hour of crisis when darkness appears to immobilise the senses. At the same time, it can signify a struggle with life, a seeking of destiny and an attempt to become more independent. As such, it is not surprising that within the context of the album, the star is associated with her lover –

> Starbright, starbright?
> You've got the lovin' that I like alright
>
> > ('This Flight Tonight')

with moments of crisis

> Just before our love got lost you said
> I am as constant as a northern star
>
> > ('A Case of You')

or impending separation –

> Let's not talk of fare-thee-wells now
> The night is a starry dome

('Carey')

Traditionally, the star is also associated with the birth of a child and 'Little Green' and 'Carey' are brought into association not simply through an impending sense of separation and loss, but equally through the immediacy of the guitar accompaniments.[9] While the gentle acoustic lullaby resonates with the folk tradition of self-expression in its fusion of the poetic with the starkly autobiographical, the funky guitar intro to 'Carey' brings the listener to the heart of the album. As Mary Routh observes:

> Everything about this song shouts 'traveller' and the opening lines,
>
> The wind is in from Africa
> Last night I couldn't sleep

suggest a tiny village called Matella, that only has one road in and out of it. It is separated from the main road by dusty and arid hills. You do not get there by accident, you go there. And you are sitting on the beach, feeling relaxed and happy ... Here is a woman who has made it to this remote and perfect village by herself, can afford to wonder where to go next, and has somewhere to go home to when she feels ready. 'Maybe I'll go to Amsterdam, maybe I'll go to Rome, and rent me a grand piano and put some flowers around my room.' The names are totemic, guaranteeing that she will indeed get there. And when she does, she can afford to rent a grand piano?[10]

The transitory nature of the 'good time' are brought into association with Carey – 'the bright red devil who's keeping me in this tourist town'. Here, the implications of staying/leaving are again focused by Mitchell's characteristic swoop to her top register which, in context, triggers a distress signal.

This lack of stability is rooted in the conflict between 'Carey' and the fact that this is 'not my home'. Again, there is word-painting. The melody is musically centred on Db (the tonic, the home key) but the word 'home' sits uneasily on the chord of Ab7 (the dominant) to effect musically a lack of resolution in the I-V cadence.[11] Carey, himself, is described as 'a mean old daddy', although it is apparent from the harmonic underpinning that Mitchell feels out of her depth

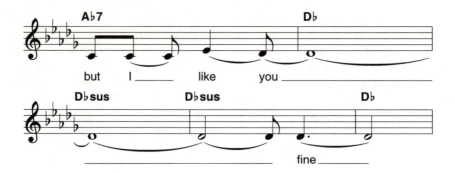

and, as the hip phrase of the 1970s 'out of sight' implies, while he has 'blown her mind' he is, nevertheless 'out of her league'.

Mitchell then plunges into the bluesness of the eponymous track 'Blue'. As the fifth song on the album, 'Blue' is pivotal, reflecting on what has gone before and informing what is yet to come. At one level, the song is a cynical commentary on the late 1960s:

> Acid, booze, and ass
> Needles, guns and grass
> Lots of laughs, lots of laughs

– the 'everyone is saying that hell's the hippest way to go' resonating with the deaths of Joplin, Hendrix, the death of optimism. It is also a recognition of defeat, of loving someone but being defeated by circumstances. She is 'at sea' with her emotions, torn between staying and leaving ('crown and anchor me, or let me sail away') but there are no answers in this soliloquy to pain. Rather the song opens out the problems, the price that is paid by those who are/were 'on the road' and this sense of anomie, this bluesness, links the song with 'California' which picks up on the continuing war in Vietnam, the dream of peace, 'the bloody changes' juxtaposed with the 'pretty people' in Spain 'Reading *Rollin' Stone*, reading *Vogue*'.

The guitar accompaniment is again pivotal in authenticating the 'truth-fulness' of the autobiographic, the pithy observations of a woman folk singer travelling through Europe, 'sitting in a park in Paris, France'. The guitar also enhances the feeling of immediacy for the stream-of-consciousness thoughts, 'still a lot of lands to see', the wandering hippy in a street full of strangers. Again, Mitchell makes use of colour to effect subtle mood inflec-tions for her thumbnail sketches. 'I wouldn't wanna stay here. It's too old and cold and settled in its ways here', for example, is accompanied by F#7 (II7) to raise the question 'Why major harmonies when, traditionally, minor harmonies would effect a feeling of bleakness?' The answer lies, most probably, in Mitchell's sense of the poetic and the way in which she uses music 'to create a precise expression of feeling'.[12] Thus, while the inclusion of a major third suggests stability, Mitchell undercuts this by the 7th to evoke both a sense of wish-fulfilment (the major third) and equivocation (the 7th). In contrast, the relationship between the I-V-I harmonies which accompany 'Ah, but California, California' are effective in providing a traditional feeling of warmth and stability. But once again, the realisation of 'coming home' (to California) is tempered by the II7 harmonies. She is not going home immediately (as the narrative of the verses show) nor giving up her right to be true to herself. However, she does get homesick and the final yearning repetitiveness of 'Will you take me as I am' with which the song ends suggests an ongoing vulnerability as it segues into 'This Flight Tonight' where the iconic imagery of the star (starbright) becomes a metaphor for the constancy of her love:

> Can't numb you out
> Can't drum you out of my mind.

However, as the lyrics unfold, it is clear that Mitchell is returning to someone who is not supportive ('you look so critical') and her awareness of the situation, the 'blackness, blackness, dragging me down' is opened out by the realisation 'I shouldn't have got on this flight tonight.'

If the songs on *Blue* reflect a sense of time, then the next track 'River' suggests that running away is no real solution. Prefaced by a moody and resolutely minor 'Jingle Bells', the 'out of tuneness' of the intro provides a musical metaphor for not belonging within the context of Christmas, a time when the awareness of being alone is particularly acute:

> They're cutting down trees
> They're putting up reindeer
> And singing songs of joy and peace.

The mood of nostalgia, of looking back over the past, is focused by an all-pervading sense of absence, of snow, of money and of her lover. The bleakness of the narrative is underpinned by the repetitiveness of the vocal line

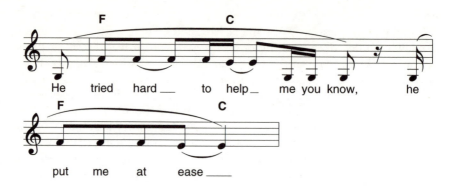

which creates a musical alignment between the 'what he did for me' and the 'why' of loss. The introspection of the lyrics, the underlying pain, is realised partly in the formal tensions of the music itself. The narrative of loss is rooted in repetition, the need to escape by upward movement, chord colouring and a lack of resolution.

The final chorus, 'I wish I had a river I could skate away on' and the reappearance of 'Jingle Bells', twisted harmonically as a musical metaphor for self-reproach ('I made my baby cry'), ends with a stark perfect fifth over D (D7 omitting the F#) to provide a final and reflective coding of emptiness. Even here, however, Mitchell does not talk of returning to her lover. Rather there is the implication of skating even further away.

The conflict between love and pain, belonging and freedom, the resultant emptiness that can accompany the 'lonely road' are clearly the unifying themes on the album and, with nostalgia constructed through the evocation of Christmas, 'A Case of You' provides contemplative insights into love and loss. Here, Mitchell muses over her obsessive love:

acknowledging her selfishness, her pig-headedness, but aware that if she were to 'go to him, stay with him', she should 'be prepared to bleed', to accept compromise. In 'Richard', the final, anti-climactic song of the album, the implications of compromise are given a specific focus.

For Richard, romanticism is a weakness. It belongs to the past, the dark cafés of youth. It feeds the anecdotes of the drunk and the boring. Mitchell, with the moon in her eyes, reminiscing about 'the last time I saw Richard ... ' knows that she is not immune, but reassures herself with the thought that 'all good dreamers pass this way some day' and while the butterfly imagery of 'gorgeous wings' and flight suggest that the mood will pass, at that moment her loss is complete. Richard is no solution, rather he personifies the end of the late-1960s' dream. He has opted out, 'married a figure skater' rather than a travelling woman. She, in turn, is still sitting in a dark café, three years on, still alone, but still part of that dream. 'And that,' says my friend Mary Routh, 'is why she despises him.'

Blue, then, is like a cycle of songs that has no real beginning, no real end.

Rather the piano outro to 'Richard' with its somewhat desolate final chord returns the listener to the lonely road where the album began. What is evident, however, is the fact that behind the experience of the songs lies the reality of the choices Mitchell had to make if she were to achieve her ambitions. In that she was a pioneer,

> actually enjoying the same rewards as men both financially and in terms of personal freedom. But unlike men, she has a female tradition behind her which sits on her shoulder and whispers, 'Capitulate.' If she is lonely, it is because she refuses to give in ... and ultimately it is the little devil in her ear that is the problem ... once other women learn from her and catch up she will not longer be the only woman with attitude.[13]

However, as Jim Miller observes, it took her nearly the course of her six albums 'to understand and accept her dependency upon men'.[14] It wasn't until *Hejira* that she could say 'No regrets, coyote.'

Nearly three decades after the release of *Blue*, Mitchell remains a significant force in popular music, having influenced artists as diverse as Annie Lennox, Prince and Seal. Her legacy is to focus attention on the personal, to express freedom of choice, to admit mistakes, unhappy love affairs, involvements with weak men, rough men and to move on – 'no regrets, we just come from different sets of circumstances'.[15] Her strength lies in her pragmatism. She was/is a realist who accepts change, a 1970s' woman who chose her lovers, accepted pain and bounced back. Her self-exploration anticipates the post-feminist emphasis of the 1990s, not least the importance for women to know, accept and explore personal feelings, to 'bridge the gap between mind and body, reason and emotion, thinking and feeling'.[16] It is a personal experience that is communicated with wit and intelligence and has certainly proved an inspiration for me.

ACKNOWLEDGEMENTS

It is always helpful to get constructive feedback from friends and fellow academics and I am especially grateful here to Mary Routh (School of Media, Music and Performance, University of Salford) and Dr John Richardson (South Bank University, London), author of *Singing Archeology: Philip Glass's Akhnaten*, Hanover and London: University Press of New England, for personal insights from which I quote freely.

NOTES AND REFERENCES

1 I would acknowledge the thoughts here of my friend and colleague Mary Routh whose feedback on my first draft provided many provocative and significant ideas that have been incorporated into this chapter. Thank you, Mary.

2 Again, I would thank Mary for her insight here.

3 Interview with Joni Mitchell. Makeover, J. (1989) *Woodstock*, London: Sidgwick and Jackson, p. 23.

4 Rycinga, J., 'Lesbian Compositional Process: One Lover-Composer's Perspective', in Brett, P. , Wood, E. and Thomas, G.C. (eds) (1994) *Queering The Pitch. The New Gay and Lesbian Musicology*, London: Routledge, p. 284. It is not suggested that Mitchell's compositions indicate a closet lesbian, rather that Rycinga's iden-tification of motion, perception, reflection etc. has a relevance to the compositional approach of the song. I would also refer here to Elizabeth Wood's article 'Sapphonics' (also in *Queering the Pitch*) which provides an interesting discussion of the ways in which women's voices cross the thresholds of register in a way that challenges the established order. As my colleague John Richardson observes, vocal and, particularly, instrumental virtuosity is a transgressive element – particularly for women performers – and the extraordinary range and power of Mitchell's voice quite literally upsets some listeners.

5 John Richardson has also contributed some relevant points on Joni Mitchell's alternative tunings which he interprets as a possible search for a different woman's voice. As he points out,

> alternative tunings also become alternative in a wider sense. It is true that people like Dave Van Ronk, David Crosby and Neil Young used similar tunings, but not with the same musical results. Mitchell herself cites Elizabeth Cotton, a black woman, as having influenced her guitar playing style, and not so much men who were working with alternative tunings at the time. Pat Metheny's frustration with Mitchell because of her use of alternative tunings (and her inability to categorise the chords) appears to lend support to the idea that these tunings are *truly* alternative and annoy people because of this.

John also notes that Suzanne Vega's unorthodox guitar style, although different to Mitchell's (Vega picks rather than strums) works in a similar way – as resisting the prevailing conditions. Thanks, John.

6 In folk music, most instruments are acoustic and portable. The important point here is that they can be carried around. As such there is an analogy with the artist's sketch pad in that they can access the immediacy of the moment through the equivalence of a thumbnail sketch.

7 Wilfred Mellors has suggested that women are successful with folk/pop because it is about 'instinct, as contrasted with the dominance of intellect and will'. This is debatable. Certainly Mitchell's songs evidence both an emotional content and a definable musical intellect. Mellers, W. (1986) *Angels of the Night. Popular Female Singers of our Time*, Oxford: Basil Blackwell, p. 141.
The examples are provided by my ex-student, Grant Shalks. My interest in Tarot provides some insight into the associations of the moon and the feminine psyche.

8 Mifflin, M., 'Barefoot and Pregnant', in *Keyboard*, p. 14, col. 3.

9 Mitchell's choice of guitar (as the accompaniment to a song) reflects her folk background. It also has strong associations with travel, the hippy lifestyle that was so significant to the late 1960s.

10 Again, I thank Mary here for her traveller's insights and the association of the riff with Stephen Stills' 'Marrakesh Express' which again highlights the exotic of travel.

11 Tonic to Dominant (I-V) cadences are associated with an interruption of expec-tations, a lack of resolution which is generally brought about by the reversal of

the V-I progression. Chord I is the harmonic 'home' of the diatonic scale and the V-I cadence implies finality. As such, Mitchell's use of the chord V on the word 'home' has an underlying irony in its musical implications of moving on.

12 As Lucy O'Brien observes, every line is carefully wrought. At times this makes her music curiously difficult to listen to – she doesn't opt for easy melody or satisfying conclusions. 'My music is not designed to grab instantly. It's designed to wear for a lifetime ... ' Mitchell said in 1994. O'Brien, L. (1995) *She Bop. The Definitive History of Women in Rock, Pop and Soul*, London: Penguin Books, p. 178.

13 Mary Routh, *op. cit.*.

14 Miller, J. (ed.) (1976) *The Rolling Stone Illustrated History of Rock and Roll*, New York: Rolling Stone Press, p. 314.

15 O'Brien, *op. cit.*, p. 178.

16 Tong, R. (1992) *Feminist Thought. A Comprehensive Introduction*, London: Routledge, p. 237.

7

DAUGHTERS OF CHAOS

Patti Smith, Siouxsie Sioux and the feminisation of rock

It is an extraordinary coincidence that punk, arguably one of the most chaotic, yet ordered sub-cultures to emerge within popular music, should coincide with the debates surrounding language in mediating socio-political relations. As Terry Eagleton wrote in 1983:

> Meaning was not 'natural', a question of just looking or seeing, or something eternally settled: the way you interpreted your world was a function of the languages you had at your disposal, and there was evidently nothing immutable about these. Meaning was not something which all men and women everywhere intuitively shared, and then articulated in their various tongues and scripts; what meaning you were able to articulate depended on what script of speech you shared in the first place.[1]

The emphasis on the text as mediating between language-users is significant, not least in asking 'why these particular groupings of statements at that time and not others'.[2] In particular the 'why' focuses a shift in emphasis from a preoccupation with the text to a new emphasis on social process, class, gender and ethnic divisions 'where the internal relations of "languages" articulate with social practices and historical structures'.[3] Whereas structuralists had stressed the primacy of structure and system in language (concentrating on the way in which the structures of visual, verbal and auditory texts produce meaning through an analysis of sign functions) post-structuralists shifted the emphasis towards the ideological implications of form. Language was seen as an active, transitive force which 'shapes' and positions the subject (as speaker, writer, reader) while always itself remaining 'in process' capable of infinite adaptation.[4]

The tensions between structuralism and post-structuralism, of fixity over process, underpins the 1970s debates surrounding the sign of 'woman' herself. If masculine and feminine are defined on the basis of their difference from each other, then woman can only be constructed as opposite, as 'other'. If, however, feminism accepts the diversity of women's experience as process, it becomes evident that different cultures fill 'masculine' and 'feminine' with a variety of characteristics and, as such, the who 'I am' as a woman addresses a multiplicity of subject positions, 'a diversity and specificity of women rather than any notional woman'.[5]

The concept of a polysemic woman focuses attention upon the relationship between experience, expression and signification. In particular the emphasis on cultural difference and diversity had moved feminist theory away from the universalising theories of capitalism and power while acknowledging the fact that although patriarchy sustains and recreates male power and female subordination, it exhibits itself in different forms both culturally and historically. Even so, while the emphasis on the plurality, diversity and difference of women avoids generalisations about the uniqueness of woman, the rejection of a unified or integrated self-identity was contentious. On the one hand it drew attention to the spilt between the conscious and unconscious dimensions of self-identity; on the other, it focused the problems inherent in binary oppositions which privileged a male/non-male distinction. As Julia Kristeva observed in an interview with *Tel Quel*,

> The belief that 'one is a woman' is almost as absurd and obscurantist as the belief that 'one is a man'. I say 'almost' because there are still many goals which women can achieve: freedom of abortion and contraception, day-care centres for children, equality on the job, etc. Therefore, we must use 'we are women' as an advertisement or slogan for our demands. On a deeper level, however, a woman cannot 'be'; it is something which does not even belong in the order of being.[6]

Kristeva's argument that 'a woman cannot be' — that she is always 'becoming' — focuses her distinction between the semiotic and symbolic order. Drawing on Lacan,[7] she identified the semiotic as a residue of the preimaginary, pre-Oedipal, pre-symbolic realm which can be interpreted as a site of resistance to the symbolic order of paternalism. For Lacan, the boy child's identification of the Symbolic Order with the anatomically similar father provides not only a sense of subjecthood and individuality, but equally an internalisation of the dominant order through language. For the girl child, her inability to fully internalise the Symbolic Order means that her access to language is suppressed. As male-defined, she can only think and speak within the confines of masculine discourse and her ability to communicate her feelings through words is denied.[8] Far from being neutral, language reveals the operation of power relations. It excludes the feminine and the woman is always the outsider.

The concept of the 'outsider' is significant in that it suggests both marginalisation and repression. For Kristeva, the misfits in society, the mad, the irrational, racial and ethnic minorities, homosexuals and lesbians, are all excluded from a dominant order which fails to take account of individuality and subjectivity. As such, there is a relationship between women's oppression and oppression in general which is not simply a matter of biological difference. 'Boys can identify with their mothers, and girls can identify with their fathers. Moreover, boys can exist and write in a "feminine" mode, and girls can exist and write in a "masculine" mode.'[9] As such, the repression of the semiotic or pre-Oedipal stage as characteristic of phallocentric thought is not necessarily inevitable. Rather there is a sense of tension between the symbolic and the semiotic whereby the latter acts as a site of resistance, undermining the rational. As such, while Kristeva associates the semiotic with the maternal it is not situated as innately female. Instead it is associated with the psychic, with irrational, rather than with rational thought and this, in turn, affects the conceptualisation of both space and time. Whereas time in the semiotic order is perceived as cyclical (repetitive) and monumental (eternal), *becoming*, time in the symbolic order is *teleological*, goal centred, linear and sequential. For Kristeva, the writers who exemplified semiotic expression, who were identified as revolutionary, were those whose often ungrammatical and disjointed writing disrupted the dialectical flow. As such, there is an emphasis on rhythm, sound and colour which displaces and disturbs syntax. It is 'fundamentally unrepressed because it has room for whatever disgusts and/or horrifies us'.[10]

While Kristeva identifies Samuel Beckett, James Joyce and Antonin Artaud as systematically dissecting language and, as such, undermining rational discourse, it is nevertheless evident that 'the play of semiotic and symbolic – the continual vacillation between disorder and order'[11] is equally evident in the seemingly contradictory texts of punk style. As Dave Laing observes, the punk listener's

> alignment with the musician's strategy of provocation must include pleasure in the awareness of how the other, 'traumatised' listener will be discomforted. That is, the identity of punk as something different depends in part on its achieving a disquieting impact on listeners whose expectations are framed by mainstream popular music and its values.[12]

As such, it is considered that Kristeva's model of 'semiotic' and 'symbolic' affective modalities provides a relevant theoretical framework for explaining the tensions between pleasure/unpleasure which characterise the punk discourse and, more specifically my analysis of Patti Smith and Siouxsie Sioux.

For women, punk can be characterised as a watershed in that it opened up a space for 'do-it-yourself' spontaneity and established individualism, discovery, change and outrage as crucial ingredients in style and image. In particular, women performers stressed both a new muscularity and a confrontational glamour that was far removed from either the introspection of Joni Mitchell, or the blues influenced rock of Janis Joplin. To a certain extent, this can be attributed to the underlying ethos of punk music, that anyone with a modicum of musical talent could form a band, that it did not involve a careful crafting of the musical sound nor technical complexity. Rather, the emphasis lay on the delivery of the vocal, the shock tactics of the lyrics and an overall emphasis on an eccentricity of self-expression. It is this identification of eccentricity, of a departure from the centre, of not conforming to common rules,[13] that provides a particular trajectory for female punk. The notorious sexism of 1960s' and 1970s' rock, which exerted both power and control and where women were the 'passive squaws of patriarchal hippy men', was replaced by a new emphasis on the woman as both 'warrior and mystic',[14] driven both by the unconscious and by social forces.

Although the moment of punk is associated with the Sex Pistols' first gig at London's St Martin's College of Art (6 November 1975), it is argued that the principal catalysts for the British new wave were MC5, Iggy Pop of the Stooges, the Velvet Underground and New York groups the Voidoids, Television, the Ramones and Patti Smith.[15] MC5's combination of a forceful rhythm section with high-energy chanting vocals provided one key element in punk style: strong, repetitious drumming with regular use of tom toms and a driving chant-like rhythm (see, for example, their 1968 album *Kick out the Jams*). There is, then, a certain comparability with Kristeva's identification of the semiotic chora[16] as vocalisation, kinetic, rhythmic, and this is equally evident in the Stooges' relentless, power-drill sound of guitarist Ron Asheton and bassist Dave Alexander and the demented vocals of Iggy Pop. In particular Pop's wild sense of depravity, his throwing up on stage, his indulgence in fellatio with members of the audience, and track after track of three chord banal rock pre-empted punk seven years ahead of time. *The Stooges* (their first LP) was produced by John Cale of the Velvet Underground. Championed by Andy Warhol, the Velvets' music was heralded as 'discordant', with 'throbbing cadences, pulsating tempos ... an assemblage that actually pulsates with menace, cynicism and perversion'.[17] More specifically, their insistent rhythms provided the raw material for groups like the Ramones whose stripped-down rock dominated the airwaves in 1976–7.

It was, however, John Cale's interest in the *avant-garde* that led him to produce Patti Smith's debut album *Horses* (1975). Smith's influences, including her 'love affair' with the nineteenth century French poet Rimbaud[18] and the political novelist and activist Jean Genet, her intellectual alignment with William Burroughs and instinctual identification with Jackson Pollock allied to such rock influences as Jim Morrison, Bob Dylan and Jimi Hendrix appear initially to be a heady mixture of romanticism, pantheism and mysticism. At the same time, there is a shared emphasis on an intuitive poetic language which stresses the 'chaos of sounds and rhythms, colour and lines'.[19] All express a sense of the intuitive through a process of disorientation. In particular, there is a heightened sense of beauty which is, at the same time, a radicalisation of form, an inherent rebellious-ness, which challenges and exposes the received languages of art, poetry, literature and music. All are visionaries, all are concerned with the revolu-tion of the mind. They are semiotic, 'embodied in poetic language' and, as such, 'disruptive of the social order'.[20]

It is not too surprising, then, that Smith's other formative influence should be her strong awareness of God. While it is tempting to suggest that her stream-of-consciousness writings and performances draw on the mythical languages of Babel, the relationship between the *avant-garde* text and the Bible is not as unlikely as may at first appear. As Kristeva suggests, there are parallels between the perfect love of the Virgin Mary, suffering with emotion, and such *avant-garde* artists as Pollock and Rothko. Mary's 'pleni-tude of signs' (as occupying all three symbolic positions of mother, daughter and bride of Christ) is an ideal which portrays separation as phallic *jouissance.* She cannot marry the flesh, but only the ideal and so remains the unique Virgin.[21] As the masculine feminine ideal she is thus analogous to the Lady, the imaginary addressee of the troubadours, who is purely the pretext for songs of love. As such, the songs are semiotic, rhythm and melody dominate the message to the Lady and, as texts of *jouissance*, presage the paintings of the *avant-garde* where rhythm and colour dominate representational or symbolic elements. In such artists as Jackson Pollock, perspective, represen-tation, clarity and order (symbolic) are challenged and even the title of his painting 'Blue Poles' is itself tenuous. The spectator is lost in the swirls of dripping colours.

While it is not suggested that Kristeva's writings influenced Smith, nor that she shared her conception of the tensions between the form-giving of the symbolic and the energy of the semiotic, her conceptual model is useful in explaining the primary *modus operandi* of the music, not least because Smith undoubtedly has a grasp of the revolution in poetic language – or as she herself explained, 'great art is seductive on various levels'.[22] In general, her musical style can be interpreted as a clash between the symbolic and the semiotic, using the language of ecstatic religion, the power of the word, struggling with the certainties of the disciplined faith she'd learnt as a child, through an often musically undisciplined semiotic babble, the uncensored traces of the unconscious. It is, in Kristeva's words, paragrammatic.[23]

Given her influences, it is not surprising that Smith's poetry moved between the real and the non-real, being and non-being. 'Piss Factory', written in 1970, merges the poetic with an underlying social realism that reflected both her experience in 'a hot, sweaty, shitty, factory'[24] and the choice to move on. Ending with the words 'I'm gonna get on that train and go to New York and I'm gonna be so bad, I'm gonna be a big star and I will

never return never return no never return to burn out in this Piss Factory',
the song provides an insight into Smith's underlying determination to leave
the suburban environment of her childhood. Moving to New York in 1967,
she began performing her frenetic poetry at St Mark's Church where she
soon attracted a cult following. Accompanied by guitarist/rock writer Lenny
Kaye, her work attracted the attention of *Cream* magazine (US) which
published her poetry in 1971. Three volumes of writings and poems
followed: *Seventh Heaven*, *Kodak* and *Witt*. By 1974 the poems had been
replaced by songs, backed by Kaye and pianist Richard Sohl. Their first
single, 'Hey Joe', with its sustained reference to urban terrorist Patty Hearst,
was funded by her 'soul twin', the photographer Robert Mapplethorpe and
has been cited as 'the first punk-rock record'.[25] With the addition, in 1975,
of Ivan Krai (guitar, bass) and Jay Daugherty (drums), the group signed to
Arista and released *Horses*, (1975), Smith's debut album. Hailed as a
powerful statement in rock, *Horses* broke new ground in many ways. The
title is an allusion to heroin, so linking it with the New York underground
scene of Andy Warhol, John Cale and Lou Reed. The back of the record
sleeve provides the space for unsung lyrics: 'only history (gentle rocking
mona lisa) seals .... only *histoire* is responsible for the ultimate cannonizing';
'me the memoire of me racing thru the eye of the *mer*'. The imagery and use
of French words foreground the hybrid nature of the album itself, fusing the
heritage of the French *avant-garde* with the harsh punk sound of the musical
delivery. It was experimental in form, combining poetry and rock 'with the
kind of intuitive brilliance that can only grow out of limited technique and
intense feeling'.[26]

Smith's style of punk was, as she put it, 'Three-chord rock merged with
the power of the word'.[27] There is, however, little of the amateur in the
skilful blend of blues, rock, soul funk and ska/reggae which underpin the
vocals. Rather the overall sound is fetishistic, harmonically static, heavily
repetitive with the momentum achieved by the build-ups to often frenetic
climaxes. Above all, the effect is *extra*ordinary. As American critic Dan
Graham observed in 1979, 'She speculated on a new definition of "female",
redefining women's subservient position in rock. Variously, she projected
herself as lesbian, androgyne, martyr, priestess, female God.'[28] Given that
Smith's only female hero, Joan of Arc, was herself a de-sexed martyr (celebrating her womanhood and fetishising her virginity), the accolade is not
too unlikely. With her emaciated look and rejection of 'a confused skirt
tagging the hero',[29] Smith was soon identified as a self-styled asexual who
refused to be complicit in her female identity. The cover image, by
Mapplethorpe, was (at the time) curiously shocking in its overt confrontation with the gendered image of the female rock singer. The photograph is
heavily posed and Smith comes across as both self-assured and sexually
ambiguous, challenging and contesting the boundaries of gender.[30]

This sense of adopting a sexual pose, of playing with, and performing different gendered identities, is picked up in the first two tracks of the album. 'Gloria' is sung from the point of view of the predatory male of the Van Morrison original, but Smith's vocals play on sexual ambivalence. She is identified as the masculine figure in a relationship that includes a feminised partner. Preceded by slow, alternating chords on the piano, Smith's opening words are a monotone of disavowal: 'Jesus died for somebody's sins but not mine'. The doxology hinted at in the title is thus subverted: this is no song of praise to the patriarchal father, but rather an exaltation of sexual desire which focuses on possession 'make her mine'.

The move into an upbeat blues 'You could say beware' is charged with increasing energy as Smith moves into the voyeuristic 'Oh she looks so good, oh she looks so fine', the vocal inflections focusing a specific link between rhyme and rhythm as the punch line 'and then I'm gonna (ah, ah) make her mine, aah, mine' shifts the narrative into an upbeat chant celebrating the arrival of 'Gloria' 'walking through my door'. Smith's vocal gestures, the declamatory 'Here she comes', the upturn of pitch on the final word of each phrase 'walking down the *street*', 'knocking at my *door*', 'walking up my *stairs*', is given an added intensity as the phrases are repeated, the piano chords responding to the 'knocking', before the celebratory 'gonna tell the world', 'made her mine' transforms the anticipatory of the first section into a celebration of possession. The power of the delivery here is due largely to the fact that the words themselves are not always intelligible. Rather the sexual rhythm dominates and the '*come*' (of 'here she comes') is charged with mounting urgency as Smith snarls out 'made her mine'. With the nuancing finally spelt out, the 'nightmares' are finally resolved as 'G.L.O.R.I.A' is subjected to vocal scrutiny, each syllable punctuated by pulsating guitar interjections before the chorus, where the gospel sound of the female backing singers echo the hymn of praise to Gloria herself, the word made flesh.

Conceptually, the juxtaposition of the choir with the pogo-like rhythm of the instrumentals, and Smith's frenzied vocals establish a sense of tension as 'rhythm, sound and colour' displace and disturb the musical syntax to create a tension between the semiotic and symbolic. There is a vacillation between disorder (Smith's vocals) and order (the gospel-like chorus with its religious associations;[31] the strong, repetitive rhythm with its drive towards resolution/climax) which is resolved by a return to the slow incantation of the reprise 'Jesus died for somebody's sins ....' and the whispered 'but not mine' which lifts to the final and ecstatic chant to 'Gloria'.

Smith's implicit masculine persona in 'Gloria' is confirmed in the second track, 'Redondo', where she describes a suicide on a lesbian beach. Sung to an upbeat jogging ska rhythm, Smith recounts the break-up with her female lover, establishing the time 'late afternoon', and the bare facts in a declamatory and largely unembellished vocal style: 'we just had a quarrel/ sent you away'. The chorus is curiously cheerful for a requiem, a throwback to the girl-group songs of the 1960s in its 'active relationship (female 'I') to the other ('you')', albeit that in this instance the active/passive is undermined by the irreversible passivity of death – 'I was looking for you (hoo hoo) and now you're gone gone'. The 'sweet suicide' draws on country codes in its references to 'little girl', 'a smiling angel', a 'victim', this time 'done wrong by her (wo)man'.[32] The fact that this is a lesbian relationship, however, disturbs the musical experience of familiarity ('heard you on the 'phone (another dimension) but you never returned') of the abandoned woman. The rock cliché 'well you know what I mean' thus becomes both extraordinary and disturbing as the listener is made aware of the dynamics of a song which narrates marginality and self-destruction, 'You'll never return into my heart/home ... because you're gone gone.'

It is, however, the classic 'Break It Up' and the follow-on track, 'Land of 1,000 Dancers', that are most indicative of what Kristeva terms the 'performative dimension of language'.[33] Whereas 'Redonda' is largely concerned with the communicative, 'Break It Up' exemplifies the scandalous, semiotic aspect of *avant-garde* poetry. In particular, Smith's lyrics have a plurality of meaning as they play on images that are both disturbing and ambiguous. To an extent, this can be attributed to the influence of the New York rock scene of the mid-1960s where there was a close relation 'between the high-cultural discourse of poetry and the angry rock style'[34] of Lou Reed, a former student of the poet Delmore Schwartz at Syracuse University, and Bob Dylan, whose self-conscious poetry was a formative influence on Smith. However, as Carrie Jaures Noland points out, the relation between poetry and popular music was equally evident in the thriving poetic communities of 1950s' New York and San Francisco.

> Jack Kerouac, originator of the Beats and a reader of those 'renegades of high culture', Celine, Rimbaud and Yeats, shared these influences with poets Gregory Croso, Gary Snyder, and Allen Ginsberg.[35]

As such, the importance of the *avant-garde* within rock music as a '*dérèglement de tous les sens*'[36] was well-established, not least in the work of Jim Morrison where non-conventional lyrics, allied to hallucinogenic experience, subverted the distinction between poetry and popular music, music and social change.

'Break It Up' has a straightforward verse/chorus format but the poetic text of the lyrics, the association of violence with spiritual salvation ('I ripped my skin open and then I broke through/I cried break it up, oh, now I understand') anticipates 'the trajectory of sin and redemption'[37] that informs *Easter*. The 'boy', nameless and part-angel/part-lover is both the subject of the song and, at the same time, inseparable from the poetic discourse and musical gesture that move to a loss of self through the *jouissance* of orgasm.

The first two lines of each verse are sparsely accompanied by piano and a sustained guitar atmospheric to create a feeling of tranquil anticipation. The slow pulse and the monotone throaty delivery of the melodic line, with its haunting resemblance to Kurt Weil's Budapest café songs and the singing of Lotte Lenya, situates the song in an altered timescape. In particular the atmospherics of an imagined reality – 'snow started falling' and non-reality – 'I could hear the angel calling' are drawn into association by the use of rhyme and a strangely Baroque musical metaphor whereby the metaphysical (lines three and four of each verse) is opened out by ascending guitar arpeggios which colour the *'break out'* (of his skin), *'turned over'* (my heart) of the lyrics.

The dynamic intensity of the third and fourth lines ('we rolled on the ground, he opened his wings') underpins a sense of urgency, a religious fervour, which is focused by the call and response of the chorus. The repeated and muted 'break it up' of the boy is initially greeted with a lack of comprehension 'I don't understand/I can't comprehend'. The need to touch if there is to be any belief ('I want to feel you') resonates with a doubt which draws on Smith's knowledge of the *New Testament* and Thomas' response to the risen Christ. This emphasis on a new conception of the physical and the metaphysical, the need to aesthetically redefine the boundaries of the self ('I ripped my skin open and then I broke through') through primal energy ('I tore off my clothes, I danced on my shoes') is equally informed by the activity of the words themselves. The verses are shaped by rhyming couplets which produce a consistent and regularised spatial framework. At the same time, the vocal nuancing plays on the lyric text. The exaggerated vowels foreground the relationship between the religious and the orgasmic 'I fell on my knees ....', the downward vocal melisma on 'I cried', the elliptical pause which precedes the sensual 'Take me please!' The eroticism of the final verse is focused by the phonetic resemblance between, for example, *'ice'*, *'I'*, *'shi*ning' and is given an added intensity as the gentle pulsating piano accompaniment is opened out for the final time by the ascending guitar arpeggios on 'melting' before the ecstatic 'I can feel it's breaking .... I can feel ... oh, now I'm coming with you ... oh feel me I'm coming' and the slow fadeout, 'break it up'.

Although 'Break It Up' has a tenuous link with the punk aesthetic in its emphasis on self-mutilation, and the fragmentation and manipulation of the lyric line (and its association with the cultural displacement of the punk sub-culture), the music itself is too self-consciously restrained to have any real sense of antecedence. Rather, it is the heroin track 'Land of 1,000 Dancers' and, in particular, the 'Horses' refrain, that most clearly situates the disruptive potential of *avant-garde* poetry within a punk musical style.

Starting with a quietly spoken introductory verse ('The boy was in the hallway drinking a glass of tea') the lyrics juxtapose the matter-of-fact with the poetic and rhythmic dimensions of the heroin experience. As Noland observes, 'if we envision poetry as a literary genre whose evolution engages other cultural practices' then the fate of a text becomes pertinent.[38] As such, Smith's contextualisation of cocaine/smack ('And I fill my nose with snow') through assonance and rhyme ('go, Rimbaud go', 'go Johnny go') identifies both the hero and the drop-out community of drug addicts within a disruptive and deviant poetic form which begins with 'the boy' (and the rock 'n' roll lifestyle encapsulated by the Chuck Berry reference) and ends with 'the man' (shrouded by sheets 'dancing around/to the simple/rock and roll/song'.)

Although the song is long, and complex in its imagery, the changing experiences are charged by a rhythmic dynamic which impels the movement from a starkly simple and unaccompanied statement of fact ('at the other end of the hallway a rhythm was generating'), through to a pulsating echo ('he pushed him against the locker and drove it home') which, in turn, informs the mechanical pulse of the second stanza. Smith's colouring of the vocal line is marked by an unrelenting rhythm which impels the narrative of events 'The boy looked at Johnny, Johnny wanted to run.' Isolation, echo, reverb and repetition: 'he drove it in, he drove it home, he drove it deep in Johnny' create an ambient mood of pulsating menace as the throbbing mechanical rhythm is underpinned by the metallic guitar riff to anticipate the sound of 'horses, horses, coming in all directions'.

Written by Smith, 'Horses' has a sense of primal energy. There is no syncopation. Rather the driving chant-like rhythm, the speech-like delivery with inflections and upturns of pitch ('suddenly', 'Johnny') and repetition 'horses, horses, horses, horses' exemplify the importance of rhythm in punk rock. At the same time there is a similarity to the chorus in 'Gloria' where stabbing piano chords move the vocals to an ecstatic high as Smith eulogises the dance crazes of the early 1960s, referencing Chubby Checker 'Do you know how to twist, well it goes like this' with its sexual *double entendre*, before moving into the dangerous territory of illicit desire – 'I want your baby sister' – that characterised Jim Morrison's classic song 'The End'.[39] The insistent rhythm continues into the fourth stanza where strong, repetitious drumming on the tom-toms creates the pogo-like feel that was later to characterise the Sex Pistols. It is, however, the delivery of the vocal that most clearly situates Smith as punk. In particular, the force and speed of such repeated phrases as 'do the watusi' contrast with the imagery and assonance of 'shined open coiled snakes white and shiny twirling and encircling' to effect a feeling of primitive violent expression and menace.

Although 'Land' is, perhaps, too self-consciously poetic in its blurring of the difference between high-cultural referents and social deviance, the rearrangement of cultural fragments ('He picked up the blade and he pressed it against his smooth throat (the spoon)/And let it dip in (the veins), dip in (the sea of possibilities)'; 'the arrows of desire'); the use of imagery ('horses') to engender word associations ('Do you know how to pony like bony maloney?'); phonetic play ('Oh, we had such a brainiac-*amour*/But no *more*';

'Do the sweet *pea*, do the sweet *pee pee*'), and the use of odd juxtapositions and figurative displacement, clearly presage the disarticulation, the *bricolage* of the punk aesthetic.

The concept of a self-consciously subversive *bricolage*, as discussed by Hebdige, refers to the ironic and impious way in which punks 'cut up', 'plundered' and juxtaposed apparently unrelated items and signifiers to create a kinetic, transitive culture which concentrated 'attention on the act of transformation performed upon the object'.[40] Connected with Barthes' concept of *significance*, it is distinguished from signification by an emphasis on process, it

> struggles with meaning and is deconstructed 'lost' .... Contrary to signification, *significance* cannot be reduced therefore, to communi-
> cation, representation, expression: it places the subject (of writer, reader) in the text not as a projection .... but as a 'loss', a 'disap-
> pearance'.[41]

As Hebdige observes, 'the ideas of *significance*' and 'obtuse meaning' suggest the presence in the text of an intrinsically subversive component. As such, punk style can be considered to be in a constant state of assemblage, of flux. This is clearly evident in the penultimate stanza of 'Land' where Smith engages in a sepulchral self-dialogue against the mechanical and train-like rhythm of the guitar and kit. Against an ecstatic and repeated 'I feel it', Smith moves into a narration of death, 'the butterfly flapping in his throat':

> Your nerves, your mane of the black shining horse
> And my fingers all entwined through the air
> I could feel it, it was the hair going through my fingers
> The hairs were like wires going through my body
> That's how I died

The musical arrangement is obtuse, a radical *collage* of sounds that 'babble' and 'battle', going beyond the 'full stop' – the ultimate sign of closure – through an often incoherent speech that privileges confusion ('At that Tower of Babel they knew what they were after'), violence ('his vocal chords shot up' (possibility) like mad pituitary glands'), and death. Above all, the sound is disruptive, chaotic, and, I suggest, demonstrates the way in which Smith feminised the sound and style of rock through an emphasis on the negative side of the chora.

As such, it is disturbing to note that so many critical evaluations of punk (by leading British academics) fail to discuss her influence. To an extent, this can be attributed to the way in which British writers have staked their claim on punk and, as such, my reading of Patti Smith provides what I hope will be interpreted as a challenging feminist critique. In particular, I would

105

point to her injection of the poetic *avant-garde* into both her songs and record sleeves. This is later evidenced in the British punk scene where obscenities are laced into record notes and publicity releases, interviews, and songs, something which has direct parallels with Smith's practice of including unperformed poetry and tributes to Rimbaud on her record sleeves. In this connection it is argued that the heritage of British punk owed less to Hebdige's identification of 'working classness' than might at first appear. Indeed, as Dan Graham argues, Patti Smith's influence on Malcolm McLaren, the orchestrator of British punk, was significant. As manager of the New York Dolls at a time when their popularity was in decline, he had been exposed to the new wave acts of Patti Smith, Richard Hell and the Voidoids, Television and the Ramones. Both Hell and Smith regularly cited high-cultural figures in their lyrics and 'were in large part responsible for implanting in McLaren the idea that a traditionally elitist heritage could be usefully integrated in his commercial project'.[42] Interviews with Richard Hell would support Graham's observation. During McLaren's six months in New York he had seen a musical sub-culture develop that was self-generated, mutually supportive, yet potentially commercial. Patti Smith, in particular, radiated 'intelligence, speed, being connected with the moment ... she was the focus'.[43] What attracted McLaren was the sense of danger and refusal, the torn T-shirts that spoke of sexuality and violence. 'If such a thing is possible to identify, it was the origin of what would become the Punk style ... He copied the New York groups.'[44] This is particularly noticeable in the fetishistic clothing, the rubberwear, glamourwear and stagewear sold in McLaren and Westwood's shop, Sex. Quotations from situationist pamphlets were used to decorate their punk-style jackets and T-shirts, and the lintel to the shop was 'sprayed with a slogan from Rousseau, "Craft must have clothes but Truth loves to go naked." '[45]

Clearly Patti Smith is but one influence upon McLaren, and the extent to which he introduced her records to the entourage of 'cult' teenagers who frequented 'Sex' is not documented. However, while there is little evidence of Smith's love of the intellectual *avant-garde* in the music, there is nevertheless a shared emphasis on shock tactics and, with Siouxsie Sioux, an idiosyncratic and disruptive use of language. The frenetic edge of her vocal style is also echoed in the harshness and tension of Poly Styrene's shriek in 'Oh Bondage, Up Yours'. I would also identify aspects of musical style. The Sex Pistols, for example, privileged a strummed distorted guitar technique with an eight-note rhythmic emphasis – a characteristic which is present in 'Land of 1,000 Dancers'. There is also a comparability with the Clash, whose Berry-style rock 'n' roll ('Brand New Cadillac'), reggae-influenced rock ('Guns of Brixton' and 'Revolution Rock') and Springsteen-like song ('The Card Game') are genres already explored in *Horses,* and Smith's collaboration with Springsteen in the hit single 'Because the Night'.[46]

It is, however, her sense of disruption and subversion (the high-energy chanting vocals, and the disquieting impact upon the listener) that particularly marks her presence as the forerunner of the British punk scene. In particular, her innate feeling for performance as art aligns her with the art-school impetus of Glen Matlock (the Sex Pistols), Joe Strummer (the Clash), Adam Ant, and Siouxsie Sioux (and the Banshees). David Bowie, who had worked with Lou Reed and Iggy Pop, and whose character transformations as expressions of alienation were to influence the duality and pretence inherent in punk, also came from an art school background. Like Smith, he had a strong interest in the impact of theatrical performance on the popular domain of music. However, during the initial stages of British punk, when 'the ability to get an aggressive response out of the audience was (seen as) a measure of potency, effectiveness and bonding'[47] was critical, is it really so surprising that McLaren should play down the significance of a performer who was well-educated, well-read and articulate?

While Smith's influence on punk has been largely overlooked by leading academics,[48] her significance within feminism has been subject to criticism. In particular, her lack of public support for women and her entourage of successful and talented men – Mapplethorpe, Cale, Verlaine, Kaye, Springsteen – suggest a woman who was more interested in achieving a personal success than risking compromise through an explicit identification with the women's movement.[49] For the next generation of female bands, however, Smith's sense of outrage and her ability to refashion rock through an intensely personalised lyric style, transformed both the gendered identity of rock style and contemporary notions of divas and rock goddesses. 'She was androgynous, outspoken, obviously well-educated and well-read. She became like a mentor to me ..... Smith in a sense was my first teacher' (ex-punk singer songwriter Adele Berten).[50]

The scream of feminised punk

Siouxsie Sioux and the Banshees were arguably one of the most significant British punk bands and one of the few to develop a long-term career. Originally from Chislehurst, Kent, Siouxsie (Susan Ballion) was part of what was known as the Bromley contingent (Simon Barker, Steve Bailey, Billie Broad). Influenced by Roxy Music, David Bowie and Stanley Kubrick's recently released film, *Clockwork Orange*[51], they became an established part of the Sex Pistols' cult audience. Siouxsie had originally met the Pistols at Westwood's shop 'Sex' and together with Simone, Steve Severin and Simon Barker had been brought in to add a little spice to the group's now famous interview with Bill Grundy. As Jon Savage points out,

> Viewed now, the *Today* clip is one long visual loss of control ...
> rather than being the instrument of editorial objectivity, Bill

Grundy loses his temper. Rather than dampening down an obviously volatile set of guests, he challenges them with the inevitable response.[52]

Siouxsie's 'I've always wanted to meet you', her grimace at his 'we'll meet afterwards, shall we?' triggered the final ten seconds of banter, culminating in the now famous line from Steve Severin, 'You fucking rotter'. As a live broadcast, it was significant in bringing both the Sex Pistols and Siouxsie Sioux into the public arena.

Siouxsie and the Banshees made their first public appearance at the September 1976 Punk Festival. It was held at the 100 Club and was an idea dreamed up by McLaren to dupe the media into thinking that punk rock was big enough to have its own festival. Groups were asked to fill the empty spots and Siouxsie volunteered. Sid Vicious, Marco Pirroni and Steve Severin were brought in, and despite the lack of rehearsal and what Siouxsie recalls as a shambolic performance, it worked. 'It was taking the piss out of all the things we hated ... What song do you really hate? What can we mutilate and destroy?'[53] 'The Lord's Prayer', 'She Loves You' and 'Young Love' were among the songs chosen for mutilation.

Siouxsie's immediate agreement to take part in the festival was very much part and parcel of the punk do-it-yourself ethic, but as Lucy Toothpaste, editor of the feminist fanzine *Jolt* explains,

> Boy bands were getting up on stage who couldn't play a note, so it was easy for girls who couldn't play a note to get up on stage as well. By the time that they developed, women were singing about their own experiences in a way which I don't think they'd done before. I never got one Punk woman in any of my interviews to say she was a feminist, because I think they thought the feminist label was too worthy, but the lyrics they were coming out with were very challenging, questioning all the messages we'd been fed through *Jackie* comics. Punk made women feel they could compete on equal terms to men.[54]

The origin of what was later called post-punk was often centred around gender politics and a questioning approach towards sexuality. In particular, punk women were confronted with the problem of presenting their ideas with a comparable 'feel' to that of the male groups, an attitude that was confrontational, challenging and culturally relevant. As such, it is not surprising that Siouxsie's style of presentation was deeply influenced by her early involvement with the Bromley gay scene, and such London clubs as Chaugeramas, the Masquerade, and the exclusive lesbian club, Louise's in Poland Street. The catalyst for sexual excess, however, was arguably Vivienne Westwood and her inner circle of punk women performers were encouraged to act out their sexual fantasies appropriately dressed in her designer clothes.

> There was Siouxsie who was dressed in a plastic apron and tights, that was all. No knickers, nothing. And she had a leather whip. My parents had these awful polystyrene tiles, and there were whip marks all over the ceiling.[55]

Siouxsie was equally influenced by the film *Cabaret* and Liza Minnelli's white shirt, black tie, cropped black hair – a style which was to inform her own *Weimar* image.[56] She was also attracted to McLaren and Westwood's highly contradictory anarchy shirts which became associated with the punks during the summer of 1976. The original slogan 'Only Anarchists Are Pretty' was soon extended to include an (often inverted) flying swastika from the Second World War ... 'but the shirt didn't exist in isolation ... and both Westwood and McLaren ... had a stock of Nazi memorabilia'.[57] Wearing a Nazi armband was initially seen by Siouxsie as part of her shock tactics, similar in effect to 'wearing something with her tits hanging out'.[58] However, the politics surrounding confrontation and its relationship to fascism was confusing, and the brutal 'in-yer-face' music, swastikas and cropped hair was seized on by the press who reported it as synonymous with the rise of the National Front and the National Socialist Party. It was an association that took some time to live down and for a year no one would touch the band. Despite the Banshees' public disassociation with the National Front and their subsequent release of 'Israel' (1980) as a public atonement for wearing a Nazi armband, it is evident that what had started as naïve shock tactics had become increasingly damaging as the opposition between Rock against Racism and the Front's Rock for Racism became front page news.[59]

Although Siouxsie's preoccupation with theatricality persisted throughout her punk years, it is evident from her coolly androgynous persona that one of her most significant influences was Patti Smith. As her friend Berlin recalls, 'Siouxsie mirrored herself on all those pop stars, Nico and Patti Smith, and Severin modelled himself on John Cale and Lou Reed, which is where he got the name Severin from: 'Venus in Furs'.[60] It was an influence that was to remain stylistically in the final line-up of the band. In 1977 Siouxsie and Severin were joined by Kenny Morris and Peter Fenton and after a huge A&R bidding war, a contract was finally secured with Polydor. 'Hong Kong Garden' (August, 1978) reached the British top ten, and this was followed in October by their debut LP *The Scream*. The album overall is characterised by hard-edged commentary ranging from confrontations with slabs of meat ('Carcass'), through cigarette addiction ('Nicotine Stain') to fraught tensions in suburbia ('Suburban Relapse'). Above all it is unrepressed. The imagery is unpredictable, the syntax disjointed, with the effect of making the familiar (butcher's shops, door bells, holiday postcards) unfamiliar and uncomfortable. As Jon Savage succinctly observes, it was 'a cool, malevolent sweep through a landscape of decay.'[61]

'Carcass' (track four) has an upbeat eight bar introduction which establishes an aptly tight, mechanical rhythm for a song which pulsates with menace. The abundance of clichés ('Out of the frying pan and into the fire', 'By hook or by crook, you'll be first/last in his book'), and familiar everyday objects ('Heinz 58 Varieties') become both disgusting and horrifying as they are drawn into association with a predatory butcher 'craving for a raw love'. Despite the predictability of the repetitive rhythms, the bass note pedal, the constant chopping drive of the guitar, and the narrative exposition of events in the lyrics, it is evident that the effectiveness of the song lies in its denial of expectations. The lyrics are open to infinite possibilities as the meaning of rejection ('you got the chop') is scattered along a chain of signifiers. As such there is a sense of what Julia Kristeva cites as the poetic dimension of language, full of ambiguity and therefore full of meaning – in effect, the negative side of the chora. In particular, the puns provide a glimpse of the unconscious in the play on different experiences of the same words, 'meat', 'carcass', 'pork', 'endlessly in love'.

Siouxsie's clipped vocal delivery effectively dissects and destabilises both the words and the phrases through exaggerated emphasis and a savage twisting of vowels which resonate with the disarticulation of the body:

> In love with your stumps
> In love with the bleeding,
> In love with the pain
> That you once felt
> As you became a carcass

This dismantling of the descriptive elements, the mutilation of a person 'limblessly in love', is metaphorically represented by the hacking staccato delivery and musical phrasing which 'chops up' the lyric syntax. The fragmentation of 'car-cass' in the final chorus also works through semantic instability ('you became a car-cass, we became a car-cass, car-cass, car-crash') and consistency through the use of phonetic resemblance. The outro opens out the aural emotion surrounding 'dead meat' through a pig-like grunt, which is followed by a lip-smacking sound juxtaposed with a sonorous bass pedal and jarring feedback from McKay's guitar. The pedal note segues into the next track, Lennon/McCartney's 'Helter Skelter' to effect a macabre retrospective in its association with Charles Manson who, like the butcher in 'Carcass' had a taste for drinking blood, performing ceremonial flailings and robotising his women into slaves for both sex and murder. As such, the songs invoke the allusive play between presence and absence which characterises the poetic text.

The seventh track on the album 'Metal Postcard' was premiered early in

1978 at a time when the band were actively disassociating themselves from their Nazi image. Subtitled '*mittageisen*/mechanistic', the music has a strong symbolic coding. Morris's heavy tom tom establishes a repetitive march-like rhythm which is emphasised by the metallic sound of McKay's guitar. The lyrics are equally tight and 'mechanical' as they follow the metric four-in-a-bar pulse, emphasising the syllabic construction of the words:

> Metal is tough
> Metal will sheen
> Metal won't rust when
> Oiled and cleaned.

The regimented character of the words is emphasised by word-painting and inflection, the upward lift on 'tough', 'sheen', 'cleaned', the allusion to combat drill, a military tattoo – 'Reunion begins (Hup!) with a glass of mercury (Hup!)'. The abrupt rise and fall on 'jerk' ('with a clockwork jerk'), the use of an abrasive staccato on one syllable words which have a similar hardness in their final consonant ('jerk', 'pluck'), creates an aural spectacle which places the listener alongside the seated family, watching as the 'television flickers with another news bulletin'. Above all, the song is mimetic in its reproduction of a mechanised world, nihilistic and noisy in its emphatic delivery. As such, it is not too surprising that the band were careful to locate the inspiration for the song as John Heartfield's collage 'Guns and Butter'. 'It took a long time to live down that Nazi thing,' says Severin[62] and 'Metal Postcard', with its references to 'commanding loud speakers' and 'master-scheme' was clearly too fascist in its imagery to escape some association with the National Front.

If 'Metal Postcard' highlights the tensions surrounding the re-emergence of British Nazis, under the banner of the National Front, then 'Nicotine Stain' deftly kills the romanticism of the 'cigarette with lipstick traces', the 'smoke gets in my eyes' which typified 1940s' *cinéma noire*. The effectiveness of the lyrics lies, once again, in their use of poetic devices, most specifically rhyme and phonetic resemblance:

> then my hand sh*a*kes
> but it's just driving me ins*ane*
> when the smoke gets in my *brain*

with the final line of the verse

> I can't resist *it*

reaching back to the first couplets

> It's just a hab*it*
> when I reach to the pack*et*

to effect a sense of repetition which is both poetic and apt: 'tell it like it is'.

It is, however, 'Suburban Relapse' that engages most directly with what Hebdige calls 'the experience of contradiction expressed through visual (and in the song, aural) puns'.[63] Above all, the song is characterised by a sense of elastic tension which is initially established by the counterpointed guitars of John McKay and Steve Severin, and a *pastiche* of the theme song to the movie *Goldfinger*. The juxtaposition of jangling metal with the association of James Bond in this unusually long (18 bar) introduction suggests 'the big number' performance of Shirley Bassey, but the lyrics situate the extraordinary within the commonplace of suburbia in a song which is characterised by an underlying hysteria.

Siouxsie's dissection of the lyric line is particularly effective in preventing the familiar from being one-dimensional. Words are stretched to their musical limits before they ping back, providing a metaphor for the psychological tensions, the breaking point inherent in a nervous breakdown. As prose they have a matter-of-factness, 'I'm sorry that I hit you but my string snapped. I'm sorry I disturbed your cat-nap.' On the lyric printout (on the record sleeve, CD) the words are arranged into three lines

> I'm sorry that I h*i*t you
> but my st*ri*ng **sn**apped.
> I'm sorry I *di*sturbed your cat-**nap**

which provide an initial glimpse of her use of assonance and rhyme. The vocal delivery, however, exposes the nervous tension through musical phrasing and vocal gestures which colour and disrupt syntax:

1	2	3	4
			I'm
Sor-	ry	that	I
HIT	chu	but	my
Strin	... ...	... ...	.g
Snap't			I'm
Sor-	ry	I	dis-
Turrrrrrb'd			your
Ca	... ...	... ...	...t
Nap			

Everyday phrases, 'I'm sorry that I' are delivered in a matter-of-fact tone; 'string', 'cat' are elastically stretched, snapping back to a rhyming staccato on 'snapped', 'nap' which are given an upward inflection. In contrast, the 'turrrrrb'd' (of 'disturbed') is onomatopoeically linked with cat. This dismantling of the signifier, the engendering of the text at the phonic level of sounds continues through the song to effect what Kristeva identifies as *sensesound.*[64] Individual words are subjected to vocal scrutiny. 'Relapse' is dislocated (re/lapse ... ... a/re ... ... /lapse'). The dip shapes (on 'lapse', 're') lurch, and the feeling of panic is heightened by an increased volume and speed. It is this focus on what Roland Barthes' identifies as 'the voluptuousness of its sound-signifiers, of its letters'[65] that underlines and informs Siouxsie's lyric strategy, aligning her most closely with both the semiotic text and Patti Smith. 'It goes back to pre-Grundy, everything being more complex, all those bands that were taking things from the Ramones that fuelled an imaginary torture.'[66]

Like Patti Smith, Siouxsie Sioux brought a new sense of individuality, a feminisation of rock, in her confrontational style and image. Her songs – not least those that questioned sexuality – were aggressive, full of brutalities, characterised by what Savage calls 'controlled hysteria'[67] and what Kristeva would identify as the negative side of the chora. More specifically, her lyrics and vocal delivery provide a particular insight into the poetic dimension of language. Her aural puns, repetition, and intensive vocal energy breaks through and distorts the *symbolic* metric flow of the 4/4 beat to effect a *semiotic* deconstruction of rock which forces the listener into a different way of listening. Although this sense of shock value is also present in male punk bands, not least in their challenge to the vocal styling of mainstream rock and their provocation of dislike (rather than identification), it is evident that Siouxsie's defiance, hardness, and position at the epicentre of punk, was a landmark in the battle for equality in rock. As Lucy O'Brien rightly points out, 'As well as celebrating a vague anti-social anarchy, punk values were about identification with the disadvantaged, the dispossessed, the sub-cultural' and as such they 'offered women permission to explore gender boundaries, to investigate their own power, anger, aggression – even nastiness'[68] – a statement that curiously echoes Kristeva's identification of the outsider, the marginalised, the repressed, as discussed earlier.

Even so, while punk celebrated assertiveness, women performers generally continued to exhibit an underlying uncertainty about their musical direction. Thus, despite the success of such bands as Siouxsie and the Banshees, the Slits, the Raincoats and the Pretenders' Chrissie Hynde, most British female punk bands retained a cult-level status. In America there were few women involved in the punk scene, despite the influence of Patti Smith, and in general music was more focused on experimentation, or in revamping rock 'n' roll roots than in shock politics. The Cramps (with Ivy Rorschach on guitar) fused rock 'n' roll with an interest in B-grade sci-fi and horror movies; Talking Heads (with bass player Tina Weymouth) focused satire and were dubbed literate rock by the critics. Debbie Harry (lead singer of Blondie) was arguably the most successful of the punk and new wave acts, but her power-pop sound veered towards commercialism rather than overt confrontation and, despite the attack of such songs as 'X Offender', 'One Way Or Another', and 'Heart Of Glass', she was largely viewed as a rock sex symbol rather than as a ground-breaking front-line singer. The traditional emphasis on 'prettiness' was equally a contributory factor to the commercial success of the Go-Go's, the first women's band emerging from punk to attract a mainstream audience. However, although their sparkly pop style was far removed from their original punk roots, they proved conclusively that all-women groups were a viable proposition.

Despite the uncertainties, then, punk opened up a specific space for women to explore and sell their own creativity and to exploit the opportunities inherent in a do-it-yourself musical culture. At the same time, it has to be recognised that in terms of commercial success, the music industry continued to exploit and promote safe and sellable images. In particular, the significance of MTV in promoting bands led to a demand for slick, sexual presentations which, at first, signalled a return to the conventional image of women performers as glamorous, front-line singers. Paradoxically, it was this demand for visually impressive women that was finally to provide an alternative space for women performers, one which bridged artistry with androgyny, alternative sexual pleasuring and lesbianism.

Acknowledgements

I would like to acknowledge the helpful advice given by my long-term friend Sharon Lowenna (Falmouth College of Art and fellow tutor on the Open University Arts Foundation course (A102) summer schools. I would also thank Thomas Swiss, Professor of English at Drake University, Des Moines, who introduced me to the writing of C. Jaures Noland, and John Richardson, whose feedback on my ideas was both constructive and full of insight.

NOTES AND REFERENCES

1 Eagleton,T. (1983) *Literary Theory. An Introduction*, London: Blackwell, p. 107.
2 D'Amico, R. (1982) 'What is Discourse?', in *Humanities in Society,* 5:3/4, p. 304.
3 Traditional semiotics privilege an emphasis on 'dig deeply enough and you will find truth' but, as Stuart Hall observes, while

> Semiotics has greatly contributed to our understanding of how signification systems work, of how things and relations signify ... it tends to halt its investigation at the frontier where the internal relations of 'languages' articulate with social practices and historical structures ... it lacks an adequate theory of representation without which the specificity of the ideological region cannot be constituted.
> Hall, S. (1978) 'The Hinterland of Science. Ideology and the Sociology of Knowledge', in *On Ideology*, Centre for Contemporary Cultural Studies.
> London: Hutchinson, p. 28

4 Hebdige, D. (1979) 'Style as Homology and Signifying Practice', in Frith, S. and Goodwin, A. (1990) *On Record. Rock, Pop and the Written Word*, London:

Routledge, p. 60.
5 Gunew, S. (ed.) (1990) *Feminist Knowledge, Critique and Construct,* London: Routledge, p. 29.
6 Julia Kristeva, from an interview with *Tel Quel*, in Tong, R. (1992) *Feminist Thought. A Comprehensive Introduction*, London: Routledge, p. 230.
7 See Lacan, J. (1970) 'Of Structure as an Inmixing of Otherness ... ', in Macksey, R. and Donato, E. (eds) *The Language of Criticism and the Sciences of Man. The Structuralist Controversy*, Baltimore, MD: John Hopkins University Press; Lacan, J. (1977) *The Four Fundamental Concepts of Psychoanalysis*, London: Hogarth Press; Lacan, J. (1981) 'The Oedipus Complex', *Semiotext(e)*, 10, pp. 190–202.
8 Lacan's emphasis on language, law and symbolic exchange as founding structures of society and, as such, key points in patriarchal culture may account for why so many feminist texts examine mother–child relationships, infantile development.
9 Tong, *op. cit.*, p. 229. This is exemplified in rock culture where women performers all too often accept the discourse of hardness, virtuosity and toughness and become 'one of the boys' as reflected in my earlier discussion of Janis Joplin and Suzi Quatro.
10 *Ibid., p. 231.*
11 *Ibid.*
12 Laing, D. (1985) 'Listening to Punk' in Gelder, K. and Thornton, S. (eds) (1997) *The Subcultures Reader*, London: Routledge, p. 419.
13 While the dictionary definition of eccentricity as 'taking an alternative rectilinear movement from a revolving shaft' suggests a certain metaphor for the phallocentric nature of rock and the need for women to create an alternative frame of reference if they are to challenge the male demarcation of territory, it is also apposite to the identification of alternative compositional techniques identified in my discussion of Joni Mitchell (cyclical, repetitive, etc.). Kirkpatrick, E.M. (ed) (1985) *Chambers Dictionary*, Edinburgh: Chambers, p. 394.
14 Bracewell, M. 'Woman as Warrior', *Guardian Weekend*, 22 June 1996, p. 18.
15 This 'colonisation' of punk by academics will be examined in more detail on pp. 105–7.
16 Julia Kristeva locates the semiotic within the *chora*, a non-geometrical space where both positive and negative, creative and destructive drive activities are 'primarily' located. Sounds (speech acts, timbre, rhythm, gesture) draw attention to the semiotic pre-symbolic in language through exaggeration. As such, the chora is mobile and is analogous to vocal or kinetic rhythm which, in turn, constitute the pre-symbolic *significance*.
For a more extended discussion of *chora* see Lechte, J. (1990) *Julia Kristeva*, London: Routledge, pp. 127–32.
17 Edition Two (1987) *The Illustrated Encyclopedia of Rock*, Belgium: Proost International Book Production, p. 236.
18 Smith's identification with Rimbaud inspired such lines as Rock 'n' Rimbaud (the title Smith gave to her performance with Lenny Kaye at *Le Jardin*, 1973).
19 As Pierre Bourdieu writes, 'the people, or those without the specific code necessary for coming to terms with what is difficult come 'to feel lost in a chaos of sounds and rhythms, colour and lines, without rhyme or reason'. Bourdieu, P. (1986) *Distinction. A Social Critique of the Judgement of Taste*, London: Routledge & Kegan Paul, p. 2.
20 Lechte, *op. cit.*, p. 15.
21 This is reflected in Patti Smith's album *Easter* (1978), and her erotic and mystical love for the boy/angel in 'Break It Up' (pp. 102–3).

22 Bracewell, *op. cit.*, p. 15.

23   According to Kristeva, poetic language heralds the dissolution of the subject as identical with itself, and foreshadows a generalised negativity seen, in certain respects, to be reminiscent of Buddhist philosophy where a 'zerologic' subject, a non-subject comes to assume the thought which cancels it out. The subject does not depend on any sign: it is simply an 'empty' space – a 'paragrammatic space'. In poetic language this can be see in the movement between the real and the unreal, being an non-being.

Lechte, op. cit., p. 114

24 Bracewell, *op. cit.*, p. 15.
25 Parelles, J. and Rimanowski, D. (eds) (1983) *Encyclopedia of Rock and Roll*, New York: s.v. 'Patti Smith'.
26 Birch, I., 'Punk' in Collins, J. (1980) *The Rock Primer*, London: Penguin Books, p. 28.
27 Bracewell, *op. cit.*, p. 20.
28 *Ibid.*
29 O'Brien, L. (1995) *She Bop. The Definitive History of Women in Rock, Pop and Soul*, London: Penguin Books, p. 112.
30 As Craig Owen writes,

> To strike a pose is to present oneself to the gaze of the other as if one were already frozen, immobilised, suspended, that is, already a picture … pose has a strategic value: doubling, mimicking the immobilising power of the gaze, reflecting it back on itself, pose forces the gaze to surrender. Confronted with a pose, the gaze itself is immobilised, brought to a standstill … to strike a pose is to strike a threat.
> Owens, C. (1992) in Bryson, S. *et al* (1992) *Beyond Recognition.Representation, Power and Culture*, Berkeley: University of California Press, p. 198)

31 Even though the gospel-like choir becomes a signifier of religion, my colleague, John Richardson suggests that in context it implies more

> a sense of spirituality breaking through to another level of consciousness, as *transgression*, thus implying Kristeva's conceptualisation of the semiotic. The improvisatory, syncopational and bluesy elements of gospel music seem to me to be about pushing back the threshold, transgressing, more than they do upholding the law as governed by the beat, diatonic harmony etc.

32 See Pavletich, A. (1980) *Sirens of Song. The Popular Female Vocalist in America*, New York: Da Capo, p. 14, for a discussion of genre stereotyping.
33   The *performative* is '*to do*': '*to act*' on an interlocutor, to modify the situation and its relations of strength. Performatic, and not informative, language is a field of enjoyment (*jouissance*) and not of knowledge (*connaisance*).

Felman, S. (1980) La Scandale du corps parlant. Don Juan avec
Austin ou la seduction en deux langues, Paris: Seuil, p. 34

34 Jaures Noland, C., 'Rimbaud and Patti Smith: Style as Social Deviance', in *Critical Enquiry*, Spring, 1995, p. 588.

I am grateful to my friend and colleague Dr Thomas Swiss, Professor of English at Drake University, Des Moines, for sending me a copy of this fascinating paper.

35 *Ibid.*, p. 588.
36 *Ibid.*
37 As Noland observes

> Smith's references to biblical figures set up the theme of religious revisionism consistent with Rimbaud's portrait of a redeemed Cain in *Mauvais Sang* and a materialised Christ at the conclusion of *Adieu.* The allusion to Cain turns out to be a particularly rich and useful one for Smith, for it serves to mythologize not only the poet but also his double in the poem, that originator of rock 'n' roll Little Richard ... Just as Little Richard 'baptised' America and 'Arthur' baptises his siblings in the river, Smith resacralizes the world through music ...
>
> *Ibid.*, p. 594

38 *Ibid.*, p. 583.
39 Jim Morrison's live performance of 'The End' at The Whiskey contained the notorious lines 'Father ... ?' 'Yes, Son?' 'I want to kill you! Mother ... I want to ... FUCK YOU!'
40 Hebdige, D., 'Style as Homology and Signifying Practice' in Frith and Goodwin, *op. cit.*, p. 59.
41 *Ibid.*, p. 63–4.
42 Graham, D. 'Malcolm McLaren and the Making of Annabella', end-note 14 in Noland, *op. cit.*, pp. 586–7.
43 Savage, J. (1991) *England's Dreaming. Sex Pistols and Punk Rock*, London: Faber and Faber, pp. 90–1.
44 See *Ibid.*, pp. 89–92 for a full discussion of influences upon McLaren.
45 McLaren had first come across the Situationist through some of his more radical friends and had obtained his magazines from Compendium Books during the late 1960s. Situationist art was largely seen as an update on Pop Art in Britain and was interpreted as gimmicky, witty, sexy and young. By 1966, interpretation was transmitted globally by the Beatles, the Rolling Stones and the Kinks. McLaren is also loosely linked with the SI/Motherfucker mutation, King Mob, who were also involved in the Anglo-American pop culture revolution of the late 1960s. See *ibid.*, Chapter 1, pp. 3–4, for a full discussion.
46 This is not meant, in any way, to underestimate the Clash who helped to promote women's music by touring with bands like the Slits. As John Richardson observes,

> their collaborations with black musicians and association with Rock Against Racism could be seen as very timely in light of the growing influence of the National Front. The Clash's political engagement, although at times abstract, misguided or naïve, could be equated with Kristeva's arguments in 'Women's Time' that it is necessary to revert to the symbolic sometimes if real, politically tangible advances are to be made.

47 Friedlander, P. (1996) *Rock and Roll. A Social History*, Boulder, CO: Westview Press, p. 252.
48 Jon Savage and Don Grama are notable exceptions in their critique of punk.

49 Lucy O'Brien records the verdict of members of the Slits, the Raincoats and the Au Pairs at an *NME* (*New Musical Express*) 'Women in Rock' roundtable discussion, that artists like Patti Smith and Joan Armatrading were more of a threat than women who openly sold their sexuality in rock. 'They've actually denied they're feminists.' O'Brien, *op. cit.*, p. 115.

50 *Ibid.*, .116.

51 *A Clockwork Orange* was very close to the reality of the bizarrely dressed, amphetamine-driven punks. Siouxsie Sioux's bleached and coloured hair owes much to the influence of this film.

52 Savage, *op. cit.*, p. 259.

53 *Ibid.*, p. 250.

54 *Ibid.*, p. 418.

55 Descriptions of bondage party by Siouxsie's friend, Berlin. *Ibid.*, p. 185.

56 Lou Reed, Iggy Pop, David Bowie, the Sex Pistols and others all shared a fascination with pre-World War II Germany.

57 Savage, *op. cit.*, p. 188.

58 *Ibid.*, p. 195. Joy Press also makes reference to Siouxsie Sioux's identification with fascism in Reynolds, S. and Press, J. (1995) *The Sex Revolts. Gender, Rebellion and Rock 'n' Roll*, London: Serpent's Tail, pp. 301–3.

59   With skinheads and British Nazis (under the banner of the National Front conducting forays into minority communities, the Clash and others (X-Ray Spex and Sham 69 being two) participated in concerts sponsored by Rock against Racism (RAR) and the Anti-Nazi League. Paradoxically, punk's anti-anything stance attracted young supporters of the rightist organisations; some punk groups didn't care, but others rejected this audience.

Friedlander, *op. cit.*, p. 257

60 Savage, *op. cit.*, p. 184.

61 *Ibid.*, p. 186.

62 *Ibid.*, p. 514. The situation was not helped by the band's shared concert with Adam Ant whose single 'Deutscher Girls' and association with the film *Jubilee* had generated hostile reviews.

63 Hebdige, *op. cit.*, p. 64.

64 In highlighting the rhythm of phonic differences, or the *timbre* of language, there is a commonality with sound-colour melodies, timbral melodies which break out of the ossified symbolic forms (e.g. Schoenberg, Webern). As such, the texts highlight the semiotic chora which underlies the language system.

65 Lechte, *op. cit.*, p. 67.

66 Savage, *op. cit.*, p. 486.

67 *Ibid.*, p. 486.

68 O'Brien, *op. cit.*, p. 65.

8

CHALLENGING THE FEMININE

Annie Lennox, androgyneity and illusions of identity

> Masculine discourse has never been able to understand woman, or the feminine, as anything other than a reflection of man, or the masculine. Thus, it is impossible to think the 'feminine feminine' within the structures of patriarchal thought. When men look at women, they see not women but reflections, or images and likenesses, of men.[1]

Rosemary Tong's discussion of a patriarchal discourse which has informed such thinkers as Plato, Descartes, Hegel, Nietzsche, Freud and Lacan, returns the reader to the debates surrounding *sameness* and the suppression of difference. Apart from her sexuality, her biological marker of sex, the woman is merely a reflection of man, the same as man. Her sexuality, because it cannot mirror the male's, is thus a lack, an absence of the male's. *Where she does not reflect man, she does not exist, and is therefore unrepresentable.* In terms of thought there is thus a linguistic absence, and within a language system that relies on an all-pervasive masculinity, the feminine is inevitably and irrevocably excluded.

The idea that woman does not have a sex,[2] that she does not exist is clearly problematic, not least in discussions surrounding identity and representation. Political representation, for example, has relied on extending legitimacy to women as visible political subjects, identifying the customary and legal constraints that block their access to, or success in, the public domain. Gender justice hinges on equality but, as Irigaray cautions, 'Woman could be man's equal. In this case she would enjoy, in a more or less near future, the same economic, social, political rights as men. She would be a potential man.'[3] Irigaray's concern that emancipatory feminism could be subsumed within a pre-established male discourse (that 'she could be a potential man') is equally relevant to the debates surrounding the ways in which gender and sexuality have served to subordinate women to men. If representation is a normative function of language, patriarchal language systems can never adequately represent women as the structures are themselves misogynistic.

The assumption of a universal basis for feminism (that oppression has a singular discernible form) is equally problematic. For theorists such as Luce Irigaray, there is only one sex, the masculine, and as such women constitute simply the fetish of representation. They are the relation of difference, excluded by conventional systems of Western culture. Notions of binary opposition (male/female, masculine/feminine) thus conceal the power of hegemonic masculinity by constantly positioning the woman as the negative other of the omnipresent masculine subject.

Irigaray's critique of Freud (that the differentiation into two sexes depends on the assumption that the girl child must become a man minus the penis) rests largely on her celebration of the psychic and somatic dimensions of desire that Freud had either excluded or suppressed. Having insisted that women devote very little mental energy to autoeroticism, autorepresentation (and she includes here lesbians), Irigaray focuses attention on representations of representations that remind women of her sex, her sex organs, her sexes. She stresses the delights of caresses, words, of pleasures that can be sustained without being subordinated to the Freudian penis, or indeed, to the Lacanian phallus. Attention is thus drawn to the erotic, and the zone where Freud had detected a castratory lack thus becomes the site of pleasure, 'genitals formed by two lips in continuous contact'.[4]

Although Irigaray has been criticised for her essentialism, of reducing femininity to anatomy in a manner not too dissimilar to that of Freud, her defiance of the phallomorphic logic of 'sameness' is important. Arguing that women's libido is 'other' to men's, that women's language is distinct from men's, she identifies the ways in which female anatomy has been represented, articulated and conceptualised. Like Lacan, she argues that 'the acquisition of language produces desire and women's language is motivated by attempts to satisfy desire'.[5] However, the fact that 'female desire is totally foreign to male desire' (in that the female has a multiplicity of sexual organs) 'the two can only be brought together through a patriarchal repression of the female'[6] and hence female desire remains inarticulate and incomplete. Defined and represented through patriarchal discourse as having an essential essence which defines her as woman (passive, receptive, nurturant, emotional), she has no other function than to facilitate the male drive towards actualising his own inner potential. As such, sexuality, textual practice and political practice become inseparable, and philosophical, scientific and literary discourses are all exposed as primarily sexualised in a masculine way.

The need to shift the emphasis from a language which is organised around the phallus, to one which expresses the diversity of female sexual pleasure opens up the concept of the autoerotic, the plural. The plurality of the female orgasm, in particular, focuses attention on the 'multiple and heterogeneous pleasure(s)'[7] that are located in the female body. If, as Irigaray argues, it is impossible to describe these experiences within the dominant masculine mode of expression, then a new language must be found, so opening up the possibility for an *écriture feminine* which will encourage women to experience themselves as something more than excess within the dominant ideology.

Irigaray's affirmation of the 'feminine feminine' and, in particular, her identification of the interconnectedness of sexuality with language and power, provide the intellectual axis for her challenge to patriarchal power. Recognising that words are male defined and that 'the passive voice simply hides the identity of the speaker from the listener/reader',[8] she urges women to speak in the active. Given that the dominant discourse is based on a privileging of the phallus and is thus single, unified, visible and definable and thus analogous to 'the erection (which is the becoming in a form)',[9] a feminine use of language would have a comparability to female sexual morphology. It would play with itself (with the analogy of the labia, two lips in constant contact), so involving a plurality, an ambiguity, a sense of the polymorphous. 'Female genitalia' could thus 'be positively represented in terms quite distinct from their patriarchal representations'[10] where the clitoris and the vagina posit two distinct zones. As Irigaray observes, 'There is indeed a visible exterior of the female sex, but that sex can in no way lend itself to the privilege of the form: rather what the female sex enjoys is not having its own form.'[11] A feminine language, then, would correspond to feminine pleasure, feminine sensuality, feminine creativity, multiple in differences, complex and subtle. Rather than unity, the emphasis would lie on heterogeneity, play and difference.

The stress on plurality, play and difference is rooted in Irigaray's second strategy which is related to female sexuality.

> Fondling the breasts, spreading the lips, stroking the posterior wall of the vagina, brushing against the mouth of the uterus ... pleasure(s) which are somewhat misunderstood in sexual difference as it is imagined – or not imagined, the other sex being only the indispensable complement to the only sex. *But woman has sex organs more or less everywhere*. She finds pleasure almost everywhere.[12]

Arguing that libidinal pleasures are extended to all forms of human expression, Irigaray proposed that adult women should confront patriarchy by engaging in autoerotic practices, in lesbianism, in exploring the whole terrain of the body. This would then enable them to think thoughts, to speak words that are contradictory, 'somewhat mad from the standpoint of reason, inaudible for whoever listens to them with ready-made grids, with a fully elaborated code in hand'.[13]

Irigaray's third strategy examines the ways in which the phallocentric mode of signifying female sexuality constantly reproduces counterfeit images which massage male vanity and desire. Through reflection (or specularisation), sexual difference serves only to create self-aggrandisement and, as such, reflecting back the image simply reinforces male defined power. The masking of a feminised identity through exaggeration, 'miming the miming' imposed on women, thus has the potential to challenge phallocentric discourse by 'overdoing' the stereotype.[14] If, as Irigaray suggests, women exist only in men's eyes, as images, then they should take the images, magnify them, and reflect them back. Conformity to image, to representations of established femininity can then become so exaggerated as to become confrontational.

It is evident that the importance of stereotyping, the acceptance of what Moi calls 'ineluctable mimicry',[15] underpins the traditional representations of women in popular music. The constraint to 'be young and beautiful' has little to do with the reality of women. Rather it provides an idealised and feminised reflection for the man, the masculine, 'be strong and virile'. Heterosexual markers in mainstream performance rely on a presentation of the artist as male, as female, as inhabiting a particular gendered identity. Sexual difference is therefore important, and female identity within the popular discourse relies largely on the performance of feminine stereotypes, on reflecting the images imposed on them by men (as discussed in Chapter 2, 'Repressive Representations'). That these stereotypical representations originate in the myths constructed by men about women accounts for the dichotomous pairing of active/passive, positive/negative that traditionally frames the fundamental couple, man/woman. Within popular music, then, the assumption that opposites attract provides both an explicit and implicit understanding of what is both absent and present. The 'Love Me' of traditional popular ballads supposes that the imaginary addressee is opposite sex, regardless of the fact that the gender identities are not stated, a point that will be explored in more detail in my discussion of k.d. lang.

It is equally evident that the 'Love Me' exerts a sense of tyranny when aligned with the notion of stereotyping. Within the romantic conventions of popular music, girls traditionally love their man, but do not get pregnant, or have abortions. They do not get raped, they do not get abused. Rather they are romanticised romantics and, as such, any deviation from the established norm is problematic, whether in the lyrics of a song or in real life. As such stereotypes do not only situate the body as the seat of subjectivity, they equally situate it as the target of power and social control. Janis Martin's initial success as 'the female Elvis' ended abruptly when she gave birth at the age of 18. Marriage and motherhood were considered incompatible with the image of a rockin' country girl. Wanda Jackson, arguably one of the most successful singers of the period, eventually turned to religion and gospel as her career in country and rockabilly foundered. Children and a broken marriage had again amounted to a demonstrable fall from grace.[16] More recently, Nigel Grainge and Chris Hill, the directors of Ensign Records, and the company's doctor, tried to persuade Sinead O'Connor to terminate her pregnancy: 'I couldn't have my baby because my record company had spent £120,000 on my album and I owed it to them not to have it.'[17]

Although success has largely depended upon following the norms of the music business, direct confrontation with the established codes of feminised representation became more explicit in the 1980s. Clearly punk paved the way but the emphasis on overt shock tactics undermined the seriousness of non-conformism. Patti Smith may have come across as androgynous, flirting with bisexual and lesbian identity in 'Gloria' and 'Redonda', but her marriage and subsequent withdrawal from live performance, her dissent from feminist politics, initially detracted from her importance to a feminised popular music. In contrast, Siouxsie Sioux's outrageous sexuality, her fetishistic image and 'control' of her three pretty boy musicians established a precedent for self-exploration and self-invention, the two major strategies in the subversion of traditional images of femininity.

Although image has always been important in popular music, not least in live performance, film clips and promos, the advent of cable television provided a new outlet for marketing bands. As Will Straw points out, MTV, a 24-hour video channel, intensified 'the discourses of celebrity around pop music', 'giving high definition to the individual images of ... star performers' and making 'the 45-rpm single and the individual song ... the basic units within the marketing of rock music'. He continues, 'the dominant form through which popular music was heard and understood within this mainstream was that of the song, and its place within a sequence of songs in dance clubs'[18] and, as such, women who stressed creativity and depth, rather than image, were initially under-represented.

It is not unrealistic to suggest that under-representation and misrepresentation have been the catalysts in instigating change both in feminist politics and popular music. If visual identity allied to dance/disco was the dominant mode of expression in the early 1980s, then the task of imaginative women performers was to subvert the traditional images of femininity, 'to make gender trouble'.[19] MTV may have appeared problematic in its insistence on the visually impressive, in focusing on appearance rather than musicality, but it provided both a challenge and a unique forum for exploring and questioning gendered identity. Eurythmics' vocalist Annie Lennox was among the first women to destabilise the traditional notions of sexuality and desire, playing with androgyny and wearing a man's suit to play down her femininity and, by inference, gain access to the male domain of artistic control.

Annie Lennox was born in Aberdeen, Scotland, in 1954 and studied piano and flute as a child before enrolling at the Royal Academy of Music, London in 1972. As a fan of Motown artists such as Marvin Gaye and the Supremes, it is not too surprising that she found the entrenched traditionalism of a classical academy stifling, and after three years she left to follow her own career as a singer songwriter. Initially performing with a folk rock group,

Dragon's Playground, she then joined singer Joy Dey to form the Stocking Tops before moving in with guitarist David Stewart. The Catch, their first group, was formed with Peet Coombes and after the release of their single 'Black Blood'/'Borderline' in 1977 they were joined by Jim Toomey on drums and Eddie Chin on bass, renaming themselves the Tourists. Their first single 'Blind Among the Flowers'/'He Who Laughs Last' (May 1979) and the self-titled LP *Tourists* was largely 1960s'-influenced rock and, while the band enjoyed some success with their two subsequent albums, *Reality Effect* (1979) and *Luminous Basement* (1980), Lennox is best remembered for her cover version of Dusty Springfield's 'I Only Want to Be with You', which reached no. 4 in the charts. The group toured the US in 1980 and were signed with RCA, but by 1981 they broke up and Lennox and Stewart formed a new group, Eurythmics.

The Eurythmics' experimental electronic sound was matched by Lennox's dramatic change of image.

> I've always been an outsider. So how do I show people who I am? I thought about that quite seriously because I didn't want to be perceived as something I wasn't. I wasn't a cutesy girl and I'm not ... but I think I'm probably representative of my generation ... we're a little more independent thinking ... I had to think how best to present myself and the idea of becoming ... androgynous ... horrible term, it's become so abused ... but it was a very useful tool for me.[20]

Lennox's slicked-back crop was first discovered when a member of the audience pulled off the bleached white wig which had signalled her first experiments with the illusions of identity. Her adoption of the male suit, historically the point of rebellion for rock stars,[21] provided a further challenge to the cultural construction of sexuality and power dynamics. As Lennox points out 'Almost putting on the male suit gave me more power.'[22] However, as Lucy O'Brien has pointed out,

> Neither the insight nor the activity is new, of course. Murray Hall died in 1901. A respected politician for 30 years, he married twice, and it was not until his death that his secret was discovered: he was a woman. Women weren't allowed to vote at the time, let alone stand for government.[23]

Cultural politics equally barred women from entering the public arena and the adoption of a male pseudonym, or posing as a man (Georges Sand, George Eliot) provided a covert access to the nineteenth century literary world. Within the tradition of music hall, Vesta Tilley's play on androgyny, dressing like a man and flirting with sexual ambiguity ('Following in

Father's Footsteps') established a tradition of 'women as men', not least in Dietrich's white tuxedo performance in *Blonde Venus* and Grace Jones's feature-length video *One Man Show* (dir. Jean-Paul Goude) where she appears with several hundred masculine cloned versions of herself.[24]

As such, it is not too surprising that Lennox perceived the male suit as a symbol that would allow her to assert the more masculine side of her sexuality. Clearly the associations of mind with masculinity and body with femininity provide one possible reason for cross-dressing. As clothes designer Carol Semaine observed, Lennox had a stated aversion to flaunting her body. 'You'd never see her in a low-cut dress. If she was whistled at in the street, it'd make her hackles rise.'[25] Lennox equally perceived the suit as an expression of control, both in her own life, and as symbolic of the Eurythmic style 'signalling music with irony. There was new technology with drum machines and synthesisers ... this was a proper production business, hence the suits'.[26] Her suit, her cropped hair, can thus be interpreted as a statement of business, female artistic control and disco style. As a woman conventionally defined by her body, her wearing of the male suit masked her femininity but, rather than constituting a denial of her identity, it was an assertion of autonomy.

The general public first became aware of Lennox's assumed androgyneity with the release of the video *Sweet Dreams (Are Made of This)*, the title track of the Eurythmics' second album, directed by Dave Stewart and Chris Ashbrook. (January 1983) Although driven by an omnipresent synth riff, the song, like the video, moves between a coolly appraising present and a dreamlike surrealism. The introduction is spiky, repetitive and memorable. Simple broken-octave synth stabs create a sense of circularity, as the harmonies move from C#minor to A/G#sus4 and back to C#minor, in an endlessly repeated phrase without closure. The rhythm is equally consistent, a pulsating drive which is inflected by whiplash stabs on the second and fourth beats as Lennox colours the harmonies with a soulful 'aaah' and a gentle scat around the basic melodic shape of the opening vocal line.

The opening shots in the video situate Lennox as a 'woman in charge'. Standing at the head of a long table, she is poised as if ready to address an absent Board of Directors. A long panning shot shows her dark silhouette against a blank screen before she swings round, using her riding crop as a gavel, to call attention to her commentary on motivation. Cropped red hair, a tie, suit and black gloves situate her as 'in control' as she moves into the opening words of the song, 'Sweet dreams are made of this ... ' Lennox's cynical commentary ('everybody's looking for someone') is, however, addressed to both a global audience (as connoted by the screened view of the world, the spinning globe on the table, and the crowd shots) and to David Stewart who, as director/producer, controls the console and, by inference, the screened image of Lennox herself. Her 'some of them want to use you' is addressed directly to him, in a shot/reverse shot which frames the relationship through a cinematic code of narration that structures the protagonists through an exchanged look, albeit masked by Stewart's dark glasses. Although Lennox's direct gaze at the camera suggests both confrontation and control, attention is refocused on the screen and a right-hand profile shot of Lennox's red-lipsticked mouth as she sings 'Some of them want to be used by you'. Who controls who, then, provides an under-lying enigma.

Like the constant synth accompaniment, the melody is narrow-ranged and repetitive, following the natural rhythm of the words. The play on minor/major (in the regular move between C#m/A:G#sus4) heightens the effect of searching/looking in the vocal motif through a lack of cadential resolution, a musical coding which equally informs the video narrative

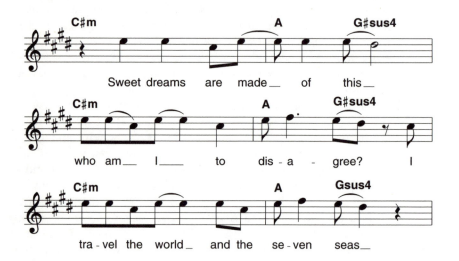

Although the final part of the verse retains the basic structure of the vocal line, the phonetic resemblance between 'use', 'you', 'abuse' draws the words into direct association. The effect is heightened by Lennox's shift to a more declamatory style of delivery which underpins the realistic mode of the song before the shift into the fantastic.

The cynical commentary of the verse, which was enhanced by the sharp focus of the camera, is now replaced by a soft focus framing of Lennox's closed eyes on the Board Room screen which dissolves into a full frame of her still-closed eyes, her mouth, Lennox and Stewart holding hands against a backdrop of framed golden discs. The connotations of daydreaming are enhanced by the change in vocal timbre, where a soulful fragility replaces the rhythmic emphasis of the verse. Reality is reasserted by her fisted hand striking the table and a repeat of the verse. This time the 'dream sequence' is extended. Accessed initially by the Hindi red spot of womanhood on her forehead, the image segues into a blue gun-sight centred on a masked, cello-playing Stewart. This time the emphasis is on masquerade but Lennox moves into the chorus: 'Hold your head up, keep your head up, moving on', her wide-awake eyes underpinning the necessity for a realistic appraisal of 'sweet dreams'.

The bridge back to the verse is opened out by unison synth strings to impart an underlying romanticism to the images of Stewart and Lennox (this time with a long black wig and red ballgown) miming the string line on cellos and seated in a cow pasture. The bovine nature of romanticised love is then refocused in the final reprise of the verse. Cows become the backdrop to both reality and fantasy as Stewart and Lennox (dressed once again in a formal suit, tie and black gloves) walk separately into the pasture before a repeated 'sweet dreams ... ' situates them on a metaphorical dream boat. This time, Stewart is in the prow, playing the cello, Lennox a passenger, hand on head, as the boat glides down the river. Romanticism, however, is tempered by realism, the dream sequence is nothing more than a yearning 'looking for something'. As Lennox awakens in bed, the camera pans on to her bedside table, following her hand as she reaches for her paperback copy of *Sweet Dreams*, with its photo of Lennox, back to the camera, facing Stewart.

Clearly, pop videos are not meant to be read as revelatory. However, the fact that 'Sweet Dreams' reads like a video *roman à clef* in fronting Stewart as a Svengali, programming computers and manipulating Lennox's image, does impact upon the viewer. The song is bittersweet in its juxtaposition of a woman in control yet immersed in a romanticised love, but the very fact that it comes across as somewhat autobiographical, albeit framed by surreal-istic images, provides a sense of authentication for the play on identity which was equally a part of Lennox's reality. However, it is suggested that *looking like you're being yourself* can be as problematic as figuring out who you are. As such, I consider it important to examine briefly the ways in which Lennox destabilises traditional notions of sexuality, gender and desire by breaking out of the male imaginary and 'miming the miming' imposed on woman.

As discussed above, the video moves between two modes of representation – the 'real' of the RCA Board Room (symbolic) and the imaginary of the 'dream' sequences (semiotic). The two dream sequences are critical to the narrative structure. The first disrupts the flow of the Board Room address; the second is similar, but its effect is to bring the flow of images to a conclu-sion which suggests that the 'real' and the 'imaginary' are all part of a dream which posits choice through a play on identity. As such, the central axis of the video revolves around the manipulation of the image. The omnipresent Stewart (as both ex-lover and professional partner) is also critical to the underlying discourse of sexuality, language and power. Initially, Lennox appears in control as she looks directly into the eye of the camera, but her masking of a feminised identity through the adoption of a male suit, tie, black gloves, reflecting back the stereotypical image of masculine power, is disrupted by the screened image of her red lips.

Stewart's control of the console, and by inference, the projection of Lennox's mouth onto the screen, is intriguing. At one level it focuses attention on the words 'some of them want to be used by you', a recognition of mutual manipulation, linking orality to sexuality. However, the fact that it interrupts the image of Lennox as powerful and in control suggests more the fetishistic, that her commanding presence is threatening and that her mouth represents the *vagina dentata*, the castrating female organ that Stewart, as the omnipresent male, wishes to disavow. There is thus the implicit suggestion that a powerful woman, is unnatural, castrating, that the sensually parted lips can both excite and threaten.

The dream sequence is thus reassuring. Here the screen reveals Lennox with eyes shut, no longer challenging, but side by side with Stewart, mirroring the male. The rapid return to the male persona thus works as a subversive discontinuity. This is reinforced by Lennox's commanding presence and wide-awake eyes before the second 'dream sequence' which juxtaposes subordination and control through the segueing of the red spot/gun sight on to Stewart, whose cello playing suggests 'calling the tune', before the wide-awake chorus 'moving on'. The bridge, with its romantic imagery, then resituates Lennox as a passive reflection of the male, playing the 'cello in unison, her long hair, long dress providing an idealised representation of sexual difference, an image which massages male vanity and desire. Controlled, her male suit is thus shown to be little more than a flirtation with the image of power as she sits passively in the boat with Stewart in the prow. Or does she?

Lennox has frequently been cited as fronting a scene saturated with manipulation and irony, where meaning (generally satirical) is conveyed by words or gestures whose literal meaning is the opposite. As such, the dream sequences can be read as essentially a witty criticism of the folly of romanticised love. This is certainly suggested by the use of cows as both bovine and as a metaphor for subduing the spirit (cow, cowed), as implied by the intrusion of cows into the Board Room before they are relegated to their appropriate place within the pastoral of Romanticism.[27] Lennox's commentary on the romantic (the long hair, the long dress, the playing of the cello in the pasture) can thus be interpreted as 'miming the miming' imposed on women, challenging the phallocentric discourse by exaggerating the stereotype. This is also implied in the wearing of masks which both underpins the conventions of Romanticism while hiding her true identity. The boat scene thus assumes an alternative meaning. There is an awareness of being a passive traveller, of simply reflecting back an image that reinforces male defined power, but her hand on her forehead implies a mindful interjection which can only be resolved by waking up to reality, of confronting the manipulative potential of 'sweet dreams'. The play on images, on representations, thus creates an ambiguity, a plurality of meaning which is both subtle and complex. Lennox has simply mimed the negative other of the omnipresent masculine subject and, as such, there is a recognition that any attempt to satisfy male desire can only be brought about by self-repression.[28]

The success of *Sweet Dreams* in both the UK and America led to the re-release of *Love is a Stranger*. Boosted by a video where Lennox performed a variety of gendered identities (a glamorous, long-haired blonde, a leather-clad brunette dominatrix and, briefly, an androgynous figure in a suit), MTV initially assumed her to be a male transvestite. The metamorphosis from woman to man, as Lennox pulled off her wig to reveal her cropped hair, was too convincing and she was forced to provide documentation to prove her true identity. By 1983 Lennox and Boy George had been cited as the main 'gender benders' of their generation. The accolade, however, proved problematic when Lennox appeared on the 1984 Grammy Awards to sing *Sweet Dreams*. America, it appeared, was less than willing to take on board her Elvis look. Fake sideburns and greased-back hair were greeted with hostility and her identification with an androgynous image was soon supplemented by more diverse feminine images which revealed that being a woman necessitates a constant negotiation of different constructions of femininities. *Touch*, the Eurythmics next album, was released in 1984. The sleeve featured a bare-armed Lennox, flexing her muscles, staring out from behind a mask to posit an enigma which is opened out in the video for 'Who's that Girl' (a Top 30 single in the US).

The song opens with an unaccompanied 'Who's that girl?', the minor tonality, echo and reverb effects, creating a musical metaphor for loneliness. Musically, the absence of instrumental backing, the singing alone, the thin flanged vocals, provide a sense of passive female space, a void waiting to be filled. The fragile tone of the voice enhances the feeling of aloneness. The question presupposes an answer which will give substance, meaning to the unknown.

The sense of space is an important element in the song. The auditory space of the opening phrase functions as a dynamic, creating its own dimensions through the timbral quality of Lennox's voice. At the same time, the reverb effect underpins its evanescence while acting as a metaphor for the singer as the keyboard synth. takes over, playing on the minor inflections in a melancholic rising sequence over a simple, syncopated bass line.

Who's that__ girl?

The

The video picks up on the enigmatic. Lennox's full frontal face, blue eyes, pink lipstick, blonde wig, is shown peering through her black-gloved fingers, a symbolic pose which suggests a veiling of identity. 'It suggests the possibility of access to another sphere, another sexuality, another self (which) … reflects the ambiguity and transparency of sexual difference.'[29] The initial 'Who's that girl?' is thus given an ironic twist in its questioning of identity and, as the camera focuses on the keyboard player, Lennox is revealed as a singer in a nightclub. From the onset, then, the video positions Lennox as performer, miming the mime of a glamorous torch singer.

The verse retains the minor feel of the introduction in a dreamy ballad style vocal which is underpinned by a sense of torment by the remembering of a past love. A subtle whiplash kick on the third beat of the bar suggests self-flagellation as the image of an engagement ring slipping onto her finger ('warmer than the sun'), and three wine glasses clinking together ('broken, just like china cups') focuses the bittersweet of 'the language of love'. The dreamy melancholy of the verse, which establishes the mood for the first section of the song, is then interrupted by a more assertive and rhythmical passage. Lennox confronts both the problem and the camera as she moves into the bridge via a full-face shot. The vocals move to the foreground to effect a dynamic shift in emphasis which is reinforced timbrally by the kit line. The subtle whiplash of the verse is given added intensity as it reinforces the narrative of the vocal melody which is, itself doubled by the piano to effect a sense of assertiveness:

and I real - ly wan-na know

The video picks up on the musical structures as images of Lennox are juxtaposed with Stewart, drinking at the table with two women to resolve the initial enigma of the three glasses. The whiplash of the kit line provides a musical metaphor for power as Stewart first moves to the woman on his right before caning his other companion (neatly synced to the rhythm) who, in turn, dissolves into a third to represent the unrepresentable, unknown others of her lover's affection. Opened out visually by images of Lennox's face and lips which segue into Stewart with yet another woman, the sense of unrestrained hurt (Lennox's blue note swerves) and anger (breaking a chair against the torch holding figurines on the stage) moves the narrative into the chorus, refocusing the initial dilemma 'Who's that girl?'

The piano line again doubles the vocal to reinforce the need to know. The naïvety of the question is reflected musically in the narrow range of the vocal line and the way in which the initial question follows the natural inflection of the spoken delivery. 'Who's that girl ... ' is measured, initially unelaborated, but with each repeat the major Bb tonality on 'girl' (with its connotations of brightness) is musically adorned with inflection, the extended melismas effecting a sense of playing with the imaginary as the video shows Stewart 'running around' with different women. The sense of transition is, itself, underpinned by the syncopated step-wise movement in the bass line, etching out the underlying harmonies, aligning Stewart and the imaginary woman through major tonalities which disrupt the otherwise minor feel of chorus before it subsides into the second verse.

This time the poignancy of lost love is tinged with self-realisation, both in the recognition of the 'foolishness' of lovers' talk and in the first glimpse of Lennox's male alter ego, sitting alone and surveying her from a nearby table. The chorus, with its repeated images of Stewart accompanied by various dates includes a shot of the female/male Lennox entering, and later exiting a 'hotel', as the 'tell me' takes on a heightened significance. Stewart's companions, tired and bored, become the questioners: 'tell me', and the video ends with Stewart rearranging photos on the table in an otherwise deserted nightclub while Lennox kisses her male persona. As the song fades, the repeated 'Who's that girl' frames the final enigma as Lennox gazes sideways into the camera, a twinkle in her eye.

The image of Lennox as a woman (in a blonde wig) kissing her male alter ego (without a wig) is both ironic and powerfully erotic. Having explored the feminine through the fetish of representation by positioning Stewart's various dates as other to his omnipresent masculine subject, her energies (as implied by the more upbeat chorus) are directed to autoeroticism and autorepresentation. Her passivity (as initially focused by the plaintive 'Who's that girl?') is overturned through the realisation that she is something more than excess baggage and her castratory lack thus becomes a site of new and alternative pleasures. Her final glance at the camera (and hence the viewer) suggests that she is aware of both playing with gendered identity and, through the kiss, playing with herself, thus stressing the delight of pleasures that are no longer subordinate to the Freudian (Stewart's) penis. As such, the images suggest a double metaphor as she acts out both a sense of autoeroticism (in love with herself, 'two lips in constant contact') and the polymorphous.

The effect of Lennox's performance is to destabilise 'the distinctions between the natural, the artificial, depth and surface, inner and outer through which gender discourses almost always operate'.[30] The lack of a coherent sexual identity not only subverts the 'meaning' of *being* a woman through exposing the illusions of gendered identity, but equally draws attention to its construction through the metaphor of hair and dress. As such, there is a blurring of the distinction between what Irigaray defines as gender dichotomies and a rejection of oppositions: fiction/truth, sensible/intelligible, through an innovative rethinking of metaphor. The final image, in particular, challenges the initial passivity of female space as implied by the plaintive tone of the questioning 'Who's that girl?' and the inference that Lennox (as the blonde torch singer) is simply 'a place and an envelope' for her man. Rather, her desire is shown to be both articulate and complete in its play on plurality, play and difference.

It is thus rather disappointing to note that despite Lennox's acute insights into gendered identity, she directly avoided any advocacy of feminism. Clearly such 'seriousness' could have impacted upon her popularity with a mainstream pop audience, and there is little doubt that the appeal of what Jon Savage charmingly terms 'the synthetic allure of fizzy pop' lay in its 'simultaneous and uneasy status as "youth expression" and kinky commerce'.[31] Even so, Lennox's challenge to the traditional images of women in rock provided a powerful example of female artistic expression. As a musician she had the ability to both write and perform her own music (Lennox actually plays most of the keyboards on records; Stewart plays guitar and produces). As one of the first women to benefit from the exposure offered by MTV she demonstrated a cool manipulation of image that was, at the time, unique. However, as she, herself, pointed out to Lucy O'Brien, 'Being in a middle place that's neither overtly male nor overtly female makes you threatening, it gives you power.'[32]

Acknowledgements

I would like to thank Dr Stan Hawkins (University of Oslo) for his inspiring article on Annie Lennox (*Popular Music* 1996) not least, his enthusiasm for her 'infectious grooves'.

NOTES AND REFERENCES

1 Tong, R. (1992) *Feminist Thought. A Comprehensive Introduction*, London: Routledge, p. 227.
2 Irigaray, L. (1985) *The Sex Which Is Not One*, Ithaca, NY: Cornell University Press.
3 *Ibid.*, p. 84.
4   Woman 'touches herself' all the time, and moreover no one can forbid her to do so, for her genitals are formed of two lips in continuous contact. Thus, within herself, she is already two – but not divisible into one(s) – that caress each other.

                                                                Ibid., p. 24

5 Weedon, C. (1987) *Feminist Practice and Poststructuralist Theory*, Oxford: Blackwell, p. 63.
6 *Ibid.*, p. 64. This was a point that was eloquently developed in Joni Mitchell's album as discussed previously.
7 *Ibid.*, p. 63.
8 Tong, *op. cit.*, p. 228.
9 Irigaray, L. (1977) *'Women's Exile'. Ideology and Consciousness* 1, p. 64.
10 Irigaray (1985), *op. cit.*, p. 24.
11 Irigaray (1977), *op. cit.*, p. 64.
12 Irigaray (1985), *op. cit.*, p. 28.
13 *Ibid.*, p. 29. Again, this is a point that is reflected in Julia Kristeva's discussion of the semiotic *chora* and Patti Smith's track 'Land of 1,000 Dancers' – most particularly in the 'Horses' section (see pp. 104–5).
14 Moi, T. (1985) *Sexual/Textual Politics: Feminist Literary Theory*, New York: Methuen, p. 140.
15 *Ibid.*, p. 132.
16 See Sanjek, D. 'Can a Fujiyama Mama be the Female Elvis? The Wild, Wild Women of Rockabilly', in Whiteley, S. (ed.) (1997) *Sexing the Groove. Popular Music and Gender*, London: Routledge, pp. 137–67.
17 See Negus, K. 'Sinead O'Connor – Musical Mother', *ibid.*, pp. 178–90.
18 Straw, W., 'Pop Music and Postmodernism in the 1980s' in Frith, S., Goodwin, A. and Grossberg, L. (eds) (1993) *Sound and Vision. The Music Video Reader*, London: Routledge, pp. 6, 7, 10.
19 Butler, J. (1990) *Gender Trouble. Feminism and the Subversion of Identity*, London: Routledge.

20 Irwin, C. (1986) 'Thorn of Crowns', *Melody Maker*, 22 November, p. 24.
21 Rock iconography is authenticated by codes of rebellion. This includes the appropriation and subversion of the bourgeois associations surrounding the male suit and its relationship to capitalism. See, for example, Teddy Boys and the Edwardian Suit, Mods and the 'London' business suit, and the use of blue jeans as a cultural affirmation of proletarianism.
22 Irwin, *op. cit.*, p. 24.
23 O'Brien, L., (1955) *She Bop. The Definitive History of Women in Rock, Pop and Soul*, London: Penguin, pp. 253–4.
24 *Ibid.*, p. 251.
25 *Ibid.*, p. 253.
26 *Ibid.*, p. 253.
27 It is suggested that Lennox's studentship at the Royal Academy of Music would have given her an acute awareness of the codes and conventions of Romanticism, not least its privileging of the imagination. In particular, the notion that an artist perceives and represents essential reality by virtue of 'his' master faculty imagination, provides a specific insight into her manipulation of reality/fantasy and her adoption of the male suit – as clearly such nineteenth-century Romantic critics as Ruskin would not have recognised the woman as 'the genius' (or autonomous creative artist). However, the Romantic Movement also embraced a vision which included the abolition of slavery, the emancipation of women, the reassertion of the erotic life and the reclamation of nature. This movement included such artists and thinkers as William Blake and Mary Wollstonecraft, Rainer Maria Rilke and Elizabeth Barrett Browning. In contrast, the desire to know the power of nature and eros was accompanied by a fear of these forces. This was focused by the association of nature with the body of women and led to the decadent school of art and poetry including Byron and Schiller. It is suggested that these diverging directions are equally present in the tensions between the pastoral and its contrasting image of the emancipated yet erotic figure of Annie Lennox in the video. It is not insignificant to note, in this connection, the adoption of a male persona by such figures as Georges Sand and George Eliot.
28 Showalter, E., (1991) *Sexual Anarchy. Gender and Culture at the Fin de Siècle*, London: Bloomsbury, pp. 148–9.
29 Butler, *op. cit.*, pviii.
30   Irigaray notes that woman is not only rolled up in metaphors but that concepts are 'rolled up' in the body matter of woman: '(man) envelops himself and his things in her flesh' so drawing attention to the way in which space constitutes woman.
        Best, S., 'Sexualizing Space', in Grosz, E. and Probyn, E. (eds) (1995) *SexyBodies. The Strange Carnalities of Feminism*, London: Routledge, p. 188

31 Savage, J. 'Androgyny. Confused Chromosomes and Camp Followers' in *The Face* (1984).
32 Annie Lennox, in an interview with Lucy O'Brien. In O'Brien *op. cit.*, p. 241.

9

MADONNA, EROTICISM, AUTOEROTICISM AND DESIRE

If Lennox's play on androgyneity underpinned control and power, then Madonna's sexuality was perceived as 'whorish ... very very whorish. It was like she was fucking the music industry. It may have been parody on her part, but I thought it was very low' (interview with Annie Lennox in *Melody Maker*, 1986).[1] The debates surrounding Madonna have been extensive, with competing viewpoints that have situated her as a feminine icon, a feminist, an opportunist. It is not intended to examine these debates in any detail here.[2] Rather, I will discuss two key videos, *Express Yourself* and *Justify my Love*, relating them to the discussions of plurality, play and difference which inform Irigaray's discussion of autoerotic practice and its relationship to the confrontation of patriarchal power.[3]

Madonna's early image fitted neatly into what O'Brien terms 'the power of advertising and its shadow sister, the soft-porn industry'.[4] Having made her film debut in 1980 in a low-budget softcore film, *Certain Sacrifice*, it is not too surprising that her first video, *Like a Virgin* (1985, with musical director Patrick Leonard), exhibits a professional confidence in its play on pornographic imagery and metaphor against a lightweight disco pop format. Set in Venice, Madonna performs the role of the knowing virgin, a figment of the pornographic mind, as she romps through marble rooms dressed in a frothy white wedding dress. Her image signifies a denial of sexual knowledge but her simulated writhing on a gondola underpins the simulation of deceit (like a virgin, with the soul of a whore) and the intrusion of a male lion confirms the underlying bestial discourse of both mythological fairytale and pornographic sex.[5] Cavorting with her masked dream lover who, not surprisingly, wears the lion's head, she sheds the veneer of innocence and shows her propensity for wild animal passions. Having instilled desire, she has turned her love, metaphorically, into the Beast.

In 1985 it was, perhaps, rather too early to take the pornographic imagery to its logical conclusion and end with a shot of Madonna's naked body. Nevertheless, the connotations of stripping are invoked by her removal of the chaste petticoats of her wedding dress to reveal her legs, before she subsides onto an ornate bed with the shadow of her lover passing over her.

There is also the use of the wedding veil itself which she draws erotically across her face in a simulation of striptease, and her inviting 'come on' look, signifying sexual invitation. As such it is not too surprising that Madonna quickly attracted hostile attention from some feminist writers who saw her as 'the lowest form of popular culture' (commercial, formulaic, trivial and shallow pop), and as corrupting 'the meaning of womanhood'.[6] In retrospect, it is evident that any interpretation of Madonna relies on either an acceptance, or a rejection, of her videos as *ironic*, as destabilising traditional representations of sexuality and gender by playing on the inflections of feminised images. If there is acceptance, then such videos as 'Material Girl', (where Madonna accepts wallets and jewellery from a chorus line of adoring men, before physically ejecting them) show her as the 'heroine of self-actualization', playing with 'her own persona, to indicate that she is the author of her image, that she constructs it to suit her desires, that she can change it as she likes'.[7] As such, the initial labelling of Madonna as a 'tarted up floozy', a 'hard hooker'[8] can be countered by that of a woman who, from the onset, has 'deliberately made a spectacle of herself'.[9] As such, her self-presentation (whether as part of her 'boy toy' phase, or as the successful 'material girl'), her 'meaningfulness', cannot be read simply from the surface of the text, but rather depends on an acceptance of the displacement of the dominant discourses surrounding gender through a fragmentation of the image. By 'miming the miming' imposed on woman and, by overdoing it, she thus undoes the effects of phallocentric discourse.[10] Or does she?

A rejection of the discourse of irony would suggest that Madonna's portrayal of femaleness and femininity (whereby bodily attributes can be reduced to a sexuality which is simply displayed for pleasurable looking) only confirms a masculine definition of femininity. Clearly her image fits the pop orthodoxy of 'sexy women', and as such, there is the distinct possibility that an audience will simply find her titillating. However, I would argue that there is a distinction between simply flirting with the camera, and consciously manipulating images through shock tactics. As such, while Madonna's early career suggests more a flirtation with gender politics (and, as such, engages with both feminist acclaim and condemnation) the 'arty, self-conscious, issue-oriented statements'[11] of her later videos are ingeniously confrontational, emanating from the mind of a woman who is fully aware of the politics of gender.

Madonna's move from a chameleon-like pop star – who adopted a new identity with each promotional video and who engaged top designers, producers, photographers, dancers and directors to mastermind images for her[12] – coincides with her 1989 album *Like a Prayer*. Following the public ordeal of her break-up with husband Sean Penn, throughout which she remained constrained and uncommunicative, the album not only heralded the debut of a maturely philosophical Madonna, but also marked her identity as a more musically enterprising songwriter. Although still characterised musically by a disco beat, *Like a Prayer* draws on more diverse stylistic influences which underpin the narrative exposition of the video. The song begins with sirens which are undercut by a heavy metal guitar to provide a dramatic urgency, evoking memories of Stevie Wonder's outro to 'Danger in the City'. The cut to flaming crosses and the narrow-ranged vocal, 'Life is a mystery, everyone must stand alone', is equally graphic in its musical naivety, presaging scenes of Madonna kissing a weeping black Christ, tableaux of Gospel choirs and the wrongful arrest of a black man. The use of images, themes and, more specifically, rhythms from black culture are important to the construction of racial tension and black morality portrayed in the video. In particular the presentation of what Ronald B. Scott calls 'the affirming and vital image of black women as an equal source and intricate part of the moral fiber and strength in the black community'[13] is focused by the strength of her gospel vocal. The juxtaposition of Madonna's 'Just like a prayer' and the soulful 'I'll take you there' within a framing of the black Baptist choir, suggests a musical encoding of cultural affirmation, a point which is supported by the narrative exposition of the video. Within the black church there is both support and an uplifting of the spirit, and the final shots – where Madonna sings and dances with the choir – suggest 'both an acknowledgement and a celebration of African musical roots and style'.[14]

Clearly, Madonna's maturation as a singer songwriter owes much to her association with Prince, not least in their collaboration on the track 'Love Song'. At the same time the album itself can be read as a reflection of past musical influences. 'Act of Contrition' features reverse tape loops and a manipulation of voices that pay homage to the Beatles' *White Album*. 'Keep It Together' and 'Express Yourself' 'are sort of my tributes to Sly and the Family Stone. "Oh Father" is my tribute to Simon and Garfunkel, whom I loved.'[15]

Madonna's acknowledgement of pastiche, of being capable of imitating musical style, is interesting but, given her ability to manipulate image, not too surprising. However, while 'Express Yourself' has a comparable musical exuberance to Sly and the Family Stone, the main point of comparison lies in the jazzy horn sections and an underlying sense of humour which also informs the tongue-in-cheek video. There is, therefore, more a sense of resemblance than a signification of authenticity, and this is equally true of the references to musical comedy and gospel which open out the disco narrative through parody and irony.

Set within a simple song structure, 'Express Yourself' plays with ambiguity through a subtle control of harmony and the avoidance of diatonic closure. The introduction suggests the key of G major but the first note of the melody – Bb/ 'don't' – implies both a minor inflection and lack of tonal stability. This is equally evident in Madonna's vocal nuance on 'express yourself' which initially centres on G before moving down a semitone to the leading note, F#, (with its feel of yearning towards resolution in the tenuously constructed home key) and finally denying any form of cadential resolution in the step down to F natural to create a musical metaphor for a shifting identity. The 'self' associated with the final F natural is equally ambiguous in that it picks up on the minor inflection of the first phrase (the Bb 'don't, identified above), so bringing a continuing sense of tension between two tonal centres (G and F major). This is also echoed in the horn interjections. Again appearing to be centred on G, the Bb pedal note aligns it with minor harmonies of the opening phrase, so reinforcing the motifs of alternative constructions of the self as Madonna plays with images, wearing a suit over her black lingerie, and sporting a monocle, with its dualistic associations of male voyeuristic power and 1920s' lesbian fashion.

The harmonic structure of the song, the play on two tonal centres, implies a sense of ambiguity which is initially opened out by the play on style. The samba style of the opening to the video, with its polyrhythmic dance feel, is traversed by Madonna's challenging 'Come on girls! Do you believe in love? Well, I've got something to say about it, and it goes something like this.' The sense of feminine space (as Madonna surveys an urban landscape from the back of a stone American eagle) is enhanced by echo effects on 'girls', 'say about it', 'like this'. The emphatic handclap on the second beat, aligned to the declamatory feel of the vocal, effects a layering of gospel over the samba rhythm before the shift to a more funky groove, evocative of the Family Stone's exuberant soul track 'Dance to the Music'. The dance feel is heightened by choreographed images of machinery and male torsos which pick up on the underlying pulse. The mechanistic feel, however, is subtly offset by Madonna's emphasis on the second beat of the bar, and the rhythmic pulse of the kit line which heightens the expressive, sinuous feel of the disco beat to effect the physicality of a 'whole body eroticism'.[16]

Madonna's raunchy delivery 'put your love to the test' complements the physicality of both the music and the video images as glistening male bodies are aligned with grinding cog-wheels and piston-shafts 'letting off steam'. The verse picks up on the eroticism as Madonna (drawing on her earlier Monroe persona and cuddling a black cat) surveys the 'workers' engaged in a choreographed display of physical exercises which play ironically on the associations of aerobics and disco. The scene draws on Jane Russell's earlier role, in the poolside setting of *Gentlemen Prefer Blondes* where the male lifesavers similarly engage in a display of physical jerks under Dorothy's powerful gaze. At the same time, Madonna's adoption of her Monroe persona (the blonde hair, the blue-eyed look at the camera) exerts an underlying duality that plays on the contradictions between Monroe-as-image, Lorelei-as-character which inform the film. The Monroe image signals innocence: she is aware of her sexuality but it is presented as primarily narcissistic. In contrast, Lorelei is definitely in control of her physicality and her wit

139

expresses an intelligent but cynical appraisal of the situation. The effect is to indicate innocent pleasure in being sexy.[17]

The play on duality, the evocation of Anita Loos' Broadway musical, is emphasised by the discourses surrounding the omnipresent disco feel, the connotations 'of the wider to and fro between work and leisure, alienation and escape, boredom and enjoyment'.[18] In particular, the juxtaposition of the Monroe image with the codes of disco picks up on a Romanticism which asserts that the limits of work are not the limits of experience and that the musical dialectic is consistent in its emphasis on whole body eroticism. As such, Madonna's off-camera vocal, 'put your love to the test', suggests less a change of direction, than a musical bridge to a new play on gendered identity. This is initially accessed by the black cat (a visual pun on the sexual *anima* of Madonna's persona), effecting a traverse shot to two male figures surveying the workers and, (by implication) the figure of Madonna, dressed this time in a black chemise, black suspenders and black stockings simulating a striptease behind a screen. The implications of voyeurism are, however, undercut by the narrative of fairytale, this time through an ironic play on the male worker's naked body as he sleeps and, by implication, dreams of Madonna's provocative body language, her assertion that 'second-best is never enough' and her challenge that to 'win her' the hero will have to 'put (him)self to the test'. With the scene set, and with Madonna's eyes gazing down on him, superimposed over the top half of the frame, the duality of the fairytale and the pornographic narrative can, it seems, get down to the real action – the physicality of disco dance and its engagement with the expressive.

Madonna's flaunting of the feminine black bra through the male attire of a suit and monocle situates the return of the verse within the discourse of gay identity. As Dyer points out, 'gay ghetto culture is also a space where alternative definitions, including those of sexuality, can be developed … the importance of disco in scene culture indicates an openness to a sexuality that is not defined in terms of cock'.[19] As such, the disco tune, which essentially drives beyond itself through endlessly repeated phrases and the denial of cadential closure, allows for an exploration of whole body eroticism. This includes both the exploration of alternative sexualities and a confrontation of 'the teleological phallic libidinal'[20] of rock within the subterranean factory of the video.

The move from striptease (which is directed largely at the male gaze) to disco dancing (within the overall framework of the omnipresent disco beat) is thus significant in focusing attention on the multifaceted terrain of the female body. Madonna's combination of the male suit with the feminine lingerie plays ironically on images of power. The earlier connotations of striptease are opened out and given a new layer of meaning as she playfully exposes her black bra while groping her crotch to challenge the myth of female castration by questioning the 'real' of the 'phallic' feminine. The emphasis on Madonna's assertive 'express yourself', allied to her visual performance, thus makes it clear that she is the 'big strong hand (that will) lift you to your higher ground'. The instrumental bridge, with its brass players symbolically imprisoned within a lifesize rotating glass box, under the monocled gaze of a Teutonic-like workmaster, is then opened out by the verse where Madonna is manacled by a dog-collar to a large white bed. Just as the suit is associated with male power, Madonna's nakedness carries connotations of submissiveness. However, as Valerie Steele has argued, 'SM adherents uniformly stress ... (that) the slave figure is very often the one "really" in command'. As such, the question is raised as to 'whose fantasy it really is'.[21]

Madonna's direct gaze at the camera, her commanding vocal tone, imply quite clearly that 'the key word to understand S/M is fantasy. The roles, dialogue, fetish costumes, and sexual activity are part of a drama or ritual ... The S/M culture is a theatre in which sexual dramas can be acted out'.[22] The emphasis on 'acting out' is important. As Irigaray observes, the phallocentric mode of signifying female sexuality constantly reproduces counterfeit images which massage male vanity and desire ... reflecting back the image simply reinforces male-defined power.[23] Initially, then, the 'Teutonic' master appears to engage with Madonna's play on the submissive, but he is excluded from entry to her room by the reprise of the horn players, and the musical accompaniment, like the video scene itself, is repeated a second time. The critical difference lies in the master's exclusion from the box. All he can do is stare through his raised monocle as Madonna sings out 'You've got to make him express himself, hey, hey'. The suggestion that some only pleasure themselves in looking, in the voyeuristic, is opened out by the instrumental break. Madonna's 'bedroom' door closes, the camera tracks the shadow of the cat, the 'master' surveys the players before the camera focuses on the 'hero' symbolically stroking the wet black cat. As the 'master' retreats the question is raised as to who is aroused, Madonna (with the visual pun on the wet black 'pussy'), or the 'hero' as he gazes upwards to the final refrain of the chorus.

The earlier connotations of submissiveness are given a new inflection as Madonna is seen crawling, catlike, across the floor as the 'What you need is a big strong hand' is juxtaposed with images of sexual power – Madonna seated on a sofa, dressed in her black suit and smoking a cigarette, gazing directly into the camera before her enticing 'make him love you 'til you can't come down' finally incites the appropriate male response. As she is seen lapping milk from a saucer, the shadow of the hero crosses the wall before he emerges, the cat slung over his shoulder, before love is 'put to the test'. The fairytale play on ordeal before winning the hand of the princess is acted out in a trial of strength as shots of two men – fighting in a boxing ring – are juxtaposed with the hero carrying off the naked Madonna (thus confirming the metaphorical resemblance to the cat) to a fadeout on 'Express yourself, whether you're ready or not'.

Although the video is itself fragmentary – playing on a bricolage of images which suggest, rather than confirm, a narrative exposition of events and a sense of resolution – Madonna's play on multiple, and often contradictory, subject positions informs the concept of a subtle and complex feminine discourse which is organised around the plurality of pleasure. This, in turn, is activated by the physicality of the rhythmic grooves which heighten the pleasures of fantasy and eroticism through the association of dance. The construction of a rhythmic and sexual body through the sexual mobility inherent in disco underpins its combination of materialism, romanticism and physicality. It is, as Dyer suggests, a celebration of technological modernity and 'its eroticism allows us to rediscover our bodies as part of this experience'.[24]

> What nudity as beautiful as this
> Obedient monster purring at its toil;
> Those naked iron muscles dripping oil,
> And the sure-fingered rods that never miss?

As Louis Untermeyer's nineteenth-century poem 'Portrait of a Machine' shows, the play on the sexual connotations of machinery is, itself, historical and cultural. *Express Yourself* plays with similar imagery as the machinery is aligned with the bodies of the workers and the technology of disco itself (multi-tracking, echo chambers, electric instrumentation, digitised rhythm). However, while this might suggest a certain fixity in the alliance of 'naked iron muscles' and 'sure-fingered rods', the suggestion that eroticism is confined to the penis is opened out by Madonna's play on gendered identity. The juxtapositions of image suggest an ironic play on the Madonna/whore binary – subordinate (crawling, catlike, lapping up milk)/dominant (in a suit, sexually in charge) – which are, in turn, underlaid by pornographic associations. However, *Express Yourself* does not simply contrast and contest the teleological phallic libidinal economy of men with the vaginal/clitoral economy of women. Rather, Madonna's play on gendered identities (overdoing stereotypes and exaggerating representations of established femininity) frees the 'feminine feminine' through the pleasures inherent in the female imaginary. Ironically engaging with the myths constructed by men about women through a capricious and contradictory eroticism,[25] her performance breaks out of the male imaginary and into the female one.

However, as Irigaray concedes, 'mimicking is not without its perils. The distinction between mimicking the patriarchal definition of woman in order to subvert it and merely fulfilling this definition is not clear. In her attempts to overdo this definition, woman may be drawn back into it.'[26] Performing representations which are often embedded in soft/hardcore – i.e. reinforcing the traditional representations of male–female differences as reducible to bodily parts which are exclusively sexual in function ... privileging the male

orgasm over the female and equating it with ejaculation; showing that pleasure can be voyeuristic – catching people in the act[27] – is problematic. The
fact that the subject's face is included (looking at the spectator and so
guiding the reading of the image) is particularly problematic, and it is here
that Madonna's inviting gaze provokes most criticism. Is she knowingly in
control? Does her play on autoeroticism challenge patriarchy or is she
simply capitalising on the allure of screened sexual activity? An analysis of
Madonna's single, 'Justify my Love' (November 1990) provides a complementary analysis which examines this question further.

Madonna's breathy vocal in the opening to the song suggests a strongly
sexual mode of address within the overall framework of a dance track This is
organised rhythmically through the repetitive mid-tempo (98bpm) pattern
which continues without variation to the end

and is overlaid with a basic 'strings' pattern which centres around the chord
of F# minor. The figure, in terms of 'traditional' harmony, uses two voices
which describe the following four chords,

$$\text{F\#m, F\#m7, B} \frac{\text{Add 9}}{\text{F\#}} \text{ and Bm} \frac{\text{Add 9}}{\text{F\#}}$$

with the bass note F# acting as a pedal point throughout the track. Both
voices are given a distinctive and continuous timbre which, in conjunction
with the unvarying tempo, dynamic and rhythmic levels and stabbing drum
line enhances the disco feel. The strings, however, move against the rhythm,
and the low pitch of the sustained F# creates a hole in the musical texture to
suggest a feeling of emptiness which is enhanced by the use of an echo
effect.

As the song unfolds, there is an increasing sense of predictability in the
musical form. This is enhanced by the introduction to each verse, where the
drum track plays alone, followed by four repeats of the parallel 5th which, in
its upward movement from E to F#,

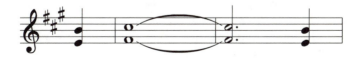

creates a feeling of anticipation, an underlying tension, which is released by Madonna's spoken delivery of the lyric line.

Although the unchanging musical structure of the song could be described as informationally closed, the contrast between the spoken verse and the sung chorus regulates the disclosure of information while posing and reposing the central enigma surrounding the title 'Justify My Love'. This is opened out by the vocal timbre of the verse where Madonna's intimate and breathy lyrics are supported by a low-volume, bluesy background vocal which anticipates the spoken 'I wanna kiss you in Paris' and provides a sense of atmosphere. Deeper in the mix, continuous slow breathing adds to the overall texture while underpinning the overall mood of sensuality.

Initially, the lyrics imply a specific relationship in the heavy reliance on I/You:

> I wanna kiss you in Paris
> I wanna hold your hand in Rome

which is enhanced by the romantic associations of the cities which are partially engendered by association with such American films as *An American in Paris, Three Coins in a Fountain* and *Gigi*, for example. The chorus, however, signals a certain change in atmosphere. Here, the breathing initially punctuates the 'wanting, needing, waiting' which prefaces the double-tracked 'for you to justify my love'. It then subsides deeper into the mix (as the voices pan between foreground/background on the repeated 'my love') to provide its own sensual rhythm as the voices duet, evoking a feel of complicity before the return to the drum track. This time it too is overlaid by breathing which climaxes with a slow, hisslike breath and an uttered 'OK' before the second verse. While the formal characteristics of the music continue, the 'OK', nevertheless, suggests a move in direction – a point which is reflected in the 'I wanna know you … no, not like that' of the second verse. As such, while the first verse suggests a certain submissiveness, there is equally a sense of struggle for control.

The chorus, with its emphasis on the incantatory present participle

> Wanting, needing, waiting
> Hoping, praying … first chorus
> Yearning, burning …. second chorus

draws initially on the connotations of the supplicant (a position also adopted in, for example, 'Like a Prayer', 'La Isla Bonita') before the explicit focus on the song's sexually unequivocal *raison d'être*, 'justify my love'. For the listener certain questions are raised: why 'justify', what is it that needs justification rather than, say, 'satisfy' or 'return'? The chorus also triggers a certain change in direction in the move from the instructive 'I want to know you – not like that' to the challenging imperatives, 'talk', 'tell' of the third verse. Here, the sexual nuancing on dreams ('am I in them?') fears ('are you scared?'), and dares ('I'm not afraid of who you are') imply more the position of a woman sexually in control, leading the 'man' (for while the 'you' is sexually ambiguous in its mode of address, the penultimate couplet would traditionally imply a heterosexual relationship) from fantasy to a sexual realisation of hidden desire. This sense of confidence is reinforced by the two final couplets:

> Poor is the man whose pleasures depend
> upon the permission of another

with its underlying connotations of domination through the imperative

> Love me, that's right, love me
> I wanna be your baby.

While the lyrics imply an overall focus on sexual fantasy, from the innocent 'I wanna kiss you in Paris' to the implicit S/M of pleasuring allied to 'permission' in the penultimate couplet – with the suggestion that certain pleasures need to be justified – there is little that invokes the diversity of sexual experience encountered in the video promo. Filmed in black and white, Madonna is first seen walking down a hotel hallway. Dressed in an overcoat, carrying a suitcase, her hand is held to her forehead.

'I wanna kiss you in Paris'	Profiled close-up of Madonna, her hands initially caressing her neck before they move down to part her coat. Camera pans left to reveal out-of-focus male figure (Ward) emerge from door on screen left. As he starts to walk slowly towards her, the camera pans right eliminating him from the frame.
'I wanna hold your hand in Rome'	Madonna plays with hair, then neck. Camera pans left to include male figure then cuts to reverse angle shot, positioned behind male figure, as he slowly walks towards her. Caresses face, mouth open, profiled. Madonna moves slowly against the wall.
'I wanna run naked in a rainstorm'	Camera cuts to reverse angle shot of male legs which frame Madonna. Camera and Ward track towards her.
'Make love in a train, cross-country'	Cuts to close-up profile of Madonna revealing bra-strap. Mixes through to shot of shoulder as Madonna slowly sinks down. Focus on hand as she appears to simulate masturbation.

'You put this on me'	Camera tracks into her thighs which part, and tilts up to reveal her looking up at male figure. She lifts her hands to him.

At this point, there is little to distinguish Madonna's play on autoeroticism from the codes of illicitness and voyeurism that inform softcore. Madonna is caught up in her own pleasure which is, at the same time, displayed for the spectator through the fragmentation of her body. She is caught unawares, and the framing of the narrative through the figure of Ward provides a point of identification for the viewer. The emphasis, as she lifts her hands to him, thus shifts to one of outcome. However, to conform to the codes of pornography, the characters are 'what they do', they operate within the established roles of pornographic fantasy – 'so now what?'

'so now what?'	Lifts her hands to Ward
'so now what?'	Camera tightens to a big close-up profile of Madonna
'Wanting'	She stands. Camera travels up with her, blurred shot as Madonna pulls Ward towards her
'Needing', 'Waiting'	Blurred shot of Madonna and Ward kissing

The use of language here, the focus on the commonplace 'so now what?' and the 'wanting, needing, waiting' again draw on both soft- and hardcore. The characters are not developed psychologically, little is demanded of the viewer, and no explanation is needed to understand what is about to happen next. Rather, the outcome is already known, but the power of pornography is to see it happen. As such, the 'for you to justify my love', and the panning shot to Ward's hand on the wall supporting them, shifts the emphasis somewhat. 'My love' may provide a momentary shot of them kissing, but there is the hint of power, and a possible scenario of sado-masochism as the camera goes beyond to the empty corridor.

'Waiting'	Cut to tracking shot down corridor down slightly open doorway. Male in black leather
'Praying'	lacing female into bustier.
'For you to justify my love'	Cut to woman in bustier who turns to camera, thrusting her breasts forward

The symbolism of tightlacing, aligned with 'justify' focuses in on the associations of S/M foreplay, fetishism, and the fantasies of dominance and submission. As Foucault writes, the body has been subject to various forms of 'disciplinary power' and these 'invest it, mark it, train it, torture it, force it … to emit signs'.[28] The alliance of 'praying' with lacing suggests physical oppression and sexual commodification. At the same time, there are the connotations of erotic pleasures, that tightlacing is both contextual and constructed: 'The dominatrix wears her corset as armour, its extreme and rigid curvature the ultimate sexual taunt at the slave who may look but not touch ... The slave, on the other hand, is corseted as punishment.'[29] Clearly, then, there is an enigma: is Madonna playing with the fetishism of fashion (as equally implied in her wearing of Jean-Paul Gautier bras); is she implying that female fetishists are sexually liberated, or is she simply stimulating debates around the dichotomous pairing of embrace/imprison inherent in tightlacing?

Drum link to chorus	Mixes to shot of door opening to reveal androgynous figure silhouetted against a window in what appears to be a hotel sitting room. Heavily posed dancing. Camera tracks towards figure then cuts to tighter shot of Ward, the back of Madonna's head blurred in the background.

The appearance of the androgynous figure, a sylph-like figure with fingers extended by long, sharp nails, suggests an allegory of fetishistic pornography – scratching, stabbing, penetration. Linked to the chorus, the figure is important in providing a central focus as, with each return, more figures are revealed: lesbian, gay, black, Latin, white, to engage with Madonna's evolving sexual fantasy which is, itself, choreographed through her vocal delivery.

The careful mixing of the music/visual draws the narrative exposition of the vocal into alignment with the images in a way that makes sense of the various scenarios. The opening vocal line 'I wanna kiss you in Paris' informs the location of the video. Madonna is there with a suitcase, in a corridor which suggests 'hotel'. The intimacy of the spoken utterance, the self-caressing gestures, the play on autoeroticism, becomes focused as Ward appears and the narrative unfolds. At the same time, the sense of enigma is teased out through the gradual revelation of information. The initial 'for you to justify my love' may suggest a partial sense of fulfilment as Madonna and Ward kiss, but the repeated line is opened out to bring into play alternative sexualities which inform the enigmatic quality of 'justify'. At the same time the images of S/M stimulate the imagination and push towards a desire for resolution which is only partially satisfied by the shots of Ward and Madonna and the sexual quest inherent in 'I wanna know you'.

The use of soft focus and the connotations of documentary, as the hand-held camera makes the viewer 'aware of its presence', its revelation of something already happening, enhances the sense of voyeurism as the hotel corridor is opened out to scenes of alternative sexuality, while the viewer picks up on the clues ('Is this what she had in mind?') and snares ('Is Ward, her real boyfriend at the time, the centre of her desire?'). Ward, former gay porn model, equally authenticates the scenes of eroticism on the video – he has done this, he knows – and this sense of the pornographic opens out the initial suggestion of a hotel – if it is a hotel, then it is more like an arranged venue for alternative sex. This is equally suggested by the appearance of the bare-breasted, black-suspendered woman in a military cap (with the connotations of both the butch lesbian and the dominatrix) who reaches across Ward's body harness to grip his crotch, the female couple drawing moustaches on each other, the male couple in drag caressing as Madonna watches.

While Madonna's live performance and videos explore a range of sexualities, the latter clearly privilege a more intimate viewpoint for the viewer by accessing eye-contact and subtleties of facial expression. There is an explicit sense of voyeurism as the viewer 'sees' with Madonna's eyes the unravelling scenes of sado-masochism and gay/lesbian eroticism, and experiences her view of Ward's body as he folds over her. The display of bodies, the feeling that the sexual protagonists are aware of the viewer in their returned gaze, Madonna's inviting 'come on' look, suggest equally a sense of exhibitionism, a perspective made explicit in the video for 'Open Your Heart' where one-way mirrors play on the duality of voyeurism and exhibitionism. Thus, while there is a distinction between a *sujet d'énoncé* and a *sujet d'énonciation* in the two videos there are also similarities. The filmed images, whereby the songs are framed by the narrative exposition, invite the viewer to look rather than listen. Sexual pleasuring is displayed for the viewer, implying that knowledge is to be secured through pleasurable looking. The exhibitionism suggests a sense of display, and is a central axis in the video's production of meaning, as facial expressions (Madonna's 'come-on' look, for example), and bodily display, sustain interest while providing a preferred reading of the lyric text.

Although the video can be interpreted as an example of the decentring of sexual objectivity and subjectivity, there is little doubt that, once seen, it stamps a particular identity, a preferred reading, upon the song itself. For some, it may come across as 'a bit of ironic exhibitionism' as suggested by Madonna's final exit, hand to mouth, suppressing a smile, winking at the camera, but the images are powerful in their assertion of a range of sexual pleasuring. As Lisa Henderson writes,

> For many lesbian and gay people, the lyrics (and later the epigram) also echo their refusal to await sanction ... to have sex and to forge their identities through the medium of sexual politics. Joining each other on the dance floors of gay clubs, where 'Justify My Love' played as song and video even while it was banned by MTV, lesbian and gay people could (and did) shimmy and sway in sexy solidarity, sparked by the song's rhythmic seductions.[30]

As such, the video provides a sense of opening up definitions of gender.

At the same time, it presents sexuality as play. It is an act, a screened perfor-mance which involves dressing up, make-up, lighting, camera styles. Madonna acts out a series of roles where she engages with the viewer's awareness that these are both choreographed images and familiar poses made unfamiliar. There is a problematising of what constitutes femininity, in its relationship to sexualities, which is expressed through a sense of fantasy which challenges stereotypical responses to what constitutes the 'male', the 'female'. As such, I would argue that the video allows both for the possi-bility of an entirely self-involved sexuality in its autoeroticism, and a complex range of identification and desire for Madonna as opposite sex/same sex. Gay black sexuality, lesbianism, androgyneity and an engagement with sexual fantasy and voyeurism (as exemplified in the choreographed shots of staged tableaux) disrupt any sense of normative heterosexuality (as implied by an unmediated reading of the song) to focus instead on themes of multi-gendering. At the same time there is an emphasis on the fetishistic in the specific focus on parts of the body (the drawing of moustaches on the lesbians, the exposed breasts, the eroticised clothing) and the returned gaze, as Madonna looks directly into the camera in the knowledge that she is being looked at, simultaneously both submitting to that inspection and controlling it. It would appear, however, that the video's explicit sexuality, its references to S/M and pleasuring, to dreams and fantasies, is at best, ambiguous. Madonna's view, as stated on *Nightline*, is that 'Justify my Love' is about two people being honest with each other, describing their sexual fantasies, 'regardless of their sex'. Her portrayal of the female protagonist can thus be equated with the Monroe prototype (innocent, heterosexual but equally becoming a gay icon). This is certainly supported by many of her fans, taken to extremes in the video: 'She shimmies into our fag imagina-tion, spreads her legs for our dyke approbation, grabs us by the pudenda and makes us face things we didn't think it was possible to learn from pop music.'[31] At the same time, the 'use' of pornography cannot be separated from its history of female suppression. The images are questionable and, for many feminists, objectionable in their association with sexuality and power. However, as suggested earlier, any interpretation of Madonna rests upon an acceptance or a denial of her sense of irony. If butch women and feminine men have attracted hostility because of the rigidity of gender definitions, then the video at least challenges sexual repression and, at the same time, forces the viewer to struggle over meaning.

Thus, despite MTV's refusal to play the video of 'Justify my Love' and feminist critiques surrounding its sexual representations, there is little doubt that Madonna's challenging stance confronted the romantic myths constructed around the feminine. Bondage, erotic fantasies and clitoral stim-ulation focus attention on autorepresentation in a celebration of the psychic and somatic dimensions of desire. Her construction of sexuality as the site of polysexual eroticism can thus be interpreted as a realisation of Irigaray's stress on plurality, play and difference. By confronting patriarchy through an engagement in autoerotic practices, in lesbianism and whole body exploration, Madonna has spoken words that are contradictory, 'inaudible for whoever listens to them with ready-made grids, with a fully elaborated code in hand'.[32]

NOTES AND REFERENCES

1 Interview with Annie Lennox, in Irwin, C. (1986) 'Thorn of Crowns', *Melody Maker*, 22 November, p. 26.
2 For different readings and debates see Schwichtenberg, C. (1993) *The Madonna Connection. Representational Politics, Subcultural Identities and Cultural Theory*, Boulder, CO: Westview Press.
3 See my earlier discussion (pp. 119–22) of Irigaray, L. (1985) *The Sex Which Is Not One*, Ithaca, NY: Cornell University Press.
4 O'Brien, L. (1995) *She Bop. The Definitive History of Women in Rock, Pop and Soul*, London: Penguin Books, p. 215.
5   Pornography is filled with associations between women and animals. We see a film in which women become animals, who are then trained with a whip ... a woman is photographed surrounded by the mounted heads of wild animals and animal skins. She opens a live lion and touches her own breasts. Over the photograph we read that 'Lea' has shed 'the veneer of civilisation for the honesty of wild animal passions ... As common as the image of woman as beast is the image of a woman in coitus with an animal, as if, when a woman is pictured as the lover of a beast, her bestial nature is confirmed.
                                        Griffin, S. (1981) *Pornography and Silence*,
                                        London: Women's Press, pp. 24–5

6 Schulze, L., Barton White, A. and Brown, J.D.' "A Sacred Monster in her Prime". Audience Construction of Madonna as Low-Other' in Schwichtenberg, *op. cit.* p. 20.
7 Tetzlaff, D. 'Metatextual Girl. Patriarchy, Postmodernism, Power, Money, Madonna', *Ibid.*, p. 246.
8 Schulze *et al., op. cit.*, p. 24.
9 *Ibid.*, p. 25.
10 Moi, T. (1985) *Sexual/Textual Politics. Feminist Literary Theory*, New York: Methuen, p. 140.
11 Tetzlaff, D. 'Metatextual Girl', in Schwichtenberg, *op. cit.*, p. 255.
12 O'Brien, *op. cit.*, p. 217.
13 Scott, R.B., 'Images of Race and Religion', in Schwichtenberg, *op. cit.*, p. 72.
14 *Ibid.*, p. 72.
15 *Rolling Stone* 23 March 1989, p. 56.
16 Disco's whole body eroticism is achieved by, for example,

      the willingness to play with rhythm, delaying it, jumping it, countering it rather than simply driving on and on ... it restores eroticism to the whole of the body and for both sexes, not just confining it to the penis. It leads to the expressive, sinuous movement of disco ...
      Dyer, R. 'In Defence of Disco', in Frith, S. and Goodwin, A. (eds) (1990) *On Record: Rock, Pop and the Written Word*, London: Routledge

17 Dyer, R. 'Stars as Signs', in Bennett, T., Boyd-Bowman, S., Mercer, C. and Woollacott, J. (eds) (1981) *Popular Television and Film*, British Film Institute/ The Open University, p. 266.
18 Dyer in Frith *et al, op. cit.*, p. 417.
19 *Ibid.*
20 Morton, M. 'Don't Go for Second Sex, Baby!', in Schwichtenberg, *op. cit.*, p. 228.
21 Steele, V. (1996) *Fetish. Fashion, Sex & Power*, New York: Oxford University Press, p. 172.
22 *Ibid.*, p. 171.
23 See my earlier discussion in Chapter 7.
24 Dyer in Frith *et al op. cit.,* p. 418.
25   'She' is indefinitely other in herself. This is doubtless why she is said to be whimsical, incomprehensible, agitated, capricious ... not to mention her language, in which 'she' sets off in all directions leaving 'him' unable to discern the coherence of any meaning.

Irigaray, *op. cit.*, p. 29

26 Tong, *op. cit.*, p. 229.
27 Kuhn, A. (1985) *The Power of the Image. Essays on Representation and Sexuality,* London: Routledge & Kegan Paul, p. 35.
28 Foucault, M. (1979) *Discipline and Punish. The Birth of Prison*, trans. A. Sheridan, New York: Vintage Books, pp. 138, 25.
29 Steele, *op. cit.*, p. 63.
30 Henderson, L. 'Justify Our Love', in Schwichtenberg, *op. cit.*, p. 112.
31 *Ibid.*, p. 122.
32 Irigaray, *op. cit.*, p. 29.

10

K.D. LANG, A CERTAIN KIND OF WOMAN

As Giles Smith wrote in *The Independent* on 3 December 1993, 'Pop stars stay on the track either by processes of radical self-reinvention or by skating blithely to avoid the ruts. k.d. lang appears to be a skater. It took her a long time to say publicly that she was a lesbian. She finally did so in June 1993, in an interview with the American gay magazine *The Advocate*. She said she was fed up with people asking.'

Smith's retrospective on lang comes across as curiously low-key. In 2000 being a declared lesbian still presents problems[1] and it is certainly worth noting that lang was, at the time, thirty-two years old and had been a professional singer since 1982. As such, the 'fed up with people asking' conceals more than it reveals. lang had persistently tantalised her fans with such statements as 'I'm a llll ... liberace fan' but she was clearly aware that 'There's a big difference between not denying it and finally just saying "I'm a lesbian." '[2]

It is a salutary fact that the identity of the music industry devolves around the structural subordination of women. The majority of decision-making positions are held by men and although women performers are the most visible examples of progress in the history of pop and rock, success often implies a shrewd awareness of the particular demands of the industry — not least its firm attachment to heterosexual desire. Thus despite the fact that many women performers are lesbians, coming out in an industry that invites fantasy, cross-dressing and camp but which predicates female hetero-sexuality is commercially precarious. Androgyneity is undoubtedly a safer option. To be a declared lesbian in country music, where representations of gender and sexuality are unequivocally heterosexual, and where performer/fan relationships depend on a shared valorisation of family values,[3] is even more problematic. It could be commercial suicide.

As suggested earlier, the relationship between gender and style is impor-tant, not least in establishing a point of communication between the performer and her fans. In particular, listeners 'find a sense of their own *iden-tity* confirmed, modified or constructed in the process. Since both performer and listener are gendered and sexual creatures, the process is over-determined by these attributes.'[4] While it is recognised that this is not a simple process, lang's 'stylising' of country, which focuses attention on both its formal and formulaic features, and her subversion of both the staged and vocal idiom through self-dramatisation, is significant – not least in raising questions about the erotics of her performance. For example, while lang constantly changed her stage persona during her 'country' years, thus implying an act, she consistently presented a problematic sexuality which suggested an identity that was gendered and only ambiguously sexed. There is thus a tension in lang's performance that expressed itself as a dissonance between her anatomical sex, her sexuality and her gendered performance and which communicated itself to her audience (in part instinctively) as different. While this may have been a source of tantalising delight to her lesbian fans, her overly dramatic presentation of country, and the playful androgyny of her butch–femme persona, posed a direct challenge to Nashville's traditional codes of heterosexual femininity.

'Big-Boned Gals!'

Kathy Lang was born on 2 November 1961 in Edmonton, Alberta – 'a date known as langmas to die-hard' fans.[5] Music was an important part of family life and lang's first heroine was Maria from *The Sound of Music*. At ten, after three years of formal piano lessons, she started learning the guitar and listening to such rock stars as Creedence Clearwater Revival, Eric Clapton, Joe Cocker and the Allman Brothers. Later influences included singer song-writers Joni Mitchell, Kate Bush, Rickie Lee Jones and jazz stars Ella Fitzgerald, Peggy Lee and Billie Holliday.

Lang's upbringing was liberal, with her mother encouraging her love of music, her athleticism, her individuality, and her 'handsomeness'; her father, in turn, liked her adventurous spirit, giving her a 50cc motorbike for her ninth birthday, teaching her to ride and shoot and calling her his 'girl-boy'. In 1979 she moved to Red Deer College where she enrolled on the music programme and teamed up with Gary Elgar (Drifter). By the second year they had both dropped out, spending their time creating experimental music and driving around Eastern Canada. Lang also established a network of gay friends, some of them other lesbians, finally moving to Edmonton where she sang lead vocal in the musical *Country Chorale*. As the play's artistic director recalls, 'Sometimes you give a performer one thing that becomes the key that unlocks the door. For Kathy it was the Patsy Cline stance. Once she had that, she had a sense of character.'[6]

Lang's introduction to Patsy Cline was through looking at album sleeves – standing sideways, hands on hips, looking out at the audience. She also discovered that 'country can be fun', and changing her name to k.d. lang,[7] she started touring. In 1983 she recorded her first single 'Friday Dance Promenade', christened her band 'the reclines' (in homage to her idol) and after a three-month sell-out tour, a forty-minute performance at the Edmonton Folk Festival, a high profile Toronto debut and launch album *a truly western experience* (Homestead, 1984), she was eventually signed by Seymour Stein, founder of Sire Records, a subsidiary of Warner Brothers.

As biographer Victoria Starr observes, 'nearly everyone who knew Kathy Lang was surprised by the emergence of k.d. ... But more surprising to those who had worked and hung out with Kathy was her new-found obsession with country music'[8] and, in particular, Patsy Cline. Although lang had earlier emphasised the point that she was growing bored with the performance art scene, and that country music came with a structure and tradition that gave her something to work for – maybe even something to conquer,[9] it is evident that country was a challenging choice of genre for a lesbian singer. However, as cultural critic B. Ruby Rich points out, lesbian androgyny was expressed quite comfortably in country and western bars in major American cities.

> In the '70s, when lesbianism took androgyny as both principle and style, the country-and-western bar was one of the only welcoming sites outside of the womyn's community. It was there, to those honky-tonk joints, that women could always go in flannel shirts and jeans and no makeup, raise no eyebrows, even dance with a girl-friend alongside all the straight country gals doing the same.[10]

Although Rich makes no explicit reference to the gay scene in Eastern Canada, lang had an established network of gay friends, partying at such local gay discos as the Flashback (Edmonton). Her ability to 'fake it 'til you make it' and her genuine love of dressing up in country clothes matched her awareness that 'the strict gender definition presented in country music provide(d) excellent material for queer drag and butch–femme role playing'.[11] It is clearly equivocal as to whether or not lang's image was calculated. Her sawn-off cowboy boots, her lensless, wing-shaped glasses, blouses with rhinestone buttons, and torn stockings suggest more a DIY country-punk approach, that she was 'making herself up'[12] and that her flamboyance was initially part of an over-enthusiasm for dressing-up rather than an overt challenge to established country codes. At the same time, her performances suggest irony and camp and as such, lang's excess of style can be interpreted as a humorous critique of country gender stereotyping. She is clearly not unique here and Dolly Parton's self-conscious femininity could equally be cited as parody and role play. However, in an industry where gendered appearance is significant, Parton's excessive femininity is both appreciated and lauded. Her wasp waist, blond bouffant hair and ample bust confirm, while exaggerating, her sexual identity as a heterosexual 'country gal'. In contrast, lang's image of a 'big-boned gal' with an Elvis quiff, her butch vocal style and 'her ability to spray sweat on everyone within ten feet of the stage'[13] raised problems. Her 'look', her image and her vocal delivery 'implied that her sexual preference was not the way it should be'.[14]

The issues that surround gender and sexual orientation are generally linked. In country they work primarily within the codes of patriarchal binary thought which correspond to the underlying oppositions between man and woman. A girl should look like a girl, a boy should look like a boy and, under patriarchy, the male is always active and always the victor. The woman is either passive, or she doesn't exist. More specifically, the dominant cultural formation of Oklahoma/Kansas country music intersects (historically) with a class, racial, ethnic, sexual and regional modality. As a result, it is problematic to separate out country from the political and cultural context in which it was/is produced and maintained. The effect, however, is more transparent. Traditional country is situated within a particular and exclusive framework where biology equals destiny and where gender is culturally constructed as coherent and stable. As a result, gender relations are both regulated and reified within a heterosexual matrix, and the linguistic practice of country music can be interpreted as a fable that establishes and circulates the 'natural' facts of heterosexuality.[15]

As such, lang's country persona, her comic androgyny, effectively produces a subversive discontinuity and dissonance (among sex, gender and desire) that calls into question their alleged relationship. Her construction of female/femininity (as constituted through the codes of country) no longer appears stable. Rather meaning becomes troubled and unfixed as lang's excessive visibility- the sheer energy of her live performance, roaring 'around the stage like a riderless motorbike',[16] her reeling behind feigned punches, like a cowboy in drag, as she sings 'Johnny Get Angry' – problematise the hidden male/female opposition. She was, as Stella Bruzzi observes 'sublimely non-passive'[17] or, to the country purist, decidedly unladylike.

It is relevant to note, in this context, that camp style and gay-identified dressing were an integral part of the 1980s' gay scene. In particular, they articulated lesbian identity through irony while challenging, what Sue-Ellen Case identifies as the ruling powers of heterosexist realist modes. What is particularly relevant to lang's performance is the way in which camp exhibits a constantly changing, mobile quality, a 'first-strike wit' and irony 'which works to reveal the constructedness of the conventions of straight sex and gender systems'.[18] In contrast, country constructs and valorises a regulatory coherence that has resulted in an idealisation of a stable heterosexuality. The fact that this then becomes normalised implies that country artists have an unproblematic unity, whereby gender and sex are grounded in a stable identity. Performance codes (to include text, context, performer/listener behaviour, the sociological and ideological function of the music and its social image) then ensure that sex, gender and desire are demonstrably shown to be internally coherent.

lang's performance, then, could only disturb this generic stability. She flaunts her femininity, so effecting a parody of the gender identification which lies at the heart of country music – 'that a woman should be tough, but never far from the kitchen'.[19] As she observed in an interview with Giles Smith (*Independent*, 18 March 1993):

> When you have such a traditional form as country, a genre with an incubated personality, and someone comes in who has a partly satirical intent, or a desire to play with the kitsch aspects, then people are bound to be protective.

By 1987 lang was fully aware that the 'wacky, crazy, kinetic k.d. lang' was beginning to 'override the music', that her voice 'was playing second fiddle'.[20] lang's focus on her voice is significant in that it switches the emphasis from the overt to the covert in performance codes. As Bruzzi points out, 'what characterises the early repertoire is the common heterosexual reference point, either in the lyrics or in lang's presentation of herself as raucously female'.[21] In contrast, lang's vocal delivery, her musical persona, connotes a more knowing butch identity.

From the onset of her career, lang's voice was recognised as something out of the ordinary in terms of its richness, depth and range. At the same time, it is suggested that her musical influences, allied to a gift for mimicry, account for her hybrid style, her combination of 'torch and twang'. Her early love of jazz resonates in her feel for pitch inflection, joy in melody, warm, solid phrasing and lyric embellishment; her adoration of Patsy Cline and love of country and western is evidenced in the nasal twang and quasi-conversational narrative vocal style that underpins the downhome songs of romance, love and loss. Other influences are equally discernible. Her balladic vocalism suggests a light operatic influence while exhibiting the full, rounded tone that is found in early Presley who is, himself, an acknowledged source of inspiration.

For the Nashville purist, however, lang's marriage of balladic jazz and country (not least her exaggerated growls and 'cowboy' whoops) and her flamboyant performance style implied not only a foray into the stylistic conventions of country but equally a critique, a play on multiple, heterogeneous difference.

Torch and Twang

Although lang had released two major albums, *Angel with a Lariat*, (Sire, 1987) and *Shadowland* (Sire, 1988) – where she worked with one-time Patsy Cline producer Owen Bradly and which included the collaborative track 'Honky Tonk Angels Medley' with Loretta Lynn, Kitty Wells and Brenda Lee – I am going to discuss briefly two tracks from the 1989 album *Absolute*

Torch and Twang for which she won the Best Country Vocal Female Grammy in 1990.

Absolute Torch and Twang was co-produced with Ben Mink and Greg Penny and combined such lively upbeat tracks as 'Big Big Love' and 'Three Days' with more moody songs such as 'Trail of Broken Hearts'. Within three weeks the album had sold over 200,000 copies and on 17 June it entered the Billboard Top Country Albums chart where it remained for 104 weeks, reaching no. 12 position. On July 4, k.d. and the reclines set off on a 40-stop sell-out tour. The Nashville radio community, however, continued to reject her.

It is, perhaps, a truism to state that country values artists who are sincere and trustworthy, who reveal their souls through their songs. The fact that the songs may come across as 'corny', 'trite' and 'clichéd' is irrelevant. Clichés have become clichés because they are concise and evocative, because of their immediacy. The important point is how they relate to the topos of sincerity: speaking only when you have something truthful to say. To cover a song should thus imply aural homage, a sharing of the singer's point of view, not least if it is written by a member of the Nashville establishment. Clearly, truthfulness for the woman country singer can come across as somewhat prosaic and sentimental in valorising the values of middle-of-the-road America, but an exaggerated performance (as in lang's cover of 'Three Days') will inevitably cause problems. As Martha Mockus points out, lang's vocal delivery – her cries, whimpers and hiccups – reinterpret the song as physically connoting menstruation. What had started out as a tribute to Patsy Cline ends as a parody 'as lang's campy vocal manoeuvres ... the "dread", the "tears and sorrows" and the knowledge that it will "start all over again" ... form a menstrual narrative'.[22] Problems also arise when a song is written by a man, when the lyrics suggest the *double entendre* of 'a big big love', and when the performance invites a lesbian reading.

Lyrics are of central importance in country music and, allied to the forward placement of the voice in the mix and the narrative simplicity of the words, attention is firmly centred on lang's vocal which is strongly directed at the ambiguous 'you'. Given the bouncy, upbeat tempo of the song, the upward scalic movement of the opening melodic phrase and lang's mischievous rhythmic inflection on the final word 'Can't you feel my love a-growin'?' it is difficult not to read it as phallic. It is equally apparent that the persistent use of rhyme ('love a growin' ', 'ain't it showin' ') which both separates and links adjoining phrases, and the repetition of big ('big, big love') invite the expansive gesture, the suggestive challenge on the 'can't you feel' of the opening line.

At this point, it is interesting to note that although lang positioned herself (until the release of *Ingenue* in 1992) within the female domain of country, she consistently used the 'I-You' mode of address, thus avoiding masculine pronouns. It is, perhaps, somewhat unnecessary to point out that, had Dolly Parton sung this song her play on vulnerability, to include the little girl giggle and the fluttering eyelashes, would communicate the feminine, regardless of the volume and power of her voice. With lang, however, the signifier is given free play. She may be a woman, but the assurance of the vocal delivery, the confidence in her 'big big love' assumes a masculine subject-position. As Sue-Ellen Case points out, part of the responsibility of the butch woman is to convey sexual expertise[23] and lang's vocal delivery thus problematises the 'you', invoking an ironic play on the conventions of country (which would assume that the 'I/You' mode of address is heterosexual). Not least, her playful vocal style (with its parodied growls) implies that the absent 'other' (you) invites a lesbian identification, so raising the ironic question of 'penis, penis, who's got the penis?'[24]

Given the posturing of lang's vocal delivery it is difficult not to hear the song as sexually ambivalent, certainly 'anything but innocent'.[25] It is not surprising, then, that lang was denied access to radio airtime by the Nashville establishment. As Christopher Norris observes (in his discussion of Derrida), voice and speech are privileged over writing in expressing the presence of a human subject.

> *Voice* becomes a metaphor of truth and authenticity, a source of self present 'living' speech as opposed to the secondary lifeless emanations of writing. In speaking one is able to experience (supposedly) an intimate link between sound and sense, an inward and immediate realisation of meaning which yields itself up without reserve to perfect, transparent understanding.[26]

This sense of 'an immediate realisation of meaning' does appear to be confirmed in both Martha Mockus' persuasive lesbian reading of lang[27] and the reaction of the Nashville country establishment. The delivery is too playful, too aware, not to suggest a gendered twist to an otherwise straightforward country classic. In contrast the self-penned 'Big-Boned Gals' is more explicit in its narrative, not least 'in singing about another woman who is not a mother, daughter, or sister'.[28] More specifically, as Mockus points out,

> lang's vocal hiccups, yodels, quirky changes of register and growls give this tune its exuberance and inspire my lesbian reading of it. Such vocal antics upset the rigid contour of melody, thereby creating a rebelliousness that underscores the tune's daring premise of queer affection and desire.[29]

It is, perhaps, too speculative to suggest that 'Big-Boned Gal' was equally a throwing-down of the gauntlet. In its narrative of dressing up, coming out, its switch from the ambivalent 'you' to the more familiar 'she', and the butch mannerisms in its vocal style, it comes across as totally uncompro-

mising. Given that the relationship between female/woman gain their signi-
fications only as relational terms, there is a fronting of lesbian identity –
lang is a mannish or male/woman. The effect is to destabilise irrevocably the
political generic construction and regulation of country identity as heterosexual.

While other genres of popular music accept a minimal gay presence,
country makes no such concession. Rejected by the country radio executives,
and castigated by critics for mocking the honesty of traditional country
music, lang's Grammy win for *Absolute Torch and Twang* at least allowed her
to leave Nashville with some grace: 'ya, the big-boned gal was proud'.

Ingenue

As lang admitted, the big issue in her career had been her irreverence to the
political aspects of country, most specifically in Oklahoma and Kansas.[30] By
mid-1990, after six years of touring, writing and recording and despite her
collaboration with such significant artists as Roy Orbison, Kitty Wells,
Loretta Lynn and Brenda Lee, she decided to leave the country scene. Since
the release of *Absolute Torch and Twang* she had further alienated the country
fraternity by her outspoken attack 'Meat Stinks', which had resulted in a ban
of her music on country stations in Kansas, Oklahoma, Montana, Missouri
and Nebraska during the summer of 1990; participated in the 'Red Hot and
Blue' project which had provided an opportunity to produce a video of the
Cole Porter classic 'So In Love'; released a video for her 1989 single 'Trail of
Broken Hearts', and starred in Percy Adlon's *Salmonberries,* a film about
repressed lesbian sexuality. *Ingenue* (Sire, 1992) can thus be interpreted as a
watershed in lang's career, reflecting on her self-experience as a woman in
love with another woman, while maintaining her silence on her lesbian sexuality.

For many diehard fans, Ingenue was 'a big snore' 'easy listening', 'trite',
'too earnest'.[31] Certainly it was far removed from the mischievous exuberance of *Absolute Torch and Twang* in its moody introspection and lush
orchestration. At the same time, lang's soul-searching delivery communicates an inherent truthfulness which is deeply compelling. This is enhanced
by the musicality of the album, the sense of seamlessness which underpins
all ten songs as they open out the omnipresent mood of 'constant craving'
that accompanies unrequited love.

Ingenue can be characterised as torch songs within the broad stylistic
framework of the jazz ballad. Despite the ambiguity of 'who' is the subject
of lang's unrequited love, the words are personalised in their thematic reference, with a characteristic flowing lyricism and a slow/slowish tempo. More
specifically, the songs provide scope for fronting the dark lustre of lang's
voice, with the crafting of the music (the melodic contours, the sophisticated chains of harmonies, the orchestration) exhibiting a meticulous feel for

arranging which resonates with the narrative exposition of the vocal line. Vibraphones, violin, steel guitar, keyboards, marimbas, clarinets, accordions and the Bulgarian State Choir provide a heady mix of timbres which allow for a heightening of emotional impact across the ten songs. There is also a stylistic diversity in the fusion of such unlikely musical bedfellows as Kurt Weil with the exotic of Hawaiian music. Paradoxically, the overall effect is curiously homogeneous. The orchestration may suggest an excess of meaning in its eclecticism, but lang's brooding vocal delivery maintains a consistent emotional aesthetic, a musical fusion of what can be described as her private and creative melancholy.[32]

As a musicologist, I find it extraordinary that the lyric content of *Ingenue* – 'enough to make a person weep … the raw ache … the hopelessness'[33] – is applauded while the musical content is more often framed by a deprecating 'adult contemporary' un-hip tag, albeit with the caveat that 'there was something about the album that beckoned a second listen'.[34] That 'something' can largely be accounted for by the evocative arrangements and the subtlety of the harmonic language which supports an often simple melodic line to provide a nuanced shading for lang's dark vocal timbre. The lacklustre harmonies which underpin the 'tarnished dreams' ('Cleanse my tarnished dreams'), the limping rhythmic contour and the lack of wholeness in the G#7 of 'mend my wounded seams' (chorus, 'Wash Me Clean') are but two examples of Ben Mink's word-painting. His arrangements are equally sensitive in 'The Mind of Love' where a romantic 'gypsy' violin counter-melody gently probes the lyric reflection on love which, in turn, is coloured by supporting harmonies which move from equivocation to a more open resolution on the final G major chord.[35]

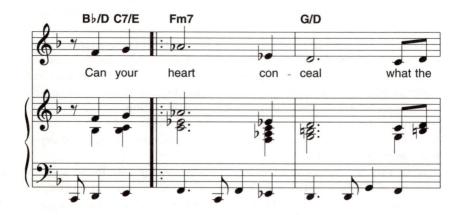

The two most lauded songs on the album, 'Constant Craving' and 'Miss Chatelaine' are equally finely honed compositions, with the latter picking up on the plaintiff mood which ends 'The Mind of Love' with a pensive violin intro. Within the popular the memorability of the opening phrase is crucial to the success of a song. Here, the violin line is remarkably simple and instantly recognisable. Its aural impact, however, is not so much reliant on its tunefulness, but rather on the arrangement and sophistication of the supporting harmonies which, once heard, impart a haunting familiarity. It seems, then, that the mood is to be one of reflection, but the pause anticipates a change in direction. With the words 'Just a kiss ... ' the rhythm switches to a Latin-tinged ballroom feel:

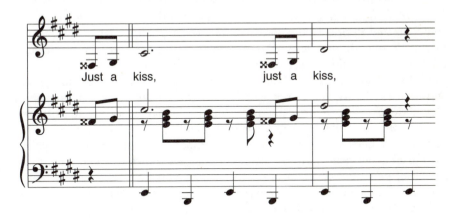

To an extent, the song comes across as curiously old-fashioned with its courtly 'just a smile', 'just a sigh', 'hold me captive'. At the same time, lang's phrasing (as she stretches out notes so that they sound behind the beat rather than on it), her pitch inflection and rubato (which create a sense of anticipation 'just a ... '), her smooth, sustained phrasing (which personalises such clichés as 'every time your eyes meet mine') effect the tonal tension and vocal nuance that earlier characterised her performance of the Cole Porter song, 'So In Love'.

For lang's fans, the parallels in the vocal delivery and the interpretation of the two songs would equally be informed by Percy Adlon's video which came out in 1989. As with all songs of the period, 'So In Love' is characterised by an 'I/You' relationship, so traditionally assuming a heterosexual mode of address. In the video, however, lang projects a boyish androgyneity and is seen wearily washing the laundry. As the song reaches its climax she is seen burying her head in a woman's slip that she has hung out to dry, 'full of grief and longing'.[36] Although lang had not yet come out, there is little doubt that her carefully highlighted masculinity allied to her subsequent appearance as a lesbian in Adlon's movie *Salmonberries* would be sufficient to inform a reading of 'Miss Chatelaine' (and, indeed, the album itself) as a lesbian text. lang could only be singing about a woman and, as biographer Victoria Starr observes, '*Ingenue* presented that woman behind the mask: Kathryn Dawn Lang',[37] hurt and full of personal angst that her feelings were not returned. Small wonder, then, that after her public coming-out and (seemingly) restored to her usual high spirits, lang was free to return to the artifice of camp, this time – significantly – as a *femme* in the company of divas Lady Bunny, Ebony Jet and Mistress Formika.

At this point, the underlying connotations of 'Miss Chatelaine' become more transparent. In 1989 lang had been nominated by the Canadian magazine *Chatalaine* as their woman of the year. With the magazine reaching one in five Canadian women its image has been described as a fusion of *Vanity Fair, Good Housekeeping* and *New York* – safe, middle of the road, fashion-conscious and decidedly heterosexual. The cover photo of lang, however, is markedly unfeminine. Despite the airbrushed lips, her hair (the traditional marker of femininity) is self-cropped and her body is angular. In contrast, the 'Miss Chatelaine' of the video is resplendent in a yellow chiffon gown and 'borrowed curls'. lang was clearly back to her witty, over-the-top self. Her masquerade as 'femme' holds femininity at bay, revealing it to be no more than a cultural mask. Gendered identity is destabilised and the distinctions between depth and surface, inner and outer through which discourses about gender almost always operate are shown to be no more than a kind of persistent impersonation that passes as real.[38] The irony of being 'woman of the year' is thus fully exploited, albeit four years later.

The *Miss Chatelaine* video also provides an interesting comparison with Madonna's performance in *Vogue*. As Sean Cubitt observes, the video extrapolates a 'camp sensibility, itself already marked by cross-gender identification … (there is) also a kind of male exhibitionism'.[39] lang's 'voguing' similarly suggests a butch woman cross-dressing as a cross-dressed man in a complex gendered performance which is quintessentially ironic and full of artifice. Her butch persona, allied to an 'excess of femininity' – familiar to traditional femmes and drag queens – thus provides another example of her complex masquerades. As one gossip columnist wrote at the time: 'k.d. lang is so butch that her concept of cross-dressing involves putting on make-up and a dress.'[40] The transition promised in 'So In Love' is thus finally realised, with the move from androgynous boy to butch dyke being achieved with characteristic lang humour.

In retrospect, the 'constant craving' with which *Ingenue* ends comes across as compellingly honest. It is widely accepted that while none of the songs on the album were completed in Alaska (the location for *Salmonberries*), 'the barren landscape served as a perfect metaphor for what was obviously going on in her life … the loneliness, and the yearning and the 'constant craving'[41] for truth and wisdom. Like the majority of songs on the album, the intro is again characterised by a chain of complex harmonies and a simple, memorable refrain which is initially introduced by a strummed acoustic guitar. The effect is uncluttered and direct. It is the yearning quality of the song, however, that impacts most upon the listener. To an extent this is due to the autobiographical content of the words, the realisation that 'even through the darkest days' there is someone inside who is drawn towards a search for truth. This sense of yearning is equally apparent in lang's vocal delivery, the way in which the words are held back, so that there is an aural sensation that the rhythm is dragging her along, carrying the heavy darkness of her mood. The supporting harmonies are equally effective in resonating with the inner conflict of the lyrics, not least in the heightened tension of the polychordal Eb/Db which aurally encodes a need, a constant craving for clarity and resolution.[42]

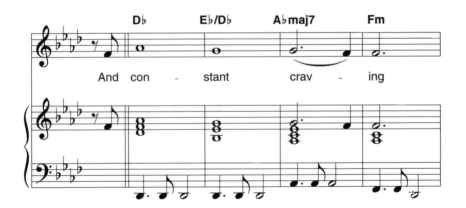

Why then, do many lang fans find the album disappointing? Clearly there is a certain 'sameness' about the ten tracks in that they all reflect on lang's self-absorbed pain, but equally her love for another woman works to proclaim women generally as the source of life, power and energy. At the same time, the melodic construction of the songs allows her to explore the more subtle dimensions of her voice 'to sing it on the border of being hungry and full'.[43] 'Outside Myself' (partly sketched out in Alaska) is almost operatic in its conception – with a mini recitative establishing the mood of the song in a strangely factual yet poetic monologue on the numbness that can accompany unrequited love

A__ thin ice__ co-vers my_ soul_
my bo-dy's fro-zen and my heart is cold and still_

Here, lang's vocal line shapes the lyric content with falling stepwise phrases which create a contemplative mood as they metaphorically reach down into her subconscious. In contrast, the chorus is heavily repetitive with a narrow-ranged vocal phrase which is spelt out with the passionate intensity of an aria. There is thus a sense of lang interpreting the song, distancing herself from the autobiographical content and focussing objectively on the nuance of the emotional content.

In terms of its musicality, then, the album is beautifully crafted and lang emerges as a mature and stylish singer who no longer needs to rely on the props and posturing of her earlier country persona. At the same time, *Ingenue* continues to play upon an implied lesbian sexuality. The songs remain genderless and, as such, the 'you' – 'grant you control of my body and soul' ('So Shall It Be') – remains an enigma. As a lesbian cult hero whose six-country tour of *Ingenue* attracted over 300,000 fans, the pressure to 'come out' inevitably mounted.

lang was not unique in masking her lesbian identity. 1960s' singer Dusty Springfield was one of the first to present an over-the-top 'excessive' femininity, modelling herself on drag queens and wearing bouffant hairdos and exaggerated eye makeup. Despite ten years of hit singles, rumours circulating about her sexuality caused her to leave Britain in 1974. During the early 1970s it was suicide to come out of the closet but by 1978 Springfield felt able to support gay issues openly in an interview with *Gay News*. Helen Reddy was similarly castigated for her feminist hit song 'I Am Woman' which reached no.1 in the American charts as well as winning a Grammy for Best Pop, Rock and Folk Vocal Performance. Tammy Wynette's late 1960s' hit 'Stand By Your Man', which was re-released in 1975, also attracted attention, this time for its adoption by the gay community for its camp connotations. As the biggest-selling single ever recorded by a woman country artist, it became an alternative gay anthem and although heterosexual herself, Wynette welcomed her status as a gay icon.

The continuing need for music which expressed the diversity of women's lives – to include their sexuality – was reflected in the success of the independent record company Olivia Records where the singer songwriter Chris Williamson's album *The Changer and the Changed* sold over a quarter of a million copies. Other women-centred record companies followed, such as Redwood, headed up by feminist rock icon Holly Near. Not surprisingly, the labels provided a space for women to write about lesbian love. At the same time, there was little real scope for cross-over, for normalising lesbian identity, and the term 'womyn's music' (singing from a woman's perspective) soon became synonymous with separatism, defined by its radical feminist politics. By the 1980s, 'womyn's music' had become an artistic ghetto with the mainstream music business unwilling to risk promoting any artist who might be gay.

As discussed in my previous chapters on Patti Smith, Siouxsie Sioux, Annie Lennox and Madonna, androgyny initially appeared to offer a space for challenging traditional representations of femininity through the presentation of a non-conforming sexuality. However, while the masquerade of cross-dressing revealed that gender identity is inseparable from its performance, lesbianism itself was still regarded with vitriolic suspicion. As Lucy O'Brien reports 'It's very glamorous to play with lesbian imagery if you're heterosexual, it's considered daring – but if you're not, it's airing your dirty laundry in public. A lot of us have discussed this over and over again, that it shows the massive imbalance of the sexes.'[44] By the late 1980s it seemed that there were three options: to remain within the relatively safe but separate domains of womyn's music, to remain on the sidelines and risk the speculation and conjecture of the tabloid 'outing' campaigns, or to come out and risk the consequences.[45]

It is interesting to speculate whether or not the new, mainstream audience who were attracted to *Ingenue* were, in part, responsible for lang's coming out. Many would have been unaware of her sexuality; others would have been attracted initially to the warmth and beauty of her voice and decided, in retrospect, that her personal life should remain separate from her public career. lang, herself, states that 'There was a part of me that really didn't think it was important to make an announcement'[46], that her music was not intrinsically lesbian and that it should be assessed solely in terms of its artistic merit. However, it is equally apparent that her wide-based appeal could demonstrate once and for all that lesbian identity and mainstream success can go hand in hand. In particular, her coming-out would not only challenge the evident homophobia of the music industry, but it would equally satisfy the fans who wanted to see a clear-cut lesbian presence in mainstream popular music. To an extent, then, coming-out could be interpreted both as a gesture of solidarity with her existing lesbian fan base and as a challenge to her new audience to recognise that while it is important for lesbians to be represented in popular music, and that while women should be able to experience different representations of gender and sexuality, the main focus should remain on the music itself. If this could be achieved, the music business would surely have to reassess its position. For lang, it appears that the question was 'when'.

It is interesting to note that lang's announcement in *The Advocate* (June 1992) anticipated the striving for racial, social and sexual equality promised by presidential candidate Bill Clinton. Nominated in July 1992, Clinton's campaign was directed (in part) at attracting the gay vote. For the gay community generally Clinton was seen as a positive force for change. The Reagan/Bush years had reflected an extreme American traditionalism characterised by a fostering of traditional (Christian) family values, a commodity-driven culture and the emergence of a right-wing hegemony which resonated in the friendship with Britain's Conservative Prime Minister, Margaret Thatcher. The Democrats promised a more tolerant and thoughtful approach to tackling inequality and in January, 1993 Clinton was inaugurated as the 42nd President of the United States. The following night lang was a guest at two celebratory parties: the MTV Ball and the Triangle Ball – the first lesbian and gay event of its kind. 'Calm, cool and extremely sexy with her tailored suit and tousled hair, k.d. lang leaned over the railing to gaze proudly at the crowd below. "You know," she said, addressing her fans, "the best thing I ever did was to come out." '[47]

Coming out certainly did nothing to harm lang's career. By September 1992 *Ingenue* had sold nearly one million records worldwide. In November she won a Billboard Music Video award for Best Female Artist and in December was nominated Best Female Artist (Adult Contemporary). By January she had taped a segment for MTV *Unplugged* and had been nominated for five Grammy awards, winning Best Female Vocal Performance. *Ingenue* accordingly moved to no. 18 on the Billboard 200 charts and with sales moving past the million mark, it became lang's first platinum record. In England she was nominated for Best International Solo Artist and performed on *Top of the Pops* – primetime television aimed at a teenage market. Then, in the summer of 1993, she posed for a cover of *Vanity Fair*. Wearing a man's pin-striped suit and with a white workshirt and tie, she was photographed reclining in a barber's chair, her cheek and neck covered with shaving cream, smiling as Cindy Crawford leaned close to give her a shave. As her biographer Victoria Starr observes, 'It was a drag scene, a gender bender, set to a Norman Rockwell theme, and it was k.d.'s own wild fantasies that had inspired it.'[48] With lesbian chic firmly established in the public eye and with the seeming indifference of fans to her sexuality, the bigotry of the music industry was finally being challenged.

Since lang's coming out, there certainly appears to be a more marked tolerance towards gay artists. Indeed, it is significant that Elton John was chosen to sing at the funeral of Princess Diana (September 1997) and that other well-known artists – Melissa Everidge, Janis Ian and David Geffen – have also gone on record as being gay. On the positive side this does ensure that radio and television programmers find it increasingly difficult to refuse airtime to artists simply because of their sexuality. At the same time, although it would appear that there is little to lose in backing musicians who have already made money and won grammys, it has taken a public scandal for George Michael to acknowledge his sexuality. As Boy George stated in an interview with Jancee Dunn (September 1998)

> I think it's important that he finally got caught with his trousers down ... There's no excuse in this day and age, especially for someone with £50 million in the bank, to be in the closet.[49]

The question clearly arises as to whether or not the issues are so cut and dried. Much, it would appear, depends on the 'packaging' of the image. Within mainstream culture, cuteness and/or effeminacy is still the most acceptable option for a man ('radiant in a black Versace suit and tasteful eye make-up, porcelain skin glowing with health (how does the man looks so fab when he's taken mountains of drugs?' as Jancee Dunn wrote of Boy George).[50] For the woman artist, it remains important to maintain a prescribed femininity – 'too competent or powerful, she'll probably be branded a dyke regardless of her sexual orientation'.[51] Androgyneity still appears to remain the safer bet – as was evidenced in the 'lesbian chic' of the mid-1990s.

For some, however, the androgynous lang remains a disappointment. Her retreat 'from her previously disruptive and troubling image' has resulted, paradoxically, in a safe compromise.[52] Being out, she no longer has to name or make visible her identity and, as such, she has left the queer dynamism of her earlier work behind. As her image and her body are brought closer together she has become, in effect, the 'universal lesbian', warm, bubbly, attractive and safe enough to show on prime time television. I wonder whether this is such a bad thing. In coming out lang has provided for many a life-affirming image, a visible lesbian presence.[53] To coin a phrase, lang is a 'certain kind of woman', a woman-loving woman, who can perform with confidence on what is arguably a heterosexual stage.

Acknowledgements

I would like to acknowledge here the friendship of Dr Stan Hawkins (University of Oslo, Norway), most specifically the pleasure of sharing a lecture seminar (Stan on George Michael, playfully entitled 'Zip Me Up Before You Go Go' and myself on k.d. lang) to the university's lesbian and gay society in April 1999.

NOTES AND REFERENCES

1 The August 1998 world congregation of Bishops of the Anglican Church meeting at Lambeth Palace, London voted by an overwhelming majority that practising lesbians and homosexuals should not be eligible for priesthood. An articulate protest from gay bishops was (angrily) overruled so raising the question as to whether it is acceptable to be repressed, in the closet, within the established church but unlawful and immoral to be honest and 'out'.

2 Starr, V. (1994) *k.d. lang. All You Get Is Me*, London: HarperCollins, p. 245.

3 In the Reagan/Bush era of the 1980s, country music represented the extolled image of American society, where the woman was sweet and uncomplaining, respectable, white and family-oriented. The traditional ethos for country singers reflected this in the unofficial rule of 'never offend your fans'.

4 Middleton, R. (1997) 'Understanding Pop Music', Open University: MA module.

5 Starr *op. cit.*, p. 2.

6 *Ibid.*, p. 28.

7 There are many stories circulating as to why k.d. lang uses lower case. These range from the sublime (in honour of e.e. cummings) to the ridiculous ('I never mastered upper-case letters').

8 Starr, *op. cit.*, p. 35. k.d. lang's adulation of Patsy Cline was reflected in her conviction that there was a link between their souls. *Shadowlands* finally laid the ghost, 'it was the whole reason for that Patsy obsession, and now I can just go back to being k.d.lang' (p. 118).

9 *Ibid.*, p. 35.

10 B. Ruby Rich, cited in Martha Mockus (1994) 'Queer Thoughts on Country Music and k.d. lang' in Brett, P. , Wood, E. and Thomas, G.C. (eds) *Queering the Pitch. The New Gay and Lesbian Musicology*, New York: Routledge, p. 359.

11 *Ibid.*, p. 260.

12 Starr, *op. cit.*, p. 72.

13 *Ibid.*, p. 51.

14 *Ibid.*, p. 134.

15 My discussion is informed by Judith Butler's chapter 'Subjects of Sex/Gender/Desire' in her 1990 publication *Gender Trouble. Feminism and the Subversion of Identity*, London: Routledge, pp. 1–25.

16 Starr, *op. cit.*, p. 16.

17 Stella Bruzzi (1997) 'Mannish Girl. k.d. lang from Cowpunk to Androgyny' in Whiteley, S. (ed.) *Sexing the Groove. Popular Music and Gender*, London: Routledge, p. 196.

18 Sue-Ellen Case, cited in Mockus, *op. cit.*, p. 265.

19 Smith, G. (1992) 'The lang Way Home', *Independent*, March 19, Arts p. 19.

20 Starr, *op. cit.*, p. 86.

21 Bruzzi, *op. cit.*, p. 196.

22 Mockus, *op. cit.*, p. 266.

23 Sue-Ellen Case (1993) 'Towards a Butch-Femme Aesthetic' in Abelove, H., Barale, M.A. and Helperin, D.M., *The Lesbian and Gay Studies Reader*, London: Routledge, p. 302.

24 *Ibid.*, p. 300. For Case (updating Joan Riviere's theory of 'Womanliness as a Masquerade', *International Journal of Psychoanalysis* 10, 1929) the butch is the lesbian who proudly displays the possession of the penis, while the femme takes on the compensatory masquerade of womanliness. The femme, however, foregrounds her masquerade by playing to a butch, another woman in a role; likewise, the butch exhibits the penis to a woman who is playing the role of

compensatory castration. Because there is no referent in sight, the fictions of penis and castration become ironised and 'camped up'.

25 Mockus, *op. cit.*, p. 262.

26 In Toril Moi (1985) *Sexual/Textual Politics*, London: Routledge, p. 107.

27 Mockus, *op. cit.*.

28 *Ibid.*, p. 263.

29 *Ibid.* p. 264.

30 Giles Smith, 'k.d. lang', *Independent*, March 18, 1993.

31 Starr, *op. cit.*, p. 220.

32 *Ibid.*, p. 222. Here, Percy Adlon argues here that there is no distinction between private and creative pain ... 'Perhaps that is why when Ben and k.d. wrote "Season of Hollow Soul" they both got physically sick from it.'

33 *Ibid.*, p. 214.

34 *Ibid.*, p. 220. Clearly many agreed as *Ingenue* went gold within five months of its release.

35 As the transcription shows, the harmonies in this four-bar phrase are complex. In the main, they are polychordal – two unrelated chords are superimposed as in the Bb/D, C7/E, G/D with the Ebm/Bb having an added complexity in its juxtaposition of minor/major. There are also complex harmonies such as the A minor chord with a flattened fifth and added seventh. Aurally, the polychords effect a tug, a tension, as neither chord is the more important and both conceal the tonic 'heart' of the music. There is thus a sense of subtle word-painting which is equally apparent in the minor inflection on 'heart' (musically encoding an underlying wistfulness) and the more open harmony of G major with which the phrase ends. This feel for word-painting is further evidenced in the repeat of the phrase where the sense of revelation is complicated by a minor 7 chord with a flattened fifth (Am7b5), so reflecting the shift in mood from 'Can your heart conceal ... ' to 'Does your heart conceal ... '.

36 Starr, *op. cit.*, p. 198–9. Although the Red Hot and Blue concert was a charity gig to raise money for AIDS victims, it is not implied that this dimension is necessarily implied in lang's portrayal of loss in 'So In Love'. Rather her performance portrays her love for another woman who is equally lost to her.

37 *Ibid.*, p. 215.

38 Butler, *op. cit.*, p. viii.

39 Sean Cubitt (1997) 'Rolling and Tumbling. Digital Erotics and the Culture of Narcissism' in Whiteley, *op. cit.*, p. 299.

40 Starr, *op. cit.*, p. 266.

41 *Ibid.*, p. 215.

42 Again, the polychordal Eb/Db encodes a tug between two harmonic centres. This is heard as a word-painting for the inner conflict of the lyrics.

43 Starr, *op. cit.*, p. 223.

44 O'Brien, L. (1995) *She Bop. The Definitive History of Women in Rock, Pop and Soul*, London: Penguin, p. 257.

45 Artists such as Tracy Chapman and Michelle Shocked adopted a semi-androgynous image as protection – 'damned if you come out and damned if you don't'. Whitney Houston and Janis Ian were both the target of outing and conjecture with the latter coming out in 1993 after lang's declaration of lesbian identity. Others include self-billed Jewish lesbian artist Phranc, who was one of the first to market her music away from the margins of womyns labels. Even so, she was initially perceived as a novelty act. It is interesting to note that lang disassociated herself from Phranc – she disliked the hardcore lesbian claims on her identity and resented being the one who was obliged to speak for the gay

community. At the same time lang appreciated the fact that when lesbians 'look' at her, they are looking for themselves and that many derive courage from the way in which she lives her life.

46 Starr, *op. cit.*, p. 223.
47 *Ibid.*, xii.
48 *Ibid.*, pxv.
49 Jancee Dunn 'George Knows Best', interview with Boy George in *Red*, September, p. 87.
50 *Ibid.*. The fact that the homoerotic image is a marketable commodity is evidenced by the success of such bands as Culture Club, Depeche Mode, Soft Cell and Blancmange. Whether or not the members were gay, the bands were marketed as cute boys.

Paul McDonald discusses the way in which 'areas of intimate flesh are offered to the viewer (through videos) by the various states of underdress displayed by the boys' in his analysis of 'The Male Body in Take That Videos', Whiteley, *op. cit.*, pp. 277–94. It is also significant that lang was signed by the one major record company headed by a gay man and that she came under the careful guidance of a small group of record company advisers – people like Liz Rosenberg and Carl Scott, who are renowned for their talent at image creation and spin control.

51 Starr, *op. cit.*, p. 229.
52 Bruzzi, *op. cit.*, pp. 201–2.
53 As Starr observes, 'her one simple but courageous act – coming out – may have been the key to unlocking the closet door for the entire pop music industry', *op. cit.*, p. xiv.

11

TALKIN' 'BOUT A REVOLUTION

Tracy Chapman, political uprisings, domestic
violence and love

In June 1988 the magazine *Musician* ran a series of articles on 'The Women's
Movement of 1988' with features on Sinead O'Connor, Tracy Chapman and
Michelle Shocked. As Gillian Gaar observes, discussing how women
performers feel about working in a male-dominated field was hardly innovatory, but the caption which appeared on the magazine cover: 'Why the best
new artists of 1988 are women: the major labels change their tune' highlighted what they felt was a new and significant development – women as
part of a new musical movement 'women in rock', serious women who
played acoustic guitars and who had a social conscience.[1]

As discussed previously, the emergence of MTV during the first half of
the 1980s had resulted in an over-emphasis on appearance. Sex appeal
equated with commercial viability, and commercial viability revolved
increasingly around a girl-pop ideal of slimness, youth and glamour. While
artists such as Annie Lennox and Madonna had exploited and subverted
sexual clichés and stereotypes through masquerade, women who were
unwilling to compete within the boundaries established by MTV faced
problems. In particular, acoustic musicians seemed somehow old-fashioned,
a throwback to the 1960s' folk movement, serious rather than fun-loving,
concerned with conscience rather than sex appeal and, as such, unsuited to a
1980s' mainstream dance culture epitomised by such megastars as Prince,
Michael Jackson and Madonna.

Although it is not suggested that folk musicians, or indeed singer songwriters, had disappeared, it is nevertheless evident that in the main they had
retired to the folk clubs, the college circuit, or to the womyn's labels which
were fostering such talents as Holly Near and Chris Williamson. Greenwich
Village, in New York, for example, had an active folk scene and had been the
home for Suzanne Vega whose song 'Luka' (1987) had become a surprising
top ten hit in the States. Sung in a quietly dispassionate voice, Vega's narrative of child abuse focused social observation within a framework of
alienation, *Solitude Standing*, alone and without support. It was an issue that
was similarly evident in the work of Michelle Shocked whose albums *The
Texas Campfire Tapes* (1987), *Short Sharp Shocked* (1988) and *Captain Swing*

171

(1989) demonstrate her abilities as a storyteller, reflecting on the anomalies between the haves and the have-nots in the supposedly affluent 1980s of Ronald Reagan and Margaret Thatcher. The last album, in particular, draws attention to the cardboard shanty towns that were emerging in such major cities as London, Washington and New York to accommodate the growing numbers of homeless. As a veteran of the San Francisco squat scene, it was an issue on which she could speak with authority. Sinead O'Connor's songs were, likewise, grounded in personal experience. Having been brought up in an abusive household where singing provided an expressive outlet for personal pain, her debut album *The Lion and the Cobra* (1987) resonated with folk authenticity – a restrained and intimate vocal delivery emphasised by a repeated use of the first person 'I' contrasting with a more declamatory nasal delivery to effect a tension between the public and the private of social commentary.

The focus on social and personal deprivation, on anomie and alienation is also central to Tracy Chapman's albums. Brought up in a tough black neighbourhood in Cleveland, Ohio, she was awarded a scholarship to Wooster School, Danbury, Connecticut via (President) Kennedy's ABC fund for the disadvantaged. Graduating in 1982 she then attended Tufts University, Boston, where she majored in anthropology. The combination of a keen musical ear, personal experience of growing up 'poor, black, working class and female in America',[2] and a university education which fostered objectivity and observation would seem an ideal background for a socially conscious musician. In particular, Chapman's personal experience of poverty, racial discrimination and humiliation, together with the insights gained on the Boston–Cambridge folk circuit provided a strong grounding for a politicised black woman. Having attracted the attention of a fellow Tufts student, Brian Koppelman, Chapman was introduced to his father, Charles Koppelman, President of SBK songs. Recognising her potential, Koppelman signed her to SBK and secured a record deal with Elektra in 1986.

It is not insignificant that Elektra had a strong association with the singer songwriter tradition. Koppelman, himself, had previously worked alongside Carole King at Aldon Music; Elliott Roberts had managed Joni Mitchell before working with Chapman on her debut album. Natalie Merchant, lead singer of 10,000 Maniacs, was also on the Elektra label. Their 1987 album *In My Tribe* included songs which focused attention on domestic violence, the environment and the US policy in Central America and, as such, it is not too surprising that Merchant invited Chapman to take the opening slot on the band's promotional tour. In return, Merchant opened for Chapman when she visited London in 1988 to promote her self-titled debut album which had been released earlier in the spring. By the summer, top 40 airplay had helped to promote it to the top of the charts, with the single 'Fast Car' reaching no. 6. To an extent the excitement generated by the album had resulted from Chapman's performance at the 1988 Nelson

Mandela 70th Birthday Tribute Concert where her performance had been beamed by satellite to 63 countries worldwide. Following an Amnesty International world tour with Peter Gabriel, Sting, Bruce Springsteen and Youssou N'Dour, Chapman was hailed by the critic Nelson George as 'Today's Black Woman', leader of a consumer group 'shamefully under-represented in record bins ... college-educated, upwardly mobile, politicised black women'.[3]

Nelson George's focus on Chapman as 'Today's Black Woman' is significant. As Heidi Safia Mirza observes

> if the black woman is traced in history what we see is how she is permitted to appear. We see glimpses of her as she is produced and created for the sustenance of the patriarchal, colonial and now postcolonial discourse (Spivak 1988; Mani 1992; Hawley 1994; Ching-Laing Low 1995; McClintock 1995; Parry 1995; Hayward 1996). She appears and disappears as she is needed, as the dutiful wife and daughter, the hard (but happy and grateful!) worker, the sexually available exotic other; the controlling asexual mother, or simply homogenized as the 'third world' woman (Mohanty 1988). In her representation she is without agency, without self-determination, a passive victim, waiting to be inscribed with meaning from those who wish to gaze upon her and name her. She is an object; not the subject of her story.[4]

Chapman's challenge, as evidenced in her self-named debut album, was to make herself the subject of her narrative, to draw attention to a country shaped by racism, observing from the sidelines the anomalies, the inequalities, involved yet dispassionate as she relates accounts of rape, death, wanting to escape yet held back by 'having mountains o' nothing at birth'.

'Talkin' Bout A Revolution', the first track on the album, establishes Chapman's agenda by focusing in on inactivity – 'While they're standing in the welfare lines ... wasting time ... sitting around' – and looking to a time when 'the poor people gonna rise up and take what's theirs'. Ideologically the song follows in a tradition that dates back to the anti-slavery songs and liberation spirituals of the nineteenth century which express a desire for freedom and, often, a total contempt for the institution of slavery itself. More recently, Gil Scott Heron's political poem 'The Revolution Will Not Be Televised', Isaak Hayes' 'Chains' and Len Chandler's mid-1960s' freedom song, 'Move on over or We'll Move on over You' express a similar revolutionary ethos, raising consciousness and energising change. As Reebee Garofalo observes, songs that were rooted in the Civil Rights movement ('We Shall Overcome', 'This Land is Your Land') were both important to activists of the day in celebrating black pride while serving as a musical background for terrifying newscasts of racial violence to the nation at large.[5]

In particular, the mid-1960s witnessed increasing unrest as the liberal Civil Rights movement gave way to Stokeley Carmichael's demand for black power. By the early 1970s, however, the deaths of Malcolm X (21 February 1965) and Martin Luther King (4 April 1968), together with the systematic repression of black radicalism, had led to a watershed in the battle for civil rights. The promotion of black pride, black unity and self-empowerment which had characterised such mainstream soul hits as 'Say It Loud, I'm Black and I'm Proud' (James Brown) and 'Young, Gifted and Black' (Nina Simone); and which offered solutions for social, economic and political oppression through a rejection of white American goals and values, had been countered by a systematic embourgeoisement of the black middle classes. For those remaining in the inner cities, however, increasing economic and political oppression led, inevitably, to an intensification of racial pressures. 'The confusion and disillusionment of the period were evident in Marvin Gaye's 'What's Goin' On?' and 'Inner City Blues'[6] and in Sly and the Family Stone's album, *There's a Riot Goin' On*, all released in 1971.

New York was the first metropolitan area to fall into virtual economic bankruptcy. The effects of overpopulation and unemployment had led to the securing of a federal loan with harsh repayment conditions. This, in turn, led to dramatic cuts in social and public services, and widespread housing problems. Initial attempts at urban renewal resulted in the upwardly mobile relocating to the suburbs while the poorer inhabitants – largely Black and Hispanic households – were forced to relocate to inferior housing, as the construction of the city's urban expressway in the 1960s and early 1970s meant the destruction of around 60,000 homes in the South Bronx. With white residents and business owners moving to the northern sections of the Bronx and Westchester, large numbers of houses were left vacant, only to be exploited by the professional slumlords. The residents who remained were, by and large, impoverished Black and Hispanic families, inarticulate, with limited community education and little or no political voice.[7]

New York was not atypical: Cleveland, Chicago and Los Angeles were other examples of societies where technological advancement and modernisation resulted in urban deprivation and instability. By the 1980s, the political separation of the black elite from the black working class had resulted in what Dyson calls 'the powers of despair, hopelessness, and genocide that presently besiege the black community'.[8] Given the context, then, and her own experience of inner-city Cleveland, it is not too surprising that Chapman should sing about the poor 'crying at the doorsteps of those armies of salvation'.

It would be misleading, however, to suggest that the tangle of social, cultural and political issues that characterised 1980s' America had resulted simply in a passive and inarticulate poor. Rather, young Black and Hispanic groups from inner-city New York had formed an alternative identity and sense of personal value through an emerging hip hop culture, uniting neighbourhood gangs through a shared identity which linked philosophy, language, fashion, art, music and dance. Emerging during the mid-to-late 1970s, rap became the major communicative force of hip hop culture representing, through 'the verbal brashness of its performers ... both the strength of street knowledge and the triumph of the street ethic'.[9] Initially limited to inner-city neighbourhoods, and particularly its place of origin, the audience for rap expanded with rap artists such as Grandmaster Flash and the Furious Five reflecting on inner-city life ('The Message', 'New York, New York') and addressing such issues as homelessness, racism, violence and drugs.

During the 1980s rap had progressively increased its commercial viability and public status and had spread from New York to Boston and to such West Coast cities as Los Angeles. Initially the 1980s marked a period of relative calm and greater racial acceptance but the increasing poverty in inner cities and the violence at rap concerts in Pittsburgh, Los Angeles, Atlanta, Cleveland, Cincinnati and New York during the mid-1980s led increasingly to a public perception that rap and aggression were linked. Aware that rap concerts had facilitated uncensored speech and cultural resistance, and disturbed by the triple platinum success of Run DMC's 1987 album *Raising Hell* (the first rap album to be featured on MTV) there was a cutback on airplay by many Black radio stations who were quick to realise that advertising space was paid for primarily by their middle-class patrons. The effect, once again, was to signal the distinction between poor Blacks and those from the middle and upper-middle classes. It was equally apparent that the problems associated with 'economic desperation, social isolation, political degradation and cultural exploitation'[10] were not being addressed, and that the 'storm of anger' that was to sweep through Los Angeles in 1992[11] was the result of decades of governmental mismanagement rather than incitement by the rap community.

As a socially aware woman, there is little doubt that Chapman would have been aware not only of the problems of inner-city ghettos, but equally of the emerging power of rap as its political voice. Although it is not suggested that all rap is enabling and productive, its focus on the political choices that reproduce poverty, racism, classism, sexism and violence is significant in speaking directly about the vicious cycle of ghetto life. 'The Message', released in 1982 by Grandmaster Flash and the Furious Five is filled with vivid images – 'Rats in the front room/roaches in the back/junkie in the alley with a baseball bat' – and an unforgettable chorus – 'Don't push me 'cause I'm close to the edge'. It is an interesting coincidence that 'Talkin' 'Bout a Revolution' was written in the same year, and while Chapman's song, like the album itself, draws stylistically on the continuing history of folk protest, not least in its identification of the underprivileged and in its radical expression, there is a similar identification of a mounting tension, when 'the poor people gonna rise up ... and get their share' and the need for activism, to 'run'.

The impact of 'Talkin' 'Bout a Revolution' lies primarily in Chapman's vocal delivery which reinforces what might be termed the poetics of musical documentary. Pitched low, the vocal line follows the 'natural' rhythm of the word or phrase, sounding quasi-conversational and restrained in its narrative of events. The verbal message is clearly centre-stage, and although the occasional use of melisma is effective in directing the listener's attention, the vocal line, overall, is narrow-ranged, simple and strongly repetitive. As such, the occasional use of word-painting – as in 'like a whisper' where Chapman uses a breathy tone while projecting her voice to create an illusion of whispering – is effective. Enhanced by a momentary pause, the words remain audible while contrasting with the harder, declamatory delivery of the contextualising phrases.

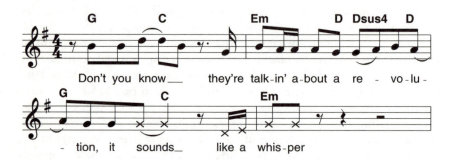

In common with the majority of folk songs, the chord sequence which underpins the melody line is equally repetitive (G-C/Em-D) and continues throughout the two bar guitar and bass phrase to give the song a cyclical feel. Initially, the acoustic guitar plays alone, first a four bar introduction and then as an accompaniment to the vocal line. Here the basic chord sequence of the second bar is extended (Em-D-Dsus4-D) to provide an underlying inflection and fullness to the central concept 'revolution'. This is enhanced by the bass line, which enters on the second verse, playing the root of each chord with a slight syncopation which works to drive the tempo, gradually moving the vocal on to the chorus where Chapman shifts to her upper register to effect a sense of urgency in the repeated 'Don't you know you'd better run, run, run, run, run, run, run, run, run.'

The second track, 'Fast Car' moves from the documentary to the personal in a song which tells of the need to escape and the hopelessness of knowing that it is simply a dream. It is a tale that speaks directly to the countless women who have cared for an alcoholic father, fall in love, plan for a better future only to find, too late, that the husband is also a drinker, that life has a horrid habit of repeating itself. 'You see, my old man's gotta problem, He lives with the bottle, that's the way it is.' The sense of being trapped is reflected in the accompanying two bar acoustic guitar riff which repeats throughout the song, relenting only when the chorus enters with the words, 'So remember...' The effect is to construct a musical metaphor of constraint. There is an emphasis on A major, the home note, and plans to escape, to get away, the 'maybe ... ' of the daydream where the guitar moves to a plaintive F# minor, are constantly thwarted by a return to the tonic in a never-ending cycle:

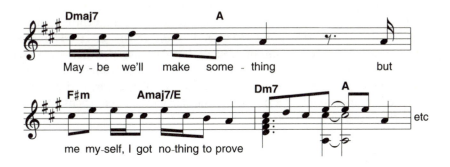

The range of the vocal melody takes the idea of being trapped further by remaining within the octave, breaking away only once, to reach F# on the melisma over the word 'I' at the beginning of what appears to be a sudden awakening of optimism in the 'I had a feeling that I belonged' of the chorus. But the F# is only a passing note,[12] and the melody is once again pulled down to the tonic A, symbolically returning the singer to reality:

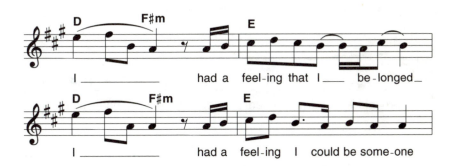

Although the song overall implies a sense of resignation in the 'I got no plans. I ain't going nowhere' of the final verse, there is nevertheless an underlying strength, an inner resourcefulness. Having supported first father, then husband and children (to conform to Mirza's discussion of the black woman as 'dutiful wife and daughter')[13] in the final reprise of the bridge she urges her man to take the initiative. He, not she, is the one with the fast car, he is the one who has to make the final decision 'leave tonight, or live and die this way'.

The emphasis on flight is picked up in 'Across the Lines' where Chapman moves back to the documentary mode, describing the onset of the riots that 'began on the back streets of America' when a 'little black girl gets assaulted ... and racist tempers fly'. Written in 1985, the song recounts the onset of riots that were to characterise the late 1980s/1990s.[14] Accompanied by acoustic guitar, Hammer dulcimer and bass, the effectiveness of the arrangement lies primarily in the snare drum tattoo which continues throughout to impart a militant feel, the people rising and taking to the streets. The vocal phrasing is also effective in communicating both a sense of anticipation and urgency. Pivotal words – 'across the *lines*', 'who would *dare*', 'under the *bridge*', 'over the *tracks*' – fall on the final quaver of the bar, and are sung across the bar lines to effect a musical metaphor which strengthens the lyric content, the need to

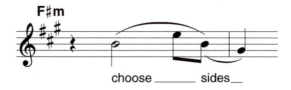

– the recognition that such a volatile situation can get out of control. In contrast, the second section of the song resolutely follows the exposition of events in a narrow-ranged, repetitive melodic phrase. The effect is one of reportage. There is no personal commentary, no elaboration:

Ending with a reflective 'Mmm ... ', the song moves into the *a cappella* 'Behind the Wall', which highlights the fact that brutality is not always inflicted from the outside, white against black. Again, Chapman's musicality is evidenced in choosing to sing unaccompanied, alone, listening as the silence of the night is shattered by screaming and the 'loud voices behind the wall' that precede marital violence. The first verse is repeated with no variation in either the lyric content or the melody line. The effect is to underpin the repetitive nature of the violence, 'another sleepless night for me' and the reflection that the police

where an extended melisma lengthens the sense of anticipation before the resignation of the final phrase. The shaping of the melodic line of the verses also reflects and constructs the mood of the lyrics. Starting on top F (at the upper end of Chapman's vocal range) and ending on the octave below, there is a move from the initial shock of waking to the screams of the abused woman and ending with the reflection on the inactivity of the police. The middle section signals a possible change of direction. The police arrive but are not allowed to 'interfere with domestic affairs' and the original verse structure returns, but this time the scream is followed by silence. As if to underpin the emotions expressed in the lyrics 'I prayed that I was dreaming', Chapman varies the melodic line, straining upwards to the very top of her range:

After the aural shock of 'Behind the Wall', the intro to 'Baby Can I Hold You' and the 'Sorry' with which the song opens has a haunting melancholy. Again, Chapman has the ability to touch anyone who has experienced a one-sided relationship and who longs for the reconciliation of 'sorry', 'forgive me' and 'I love you'. The power of the song lies in the organic feel of the music which moves the reflective of the verse into the emotional outburst of the chorus and back again to the reflective. This is largely achieved by the way in which the vocal melody follows the natural rhythm and mood of the words and an effective use of rests which creates a feeling of faltering reflection, reinforcing the sentiment that 'words don't come easily'. The verse structure works primarily through small intervalic motifs. The initial falling interval on 'sorry', is mirrored in the 'is all ... ' of the following phrase and followed by a descending sequence which is repeated twice before the return to the central motif 'sorry' to effect a cyclical mood of nagging insecurity. This is enhanced by the reflective feel of the accompanying chords which move from an assertive major under 'sorry' to an unstable Em7:

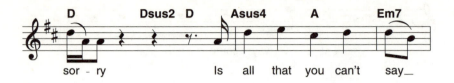

sor - ry   Is   all   that   you   can't   say__

The confined vocal range of the verse is then opened out in the chorus where a surge of emotion is reflected in the swoop to top F on 'but you (can say baby)'. The urgency of need juxtaposed with the insecurity of unrequited love resonates with the falling shape of the melodic line, the poetic use of inner rhyme 'hold/told', 'tonight/right' 'time/mine' and the faltering use of vocal silence which reinforces the plaintiff segue into the next verse

may-be if I   told__ you the right words   at the   right

__ time   you'd be mine

After the rock-ballad feel of 'Baby Can I Hold You' Chapman moves into 'Mountains o' Things' where the xylophone sound of the African marimba establishes a fluid, offbeat, rhythmic groove. The overlay of timbral cross-rhythms in the instrumental accompaniment (not least the marimba, congas and bass) works to establish an immediate memory-trigger[15] – it 'sounds' African and for the first time on the album, the musical style resonates directly with a black musical aesthetic.[16] The marimba riff is heavily synco-pated and forms the structural foundation for the song, maintaining an open-ended yet hypnotic feel that evokes the distinctiveness of African culture within a Caribbean musical format – hi-life. Stylistically, the relaxed feel of the music works to support the sentiments of the song, 'to have a big expensive car, drag my furs on the ground, and have a maid … ', those 'material things' that come with 'a life of ease', and which resonate with the lure of embourgeoisement inherent in black capitalism.

Chapman demonstrates an acute awareness of the meaning of consump-tion – 'that we base our lives on the traditional idea of the pursuit of well-being'[17] – or, as she expresses it in the first verse, 'everyone will look at me with envy and with greed' and 'I'll revel in their attention and moun-tains, oh mountains o' things.' Her identification of furs, a maid, her need to surround herself with luxury, instances the way in which 'woman is sold to woman ... while doing what she believes is preening herself, scenting herself, clothing herself, in a word "creating" herself, she is, in fact, consuming herself'.[18] There is also an awareness that consumption produces both wealth and poverty and that the tensions inherent in a 'growth' society governed by insatiable needs will lead to psychological poverty, anomie and alienation: 'mostly I feel lonely ... '.

Although it could be suggested that the chorus provides a viable alternative 'renounce materialism ... save your soul' there is again an underlying awareness that puritanism – 'and all that it implies in terms of sublimation, transcending of self and repression'[19] – is the very ethic that both haunts and drives consumption and needs. Thus, while Chapman muses over individual private needs, aspirations, drives, 'the life I've always wanted', her reflection on the exploitation of the weak ('good people are only my stepping stones'), which is accompanied by the omnipresent rhythmic groove of hi-life style, provides an attitudinal lexis of what could have been there, but is not – a move to a gospel style for example and, potentially, a feeling of redemption. Instead, the final verse of the song picks up on the paradox of consumption: 'consume more than you need', the fact that it 'make you pauper or make you queen'. Needs, as the song points out are valid: there is a need to stop exploiting other human beings, a need to belong, but conversely the 'champagne and caviar' are part of an unquenchable desire that is insatiable because it is based on a lack, a need for those 'mountains, oh mountains o' things'.

For me, the effectiveness of the song lies primarily in Chapman's choice of musical style. Hi-life is aurally engaging, it sounds 'happy' in its association with carnival and celebration. The mood, however, is as deceptive as the lure of 'the American dream' is to those who are living in poverty. Money, it would seem, can buy respectability, a house in the suburbs, a maid, 'the life I've always wanted'. Instead, the song opens with the recognition that 'I'll be working for someone else until I'm in my grave', sentiments that are not so far removed from the rural blues of slavery. It would seem, then, that this is Chapman talking as a perceptive black woman, drawing attention to inequality through an idiomatically black musical style that gradually fades with a recognition that survival sometimes depends upon imaginative escape.

dream - ing, dream - ing, dream - ing, dream - ing,

dream - ing, dream - ing, dream - ing_____

dream, dream - - ing I'll be to Fade

Stylistically, the music now switches from hi-life to reggae, so maintaining a distinctive ethnic feel. 'With historical roots in Caribbean admixtures of proto-African genres with British, French and Spanish influences, reggae and its immediate forebears emerged from an encounter with American R&B ... ',[20] itself an offshoot of black Afro-American blues. For many British-born and American Black communities, reggae became the most important link with Jamaica and with their own African roots. Its heavy repetitive bass line, its characteristic drumming style (one drop on bass and snare, the use of rim shots), its polyrhythmic complexity, and its Rasta or patois lyrics sung by and directed at black people, became central to cultural consciousness and cultural resistance. As such, Chapman's choice of style is significant in that reggae – and its association with the Rastafarian movement – is a music that is centred on 'roots', on belonging, on 'finding a place in the sun'.

In contrast to the earlier rude boy culture of West Kingston, Jamaica, and its association with hustling, rocksteady and ska, Rastafarianism condemns property, alcohol and gambling as elements of Babylon (white colonial capitalism) and looks to Africa and, more specifically, Ethiopia, for salvation. Ras Tafari, crowned as Emperor Haile Selassie (Lord of Lords and Conquering Lion of Judah) in 1930, had been acclaimed as the Returned Messiah and the Black Christ and for young Jamaicans the Ethiopian colours of red, green and gold, along with long, uncut hair worn in dreadlocks became important symbols of Africanism, representing a point of conflict with white society and a positive evaluation of being black. In 1970s' America, tee-shirts in black, red, green, yellow and the message 'By Any Means Necessary', 'Fight the Power' etc. worn with medallions in the shape of the African continent also symbolised a direct relationship with the motherland, with African ethnicity (ethnic-based action),[21]) and collective consciousness through black power and revolution.

For the Rastafarian communities, the problems associated with capitalism,

> ... Socialism, Communism, Protestantism
> Liberalism, Capitalism, Catholicism
> Too much ism and schism in Babylon system

(Lincoln Thompson and the Rassas, 'Mechanical Devices', 1980)

had resulted often in forming separatist communities, and being 'pushed into voluntary unemployment: constantly informed by a common sense of oppression and rejection'.[22] This sense of rejection, of not belonging, of being surrounded by racial 'hatred, corruption and greed' is the centre point of 'She's Got her Ticket'.

Opening with five quaver rimshots, and accompanied simply by a single offbeat on the conga, Chapman's opening vocal line 'She's got her ticket ... ' is initially enigmatic. Its downward melodic contour, the hesitancy and offbeat phrasing of 'I think she gonna use it' recall earlier songs like 'Across the Lines', where racial conflict results in death. The answering phrase 'No-one should try and stop her, persuade her with their power, she says that her *mind* is made' follows the same melodic shape. The highpoint of both phrases – the push to top G on 'fly' and 'mind' – the extension of off-rhymes (a)-way/made – suggests, however, an underlying sense of resolution and, as the song relaxes into the reggae feel, it is apparent that the lack of ornamentation, the lack of groove in the introduction, is yet another musical metaphor for the barrenness of life in America for 'a young girl with no chances'.

The entry of the reggae groove is significant, then, in establishing a collective mood of belonging, a closing of the circle. Within Afro-American, Afro-British culture the sense of be yourself but become part of the whole Black culture is symbolised through musics which allow for a similar sense of expressivity. The individual musician adds to the overall sound, but is free to come in and out according to his/her sense of contributing to the whole. It is inclusive rather than exclusive and thus provides a musical metaphor for the collective of African culture itself (as reflected in the musical blend of Clinton's funkadelic sound in 'One Nation' (1971), for example). The reggae groove, then, with its free delivery, its feel for power (the heavy dub sound) and equality in the instrumental mix of polyrhythmic timbres provides a musical symbol of and for the black community. It is sung by a black woman to the people of her own race in a shared musical language that penetrates a common sense of identity: you 'give your life and invariably they leave you with nothing'. Ironically, however, although reggae is a powerful source of symbolic protest, voicing an awareness of structural subordination and revolution through such songs as Bob Marley's 'Burnin' and a Lootin' and 'Africa Unite', it has also achieved widespread popularity in the record charts, so attracting a white audience. As such, the song has a double-edge in that its message is open to both diffusion (the spreading of a revolutionary message) and defusion for, like any other form of popular music, it also exists as an escape route from the real world. The music, then, can be interpreted as both an instrument for change, and as a placebo which is offered *instead* of real change. The coda and fade suggest the former. Aware that she will never belong 'she's shed all pretences', and after an upbeat instrumental solo which situates a sunny 'other' to the bleakness of the unaccompanied opening to the song, 'she'll fly, fly, fly, fly, fly, fly, fly, fly, fly'.

After the instrumental fade and Chapman's spacey improvisation on 'she's got her ticket' (the first of the album), the lyrics to 'Why' come across as jam-packed, spilling over each other as they reflect on inequality and the paradoxes associated with war and peace. The return to a rock feel is again interesting. Chapman is demanding answers from the outside and chooses a popular musical language that expresses a white identity.[23] The song is in two contrasting sections, both characteristic of Chapman's compositional style. The first two-bar phrase of the verse is built on the chord of Bm7, the second on G/A. This is repeated with the principal shift in emphasis being vocal, as she moves upwards from top F# to A as if to underline the ultimate stupidity of war

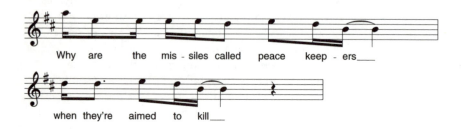

In common with the other 'documentary' songs on the album, the melody follows the natural rhythm of the words which are tightly packed, creating a punchy delivery that accuses and demands 'why … ', 'why … ', 'why … '. The chorus then moves to a more reflective mood as it focuses in on paradox and contradiction. This is reflected in the organ line which works in counterpoint to Chapman's vocal which, in turn, drops to the lower register, again symbolic of searching deep inside for some sort of solution before swooping back to an emotional F#

But __ some - bod-y's gon-na have to ans-wer____

The final three songs on the album return to the personal as Chapman reflects, once again, on the problems surrounding relationships, sacrifice and unrequited love. The first re-positions Chapman in the role of the supportive woman: 'two weeks in a Virginia jail ... for my lover, for my lover'. The song is characterised by melisma, with key words, *'lover'*, *'you'* being opened out to a range of inflections which colour, and increasingly elaborate on her feelings, making each experience ('climb a mountain if I had to', 'risk my life') fresh and new.

you,_ you,_ you,_ you,____ you,_ you,_ you,_ you,_ you,_

At the same time, as Chapman aptly demonstrates, her love is an affair of the heart and the underlying nervousness/edginess in the song – the jumpy melodic contouring which underpins the intervention of thinking about possible implications, the fragmented feel of syncopation and silence – provide a musical metaphor of uncertainty which is supported by the lack of resolution inherent in the accompanying harmonies as they move from a wistful Em to a lack of resolution in the equivocal Asus4[24]

The things we won't do for love __

'If Not Now' then moves to a reflection on the transitory nature of love and again instances Chapman's idiosyncratic use of a fragmentary vocal line and ornamentation to effect a sense of reflection. Key ideas are heightened through a contrast in register – the head tone of 'If', the chest resonance on 'then ... ' – and elaborated on as words are suspended across the bar line

If not now_____ then when ___

or punctuated by a fluctuating harmonic pulse and a downward melodic contour to suggest, once more, a feeling of introspection and searching for answers

then ___ Why_ make your prom-is - es____

which, in turn, contrasts with the overspill of emotion as the vocal line follows the natural inflection of the words 'You can wait till morning/comes you can wait for the new/day ... .'

It is, perhaps, not unexpected that the last song of the album should be accompanied simply by acoustic guitar as if to signify the ultimate alone-ness, the separateness of unrequited love. Any residual optimism is gone and the occasional intervention of common sense which emerged in 'For my Lover' has gone: 'I'm no longer the master of my emotions'. Again, Chapman makes use of word painting. 'Control', for example, begins on top G and slowly falls, the syllables extended, as if to trace the contours of the emotional experience as the melodic line slips downwards. In contrast, the 'look at my losing ... ' follows the natural syllabic distribution and is sung on one pitch as if to 'hammer it home'

look at me los-ing con - tro - o - ol ___

Chapman's compositional style is equally evident in her use of space which effectively underlines the significance of her emotions

Deep in my heart   Deep in my heart

sentiments that are effectively followed through in the instrumental 'musing', the sense of internal dialogue as the 'call' of her vocal line is followed through in the 'response' of her acoustic guitar.

It is, however, the use of vibrato that is most significant in Chapman's love songs. This creates a mood of wavering, as though the singer were on the edge of tears and, in conjunction with her arrangement of the lyrics (pausing in the middle of sentences, splitting syllables, using silence to heighten the effectiveness of particular words and phrases and, generally, confining her melodies to the interval of a fifth and reserving the wide intervalic leaps for the beginning of emotional outbursts) serves to express and communicate directly with the listener.

Clearly such musical devices are not confined simply to the love songs. Depth of tone, for example, is common to all Chapman's songs and this is achieved by using her diaphragm to support her singing, giving her voice its characteristic strength and depth. Her placing of the chest register is evident, for example, in the second track 'Fast Car', and is achieved by pushing the chest forward, directing the sound towards the nose so that it resonates at the front of the skull, so effecting a nasal but strong tone which comes across as curiously masculine. This is further enhanced by the way in which she pronounces the lyrics – her blurring of the 'i' to 'a' as in 'Mountain o' Things/Thangs', an effect which is due largely to not opening the mouth fully and which effects a characteristic lazy sound to an otherwise full and rounded tone.

However, it is possibly this lazy vocal tone and seeming lack of involvement, that led to the critique of her album as 'too anodyne for a black audience'.[25] However, the implication that Chapman's musical style is, by analogy, 'medicinal', that it 'allays pain', and 'avoids argument or controversy'[26] is, I feel, somewhat unmerited. The pain is there – at its most extreme in 'Across the Lines' and 'Behind the Wall', but equally evident in the sense of personal loss in the four love songs 'Baby, Can I Hold You', 'Why', 'For My Lover' and 'If Not Now'. The critique, then, appears somewhat misleading, but it is nevertheless true to point to the somewhat dispassionate delivery, the emphasis on narrativity which suggests that the artist is an observer rather than a participator and which resulted in her identification by *Rolling Stone* (1988) as an 'after-dinner conscience-comforter'.

As a black musician, there is little doubt that Chapman would be aware of the conventions of delivery that characterise black musical performance.

In particular, there is a stress on 'aliveness' which 'is expressed through visual, physical and musical modes' which involve an 'intensity of emotion and total physical involvement'.[27] Not least, the music is interactive, serving to 'unite Black people into a cohesive group for a common purpose'.[28] Although Burnim and Maultsby are referring primarily to live performance, such interactivity is evident in any recording of soul, gospel, r&b, funk, jazz and rap where there is scope for improvisation and an interaction either instrumentally, with backing singers or with the audience. In particular, the call and response structure is critical in allowing for a manipulation of time, text and pitch, musical change and rhythmic tension. However, 'The most noticeable African feature in African-American music is its rhythmic complexity ... (which) is organised in multi-linear forms ... patterns which produce polyrhythms.'[29]

Although the emphasis on rhythmic complexity is evident in 'Mountains o' Things' and 'She's Got her Ticket' and in her idiosyncratic crushing and expansion of words and syllables, there is little in *Tracy Chapman* which reflects this interactive groove. However, as suggested previously, Chapman's album deals largely with being an outsider, of divisions in society (racial, economic, and in personal relationships) where there is no collective support or involvement. Rather, her 'heroines' are ultimately alone, unable to escape, 'two weeks in a Virginia jail', immobilised ('Fast Car') or beaten into submission ('Behind the Wall') and, as such, the supportive 'collectivity' of black musical style seems less appropriate than the personal narrative of her solo compositions. Crowds 'disperse', the 'I have a dream' of Martin Luther King has been 'killed' ('Across the Lines') and all that remains are questions 'why, when there's so many of us, are there people still alone?' ('Why?') However, although Chapman is largely positioned in the role of narrator, drawing on the reportage characteristic of a folk idiom, her conceptualisation of the music – which involves an ability to 'translate everyday experience into living sound'[30] and where 'beauty' of tone is replaced by a vocal delivery which reinforces the musical context – is equally typical of black musical tradition.

In particular, her identification of man's inhumanity to man, the deadening of compassion, is sung in a largely flat tone with little or no elaboration other than the alternation of straight and vibrato tones which characterises such songs as 'Behind the Wall' and which gives the characteristic 'wavering' quality to her vocal line. She is equally sparing with her vocal range, using the polar extremes of her voice to highlight emotional outburst – jumping to the top of her vocal register (high A) to signal distress, pain, while remaining primarily confined within melodic contours which encompass the interval of a fifth, as though demonstrating the imprisoning connotations of ghetto life. Not least, Chapman makes extensive use of melisma to colour and generate an intensity of delivery. These are techniques that are integral to the solo style of many black performers, not least such blues artists as Bobby Blue Bland:

> All the distinctive features of Bland's vocal style are in evidence, notably the hoarse cry and his use of melisma on key words. Bland's cry usually consists of a twisted vowel at the beginning of a phrase – going from a given note, reaching up to another one, and coming back to the starting point ... Almost without exception Bobby uses more than one note per syllable on the concluding word of each phrase ... In slower tempos he will stretch out syllables with even more melisma.[31]

It is also important to note that Black peoples, since the onset of slavery, have always interacted with musical influences which have come, largely, from Europe. In doing so, they have assimilated characteristics and integrated them with more identifiable black musical techniques (e.g. fashioning Protestant psalms, hymns and spiritual songs into new compositions by altering the structure, text, melody and rhythm; producing polyrhythmic structures by adding syncopated foot-stomped and hand-clapped patterns, etc.)[32] It is not so surprising, then, that a folk idiom which was Celtic in origin but which, in its identification with first the union movement of the 1930s and second, the Civil Rights agitation of the 1960s, should be recognised by a young black woman as a musical style which could express pain, loneliness, inequality and desolation in a manner comparable to the Mississippi Delta blues. Indeed, Chapman was not alone in her recognition of the radical connotations of folk. In the 1950s and 1960s folk/gospel singer Odetta Felious had sung on the historic Student Nonviolent Coordinating Committee (SNCC) March on Washington in August 1963. As an active protest singer she had also campaigned against the US involvement in Vietnam and performed at the War is Over concert in New York's Central Park in April 1975 in the company of Joan Baez, Phil Ochs, Pete Seeger and Paul Simon.[33] Chapman's use of a folk idiom, then, can be interpreted as the assimilation of a powerful musical critique traditionally associated with the expression of marginality.

It is also true, of course, that the folk music scene was largely associated with the university campus and that Chapman's first audiences were white festival-goers who were used to folk. As such, it is not so extraordinary that she should direct her protest against racism through a shared musical vocabulary. It is also relevant to note that many of her songs were performed at all-women music festivals and that themes of marginality equally resonated with her lesbian connections – the audiences that supported her and the foregrounding of feminist issues that are intentionally ignored in her promotional material. For many, it seems that Chapman's easy passage to a mainstream audience was what was most contentious – 'Tracy Chapman ...

and K.T. Oslin singing to working class straight ladies';[34] attracting an audience of white middle-class males who are looking for 'comfortable liberal platitudes to make them feel better'.[35]

Many were more perceptive in their response and it is worth noting that half the songs on her album were covered by reggae artists – with 'Fast Car' being a hit for Foxy Brown. It would thus appear that Chapman's concern for the illusory nature of progress – social, economic, political, racial – and her identification of the worsening conditions in inner-city ghettos were more than simple conscience-cleansing.[36] Rather, Chapman can be situated alongside contemporary artists from the field of funk and rap whose lyric themes also highlight frustration, disillusionment and distress.[37] Indeed, with the release of her second album, significantly entitled *Crossroads*[38] Chapman became increasingly identified with 'the rich tradition of Black civil rights protest'[39] with her 1989 video *Born to Fight* (which announced her refusal to be beaten into a white man's drone) becoming part of a high school text on the black history of the United States. The album itself reached no. 9 on the US charts and, like *Tracy Chapman*, was also a platinum seller. *Matters of the Heart* followed in 1992 and was equally politicised in its critique of racism and poverty and sparse in terms of instrumentation and vocal style.

I would argue, then, that there can be no totalising definition of what constitutes Black music[40] – any more than there is one totalising definition of what constitutes the Black woman. Rather, both occupy a social terrain fractured by oppression, exploitation and struggle where difference and diversity are significant markers in identity politics. Chapman's music is the product of the sociological circumstances in which it was created, and this, in turn, links her with other articulate women of her generation. Queen Latifah, for example, in the 1980 music video promotion for her rap song 'Ladies First',

> drew upon the diasporic history of black people around the world to fashion an affirmative representation of women of African descent. Assisted by Monie Love, an Afro-Caribbean rapper from London, as well as Ms. Melody and a chorus of other black female rappers from the U.S.A., Latifah appeared in a video that interspersed still photos of Angela Davis, Sojourner Truth, and Madame C.J. Walker with newsreel films of women prominent in the struggle against apartheid in South Africa.[41]

As George Lipsitz observes, the achievement of 'Ladies First' was to invert and subvert the media's fixation on black women as unwed mothers and welfare queens. Instead, Latifah celebrated their historic accomplishments, as 'queens of civilisation', demonstrating that the African-American was part of a global majority who had been victimized and oppressed by Euro-

American racism and imperialism.[42] The celebration of the African diaspora is also expressed in Lauryn Hill's tribute song to her son Zion, son of Ziggy and grandson of Bob Marley. 'Free Zion' fuses a free vocal delivery with the South American Latin feel of guitarist Carlos Santana, with Jamaican reggae and Afro-American hip hop, soul, r&b and gospel in an interactive groove that once again talks directly to the collective of black peoples, the fugees (fugitives) of white colonialism.[43]

It is a link that is equally evident in the 'constant referencing and cross-referencing between music and literature ...' that took place in the 1980s and early 1990s. Alice Walker, for example, 'wrote sleeve notes for the Black female *a cappella* act Sweet Honey in the Rock, as did Ntozsake Shange for Nina Simone, and Maya Angelou received a warm dedication in a Pointer Sisters' song'.[44] As rap artist Nefertiti pointed out 'It's all about awareness'[45] and it is this awareness about difference and diversity within the African diaspora that equally links artists like Chapman and Nefertiti to the problems surrounding racialised exclusion, 'Black' identity, and social and cultural difference.

Educational achievement, for example, had become increasingly significant during the 1980s and 1990s.[46]. The ideal of self-reliance, of getting on, is reflected both in Chapman's university education and musical output and in Nefertiti's 1994 debut album *L.I.F.E. – Living in Fear of Extinction*. It is also interesting to note that her advocacy of personal achievement was taken to its logical conclusion when she made her record company, Mercury, pay $250,000 of her college tuition as part of her deal. As feminist writer Heidi Safia Mirza points out, black female educational urgency, the desire for inclusion, 'is strategic, subversive and transformative ... black women are both succeeding and conforming in order to transform and change ... Black women do not just resist racism, they live "other" worlds'.[47]

Chapman's success as an artist, then, can be partly attributed to a desire for inclusion and partly to her refusal to be contained by the notion of uniformity – not least the stereotyping of what constitutes Black women or black music. More specifically, it could be argued that she has constantly asserted a sense of both private and public self – a self that is rooted in what has been dubbed the 'holy trinity' of race, class and gender[48] but which has succeeded equally in the mainstream world of popular music. Her 'dreads' and combat gear express her personal identity as a politicised Black woman. Her songs resonate with a reflective collectivity based on common economic, social and cultural oppressions, addressing the growing numbers of the homeless, a failing education system and an ever-rising crime rate through a personal and poetic musical language. As such, she is both an icon for, and a part of the self-defining presence of contemporary black women

struggling to define
just who we are

where we belong ... '[49]

speaking out, in a world where so many black women have, for so long, been denied the privilege to speak[50] and committed both to struggle and change.

Acknowledgements

I would especially like to acknowledge my former student Clare Canty whose discussion of Tracy Chapman's vocal style informed my own analysis, and Debbie Allen for her constructive thoughts on the nature of black musical style.

NOTES AND REFERENCES

1 Gaar, G.G. (1993) *She's A Rebel. The History of Women in Rock 'n' Roll*, London: Blandford, p. 364.

2 O'Brien, L. (1995) *She Bop. The Definitive History of Women in Rock, Pop and Soul*, London: Penguin Books, p. 375.

3 Nelson George, cited in Gaar, *op. cit.*, p. 376.

4 Mirza, H.S. (1997) *Black British Feminism. A Reader*, London: Routledge, p. 6.

5 Garofalo, R. (1992) 'Popular Music and the Civil Rights Movement', in *Rockin' the Boat. Mass Music and Mass Movements*, Southend Press. p. 237.

6 *Ibid.*, p. 238.

7 Norman, U. (1998) 'Commercialising Hip Hop: Urban Rap versus the "Gangsta" Construct' (unpublished dissertation), pp. 6–10.

8 Dyson, M.E. (1991) 'Performance, Protest and Prophecy in the Culture of Hip Hop' in Spencer, J.M. (ed.) *The Emergency of Black and the Emergence of Rap*. A special issue of *Black Sacred Music. A Journal of Theomusicology*, vol 5, no 1, Duke University Press, Spring, p. 24.

9 *Ibid.*, pp. 4, 17.

10 *Ibid.*

11 This phrase was used to describe the riots in Los Angeles where twenty-three died and 900 were injured after the jury acquitted Sgt Stacey C. Koon and Officers Laurence M. Powell, Theodore J. Briseno and Timothy E. Wind of inflicting bodily harm (beating and kicking) Rodney G. King, a black motorist. The jury also announced that it would not indict any of the nineteen police officers who were bystanders at the beating. The police department later punished ten of them. The incident was videoed and the verdicts 'set off a wave of shock and anger' (Seth Mydans, Special to the *New York Times*, Thursday, 30 April 1992.

12 A passing note is a note or tone that effects a smooth passage, but forms no essential part of the harmony. It can also form an unprepared discord in an unaccented place in the bar (measure).

13 Mirza, *op. cit.*, p. 6.

14 The period is notable for the failure of the federal government's control policies over the illicit import of cocaine. Colombian producers in Medellin and Cuban-American importers in Miami had created a glut of cocaine on the streets and retail drug entrepreneurs had, in turn, developed a new way of marketing cocaine in the form of crack (cooking cocaine into smokeable crystalline 'rocks'.) Potency, and the fact that crack could be sold in small monetary packages, made it an instant hit on the streets, doing as much damage to the black community

as the Jim Crow laws of the 1970s. Tidey, D. (1994) 'Rap Music, Censorship and the Black Experience' (unpublished dissertation), p. 13. It is possible that the song refers to the death of a young black girl whose body was discovered in a black polythene sack in the backstreets of New York. Beaten up and sexually abused, it was alleged by the police that she had been scared to go home after a night out with her boyfriend and had hidden herself in the sack. The incident led to street protest and violence and, as such, relates to the lines 'a little black girl gets assaulted and racist tempers fly'.

15 The concept of timbre as a memory trigger was originally used by my friend and colleague Mark Grimshaw, (1996) 'Remix Technologies. Sound and Music' a paper presented at the Drake Conference on Popular Music, 29–30 March, Des Moines, Drake University.

16 An understanding of the black musical aesthetic requires an awareness of three primary criteria: quality of sound, and style and mechanics of delivery. Burnim, M. (1980) 'The Black Gospel Music Tradition. Symbol of Ethnicity' (doctoral dissertation, Indiana University). The issues and principles are discussed in some detail in Burnim, M.V. and Maultsby, P. K., 'From Backwoods to City Streets. The Afro-American Musical Journey', Chapter 5 in Gay, G. and Baber, W.L. (eds) (1987) *Expressively Black*, New York: Praeger.

17 Baudrillard, J. (1998) *The Consumer Society. Myths and Structures*, London: Sage Publications, p. 174. This was originally published as *La societé de consommation. Editions Denoel* in 1970.

18 *Ibid.*, p. 95.

19 *Ibid.*, p. 76.

20 Middleton, R. (1997) 'Understanding Pop Music', MA Module, Milton Keynes: Open University Press, p. 47.

21 Professor Portia Maultsby, Indiana University, from her keynote address to the 1992 International Association for the Study of Popular Music Conference, Stockton, California.

22 Muncie, J. (1981) 'Pop Culture, Pop Music and Post-war Youth. Subcultures', in Block 5 'Politics, Ideology and Popular Culture (1)' *Popular Culture*, BA Module. Milton Keynes: Open University Press, p. 52.

23 As such there is a comparability with Bob Dylan whose introduction of rock instrumentation into acoustic folk effected a more direct communication with his youthful 1960s' audience.

24 A sus chord has no defining major or minor third. As such, there is no indication as to whether it belongs to a major or minor scale or, at a connotative level, which mood is indicated (at its simplest, major/bright; minor/dark).

25 O'Brien, *op. cit.*, p. 375.

26 Kirkpatrick, E.M. (1983) *Chambers 20th Century Dictionary*, Edinburgh: W & R Chambers Ltd, p. 47.

27 Burnim and Maultsby, *op. cit.*, p. 192.

28 *Ibid.*, p. 187.

29 *Ibid.*, p. 193.

30 *Ibid.*, p. 191.

31 *Ibid.*, p. 194.

32 *Ibid.*, p. 198.

33 O'Brien, *op. cit.*, p. 376.

34 Garofalo, *op. cit.*, p. 250.

35 Pond, S. (1988) 'On Her Own Terms. Interview with Tracy Chapman', *Rolling Stone*, 22 September.

36 As Peter Dunbar-Hall explains in his paper, 'The Use of Reggae by Contemporary Australian Aboriginal Musicians' (IASPM Conference, University of the Pacific, July 1993) 'the presence of reggae as a style favoured by Aboriginal musicians is continually commented on in the sparse literature on Aboriginal rock music'.
Narogin writes:

> In the mid-seventies black music song types began to have some impact. One such music was reggae ... this music with its lyrics purporting an identity with oppressed people, portrayed itself as being sung by and directed at black people, and condemning European cultural influences ... one of the most successful Aboriginal bands, No Fixed Address, saw themselves as essentially a reggae band, and could declare at one time that reggae was Aboriginal music.
> (Narogin, M. (1990) *Writing from the Fringe: a Study of Modern Aboriginal Literature*. Melbourne: Hyland House), p. 63f

The ideology of reggae, then, is relevant to an expression of oppression by all Black peoples and is a potent musical style for identifying social, economic, political and racial frustrations.

37 George Clinton, Gil Scott Heron, Grandmaster Flash and Melle Mel, N.W.A., Ice-T, Public Enemy and Disposable Heroes of HipHoprisy are but a few examples.

38 *Crossroads* can be read as a homage to early blues artists such as Robert Johnson, one of the greatest of country blues artists in the Delta style. He recorded only twenty-nine songs, one of which was his famous 'Crossroad Blues'.

39 O'Brien, *op. cit.*, p. 376.

40 See Tagg, P. (1989) 'Open Letter: "Black Music", "Afro-American Music" and "European Music" ', *Popular Music*, 8, pp. 285–98.

41 Lipsitz, G. (1994) *Dangerous Crossroads. Popular Music, Postmodernism and the Poetics of Place*, New York: Verso, p. 25.

42 *Ibid.*, p. 25.

43 I would like to thank my friend and colleague, Debbie Allen, for her perceptive insights here.

44 O'Brien*, op. cit.*, p. 314.

45 *Ibid.*, p. 315.

46 In Britain,

> the 1993 Labour Force survey showed 61 per cent of all black women (aged 16–59) to have higher and other qualifications (*Employment Gazette* 1993). Figures for 1995 show that 52 per cent of all black women (aged 16–24) are in full-time education, compared to 28 per cent of white women, 36 per cent of black men, and 31 per cent of white men (*Employment Gazette* 1995). Similarly a recent study for the Policy Studies Institute shows that in relation to their respective popular sizes, ethnic minority groups overall, are over-represented in higher education ... This over-representation was especially apparent in the new universities. Here people of Caribbean origin were over- represented by 43 per cent, Asians by 162 per cent and Africans by 223 per cent. This compared with the white population who were under-represented by 7 per cent. But educational urgency does not stop there. As mothers black women strategically

negotiate the educational advantage of their children within the constraints offered by the decaying urban education system and access to cultural capital ... (by) the setting up and running of black supplementary schools. They invest in the education of the next generation.

Mirza, op. cit., p. 271.

47 *Ibid.*, 270.
48 *Ibid.*, p. 9.
49 Jackie May (1985) 'So You Think I'm a Mule ?' The full poem appears in *Ibid.*, pp. 1–2.
50 *Ibid.*, p. 4.

12

AUTHENTICITY, TRUTHFULNESS AND COMMUNITY

Tori Amos, Courtney Love, P.J. Harvey and Björk

It is frequently argued that the 1990s were characterised by 'the cult of the disconnected fragment, the fashion for a free-floating identity politics, in which we are all at liberty, apparently, to be who we want to be'. [1] Indeed, given the 1980s' commitment to self-expression and self-identity, and the challenges made to traditional representations of femininity by such artists as Annie Lennox, Madonna, k.d. lang and Tracy Chapman, the question arises as to whether women performers were finally freed to 'be themselves'. While this brings up problems surrounding definitions of selfhood and the framing of women as culturally imagined rather than born,[2] the turn of the decade did seem to suggest that the unitary categories which had earlier characterised 'identity politics' (female/male, gay/straight, black/white) had been replaced by cultural forms that challenged single determinate meanings.[3] As my analysis of, for example, k.d. lang's album *Absolute Torch and Twang* illustrates, popular music (in common with other cultural forms such as film and television) was 'increasingly understood in different ways by different cultural and subcultural groups.[4]

My analysis of the 1990s suggests that *musically* the period is discursively constructed by two distinguishing practices (each with its own assumptions, values and premises) and that these are contextualised by the cultural space or context from and through which (women) artists 'speak' or represent themselves. The first, relates to folk (and the singer songwriter tradition) in its emphasis on authenticity, 'truthfulness' to personal experience, and community; the second is concerned with artifice and is largely governed by the imperatives of commercial success. At the same time, both 'categories' are subject to discursive repositioning as questions are raised, such as 'what is this music trying to do, how should it be listened to, whose is it?'[5] Similarly, they provide insights into the ways in which popular music contributes to an understanding of the relationship between popular culture, sexuality and identity. In particular, I would suggest that the artists discussed provide specific insights into the relationship between subjective experience and the meaning of women's lived reality.

Adios, clichés of pigeon, ragdoll, and just a victim of her man. If they show no signs of leaving, it is we who must back away through time and turn to other women for a clearer vision.[6]

It is, perhaps, self-evident that my discussion of women artists under category one is predicated by their overall significance to the field of popular music. They are big names writ large. However, as women they are also significant in tackling specific issues – whether this is concerned with language (Patti Smith), representation (Madonna), sexuality (k.d. lang) or race (Tracy Chapman). As such, they have what Simon Frith identifies as 'a believability (and its complex relations with both realism and fantasy); coherence (whether in terms of form or morality) and a usefulness – whether at the most material level, or at the most spiritual (does this experience uplift me, make me a better person?)[7] Although the aesthetic/functional axes cited above refer to cultural judgements generally, I would suggest that such communication 'takes place only where the gesture made has the same meaning for the individual who makes it that it has for the individual who responds to it'[8] and that this sense of identification, the ability to address an audience on a one-to-one basis, is particularly important when songs express the personal experience of the artist.

'Me and a Gun', from Tori Amos's 1992 album *Little Earthquakes*, for example, can be considered a pivotal song in communicating her personal experience of rape. The song is unaccompanied, the melodic line simple and direct, with the emphasis on the words and the immediacy of the moment 'Five a.m. Friday morning ... ' Initially, the vocal delivery is hesitant, punctuated by irregular pauses as if to underline the trauma of remembering. This is also reflected in the narrowness of the vocal range – the subdued effect of repetition (which serves to confine the singer to a neverending present) and the aeolian mode itself and its association with death.[9] More specifically, the song is dominated by the interval of a fourth which not only serves to contain the vocal line, but also becomes the *leitmotiv* for the expression of the personal as it draws into association the desire to live, the horror of rape, and the talismanic of prayer.

While it is speculation to link the interval of a fourth with such well-known carols as 'Away in a Manger' (which is used extensively as a memory-aid by music students in recalling the sound of a perfect fourth), Amos's classical training as a pianist and her Methodist background would have familiarised her with the effect on the listener of such common musical devices and their associations with protection 'Be near me, Lord Jesus ... '. However, it is evident that her musings on rape ('Tell me, what's right? Is it my right to be on my stomach of Fred's Seville?') challenge the traditional guilt ('Yes I wore a slinky red thing, does that mean I should spread for you, and your friends, your father, Mr Ed?') and its historic alignment with the confessional ('Jesus ... said "It's your choice babe ... "). In so doing, Amos positions herself within the continuing history of women who campaign against sexual violence and oppression, who recognise that rape is centrally involved in a woman's sense of personal identity, that it is the kind of crime that 'threatens to disintegrate a woman – that is, to make her less of a person by depriving her of bodily autonomy. In rape – and also in incest, sexual harassment, prostitution and pornography – a man takes a woman's sexuality, as it is mediated through her body, and through his action proclaims that women's sexuality is for men – for what men want and need'.[10]

Amos's recognition of her assailants is also common to the majority of rape victims. In date rape, for example, it has been confirmed that 85 per cent of women know the attacker. Court cases, moreover, still require women to provide evidence supporting their dress sense and behaviour, and while there have been anti-rape campaigns such as that produced by Trevor Beattie, director of the advertising agency TBWA, in which images of 'beautiful' women were accompanied by the message 'This is not an invitation to rape me' and 'When it happens to your Mother – will you say she was asking for it?',[11] the strength of 'Me and a Gun' lies in its 'truthfulness' to personal experience rather than to an orchestrated media campaign. In particular, such lines as 'these things go through your head when there's a man on your back, and you're pushed flat on your stomach, and it's not a classic Cadillac' evidence a keen sense of irony and a personal insight into the innocuous thoughts which course through the mind at moments of crisis – 'do you know CAROLINA where the biscuits are soft and sweet'. Survival tactics – 'but I haven't seen BARBADOS, so I must get out of this', and the will to go on – 'I wanna live', equally define the need for strength.

There is, then, a sense of both speaking to and for others, so energising the activism which characterises, for example, such grassroots organisations as the Rape Crisis Centre Movement and the belief that women can make inroads into negative life experiences and negative self-images. More specifically, the experience of rape encouraged Amos to voice her support for the RAINN (the Rape, Abuse and Incest National Network). It is salutary to note, however, that she had first to work through her feelings of victimisation, that she had a nervous breakdown, and that her extensive self-analysis

— which involved 'freeing the attacker in yourself, tearing away all the layers'[12] — resonated with a cry for absolution from a crime which still blames the victim rather than the perpetrator of violence. The re-release of the single 'Silent All these Years' (from the *Little Earthquakes* CD) and the 'Unlock the Silence' show at Madison Square Gardens, New York evidence her personal commitment to giving and receiving support from those who have gone through similar experiences.[13]

As such, it is not too surprising that her 1992 album, *Little Earthquakes*, is largely about self-examination, reflecting on the tensions between her religious upbringing, her rebelliousness, her relationships, and the struggle to find her own voice. 'China', the seventh song on the album, but chronologically the first written, provides a key to the problems identified throughout the twelve-song cycle, the recognition that 'distance learns to grow'. In a way, the song is a personal insight into the paradox that being with someone can be more lonely than being apart — 'I can feel that distance getting close'; that attempts to build bridges cause withdrawal — 'you just look away'. The use of China, as a central metaphor for the separation and conflict inherent in wall-building,[14] and the distancing inherent in ritual — the sense of polite aloofness that heralds both the break-up of a relationship, and the breakdown of conciliatory talk — is musically reflected by the use of fifths in the bass. At one and the same time harmonically perfect yet incomplete,[15] there is an evocation of 'an ancient ceremony. This ceremony took me to China took me to the kitchen table where most wars get nurtured. I've always felt China and secrets are good friends ... '.[16]

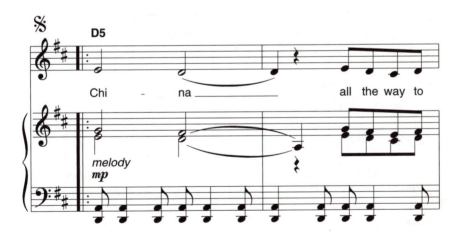

The use of metaphor is also central to the musical evocation of mood. The verse opens in dissonance, with the opening syllable 'Chi' coming on the strong beat of the bar on the second degree of the scale before falling to the tonic, D, '-na'.[17] The syllables are spaced out, tied over the bar line and followed by a reflective rest before the narrow-ranged 'all the way to' which completes the minimalistic motif on which the verse is built. The effect is to create a feeling of confinement (the repetitive, narrow ranged motif) and distance (the slow tempo, the use of tied notes and rests which impact on the spacing of the syllables, and hence, the sensibility of the words) which together provide a musical synonym for estrangement:

The metaphorical significance of the interval as a distance between two notes/two people is maintained in the chorus where the bass moves between the octave unison (symbolic of 'oneness') and the fifth (with its feeling of emptiness and its association with the 'primitive', the 'exotic' especially when given rhythm articulation as in the bass accompaniment):

and this sense of trying to close the distance, of struggling to recapture the oneness of the relationship, is reflected in the piano accompaniment where increased movement and shifting metres are frustrated initially by a return to the verse ('China decorates our table, funny how the cracks don't seem to show') and, more specifically, the coda where it is finally acknowledged that 'in the distance, a Great Wall around you … ' and a gradual fade over the omnipresent starkness of the open fifths.

Her sense of personal struggle is also there in 'Crucify', the opening song of the album, and again this is characterised by the interval of a fifth, this time within the dark framework of G# minor. The vocal line is even more constrained – with accusatory lyrics delivered on a stabbing monotone over slowly moving parallel fifths. The effect is one of recitative, a narrative freed from melodic constraints:

1. Ev-ery fin-ger in the room   is point-ing at   me_

I wan-na spit in their fac - es

Although the song might suggest the penitent, the sensuous vocal tone denies any real desire for redemption. Rather, there is a sense of tormented self-recognition, a realisation that the relationship between God and the victim is one of reciprocity – 'God needs one more victim … I gotta have my suffering so that I can have my cross', and an awareness that the 'search for a saviour beneath these dirty sheets' reflects more a need for sexual release than a resolute cry for absolution. The chains, the sense of self torment, is opened out in the chorus 'nothing I do is good enough for you … ' and further clarified by the video which zooms in on high heels, a metal choker, a formal evening dress and reddened lips. Amos's stage/video performance shows her to be full of feminine wiles, an illusionist, capable of faking 'lightheartedness, girlishness and orgasm … the roses in (her) cheeks, the thickness, colour and curliness of (her) hair; the thinness of (her) waist, the longness of (her) legs and the size and shape of (her) breasts'.[18] 'Chains.' At this point the vocal line shifts to a sinuous, high-pitched descending motif that suggests the exotic, evoking the imagery of the geisha, the quintessential courtesan trained to entertain men through dance and conversation. 'Sick of being in chains'.

As Tori Amos explains, in the now famous interview with Björk and Polly Harvey, 'I have stuff to deal with in the intimate sex realm',[19] and this is particularly evident in the tussle with her own sexuality and the conflict inherent in her desire to please others (her lover, her father – himself a Methodist minister). This sense of personal struggle is reflected in the use of counterpoint and echo on 'please save me' (with its connotations of church litany) and the more sensuous delivery on 'beggin' for LOVE'. Amos's personal battle against guilt ('drive another nail in', 'got enough guilt to start my own religion'), and her rejection of the established teachings of the Church on female sexuality is significant. As feminist theologian Mary Daly observes, the 'original sin' of women is the internalisation of guilt and blame. Among its side-effects are psychological paralysis, feminine anti-feminism, false humility, and emotional dependence. As victims of the 'scapegoat syndrome', women can never win. Being 'good' or 'bad' within the system is equally destructive. The way out of the imposed 'innocence', or lack of knowledge and choice, of both the good and the bad women is through experiential knowledge, a 'fall from innocence into a new kind of adulthood'.[20] Small wonder, then, that the omnipresent bumblebee tinkle of the piano that underpins 'Silent All these Years' homes in on the personal, the urgency of bleeding 'real soon', the scream that got lost 'in a paper cup', and the final realisation in 'Little Earthquakes' that it 'doesn't take much to rip us into little pieces'.

The crusade against personal guilt continues in Amos's second album, *Under the Pink*, this time exposing the hypocrisy surrounding female masturbation.

> Icicle, once again, explores conflict – this time the pleasures of autoeroticism and the moral imperatives of the established church. Most specifically, the song rejects her Methodist upbringing 'Father says bow your head like the good book says ... ' and the realisation that 'As a child she was surrounded by women who hadn't been wet between their legs for twenty years.'[21]

The music itself underpins the images, beginning with a changeable motif in the upper register of the piano, reminiscent of a child's musical box, hinting at innocence through a timid dynamic. As the volume increases, the chords become harsh and dissonant, a persuasive metaphor for inner conflict 'getting off, getting off while they're downstairs singing prayers'. The repetitive drive of masturbation is reflected in the ostinato figure played by the right hand which gradually builds throughout the verse, finally resolving into full chords as Amos sings 'Getting off ... '. The vocal line also imitates the gathering momentum of orgasm, the pitch rising, the dynamic level increasing so that each individual phrase becomes an ecstatic rush until the moment of release when the voice soars climactically to the octave.

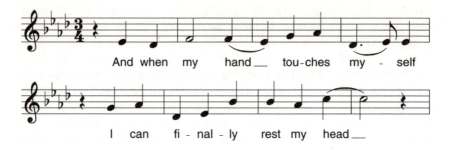

And when my hand — tou-ches my - self

I can fi - nal - ly rest my head —

Tori Amos's attitude towards female arousal, and her challenging stance against Holy Communion ('and when they say "take of his body" I think I'll take from mine instead ... ') remains controversial yet the issues surrounding autoeroticism and its relationship to morality are still problematic. In particular, the association of masturbation with hysteria which characterised the Victorian attitude towards female sexual arousal (and which led to the removal of clitorises from women in both the UK and the US) has not disappeared, and autoeroticism continues to be regarded as sinful by, for example, Christians and Muslims. Further, while such extreme cases as the removal of clitorises from 600 women, without anaesthetic or antiseptics, in the Grafton Camp for displaced persons, Freetown, Sierra Leone makes, quite rightly, headline news, it is a salutary fact that some 120 million women alive today have suffered genital mutilation. The American Academy of Paediatrics, for example, 'recommends that clitorises of more than three-eighths of an inch in length should be removed from baby girls before they are fifteen months old. Five such procedures are performed every day in the United States.'[22]

As Germaine Greer observes 'A woman's body is the battlefield where she fights for liberation. It is through her body that oppression works, reifying her, sexualizing her, victimizing her, disabling her.'[23] Amos's open-legged stance at the piano, her reverence towards masturbation, her independence, would certainly have aligned her with the out-of-control carnal lust that historically characterised witches,[24] a point she tacitly acknowledges in 'Thoughts' (*Little Earthquakes*) – 'what would become of me?' In the 1990s, however, her ability to address the problems inherent in sexual desire, and her defiance of sexual oppression, have earned her respect. More specifically, she has given women a voice for their anger:

> Believe in love and peace, my child and it'll all be over
> Well, fuck you
> – that isn't the answer.[25]

What makes Amos special for me, however, is not simply the power of her lyrics or her personal confrontations with tenets of outmoded morality. Rather it is her ability to communicate intimately with her fans. As Thomas Crayton Harrison explains,

> In the pre-band days, a Tori Amos show meant a meandering trail down whatever emotional road she was travelling that particular evening. She told a lot of stories, in between numbers, personal stories of her childhood and her friends and her experiences with drugs ... . It was that side that made her more personal and real to a lot of people ... . Her between-song interruptions used to serve as a break, a kind of comic relief, from the heavy drama of her music ... In her recent performance with the band (Oklahoma City, September 28) 'her songs came rushing in blow by blow, never slowing down to take a breath. One was assaulted by the visual imagery of Ms. Amos clutching her belly – which once held the child she miscarried, as she sang mournfully 'Why has it got to be a sacrifice?' and then knocked back again at the sight of her arching back in erotic ecstasy with one hand playing the piano and one the electronic keyboard as the 'Raspberry Swirl' beat pulsed through the auditorium. It's a tough experience to be drowned and electrocuted and thrashed about, and that's how I felt when I left Oklahoma City that night ... .[26]

It is interesting to note that public performances of 'Me and a Gun' are now a rarity. For those who have seen Amos perform live, this is regrettable.

> On the last tour, it was in virtually every show, and it was the most personal and terrifying moment I've ever spent in a concert, watching a woman look directly at me and tell me what went through her mind as she was sexually attacked ... . It is probably one of the most important contributions to the movement against violence against women, and it deserves to be heard.

Crayton Harrison, who sent me his feedback on the concert, is majoring in journalism at Southern Methodist University, Dallas. His opinion is shared by many male colleagues and friends and is a contributory factor in my choice of Tori Amos as one of the most significant artists of the 1990s. My other reason is her musicality. Her compositions are 'minimalistic', often centring around two contrasting ideas which are thoughtfully developed to form an impressionistic support to the lyrics. These, too, have a suppleness, a refusal to be bound by such traditional confines as metre and rhyme. Rather they are led by the process of thought, sometimes stumbling, sometimes tumbling over in an attempt to 'tell it as it is'. At its most extreme, Amos resorts to wordless singing, the last refuge of a desire or despair that can't be communicated through language. As Reynolds and Press observe, 'Usually, such non-verbal singing has surfaced as outburst or breakdowns in a song, points at which inexpressible longing suddenly asserts itself at the libretto's expense' [27] as in 'Little Earthquakes' where an incantatory 'Give me life, give me pain, give me myself again' is followed by a wavering yet intense passage of wordless singing. The reason why this is so powerful lies, once again, in Tori Amos's compositional techniques. The vocal ('Ee ... .'.) is based on the unstable semi-tone motif (A#/B) which had earlier provided a sense of numbing uncertainty to the lines 'I can't reach you'. The scary reali-sation of aloneness is then heightened in the piano accompaniment where the right hand initially follows the vocal line in parallel thirds before a dramatic move to the octave:

Tori Amos's thoughtful approach to composition is matched by her ability to draw on a diversity of styles which develop the feel and direction of the lyrics – the *a cappella* of 'Me and a Gun', the vamping chorus of 'Leather'. More importantly there is a sense of musical growth, where she

actively stretches her sound by incorporating a broader approach to instrumentation, as in, for example, the remix of 'Professional Widow' from her
1996 album *Boys for Pele*. Released as a chart-topping dance track, there is
an effective contrast of heavy four-on-the floor sections, with aptly anthemic
lyrics – 'Honey bring it close to my lips'/'It's gotta be big' – and ambient
breaks with panned synthesised swirls and a characteristic move to a high
vocal register – 'Mother Mary, China white ... '. In summary, then, there is a
move to a contemporary dance feel which, nevertheless, reflects her characteristic compositional and vocal techniques.

In contrast, 'Hey Jupiter' reflects Amos's love of words and her ability to
play with nuance. The result is a confusion of pronouns – 'No-one's picking
up the 'phone guess it's me and me.'; and this ambiguity, the 'who is the
we?' informs the play on gendered identity and sexuality ('are you gay';
'sometimes I breathe you in and I know you know ... ') and the final enigma
of the extended coda with its orgasmic 'ooh ... yes'. For her numerous fans –
both gay and straight – the esoteric quality of the lyrics is an added bonus.
There is no one right interpretation, and Amos herself rarely reveals the
meaning behind the words. As evidenced on the numerous web-pages and
discussion groups dedicated to Tori Amos, 'Hey Jupiter' is seen by some as a
personal revelation. It is about the discovery of a female friend's romantic
attachment for her. Others situate it within the reality of Amos's life, as a
biographical song about the break-up of her long-time relationship with
Eric Rosse. The 'who it is', however, is not the real significance of the track.
Rather, it is about the emotions surrounding relationships and this, together
with the thoughtful sparseness of her arrangements and her powerful vocal
lines, remains a defining characteristic of Tori Amos's musical output.

Arguably, Tori Amos is one of the reasons why such artists as Alanis
Morissette, Fiona Apple and Natalie Imbruglia have subsequently achieved
popular appeal in the late 1990s. Certainly, few had sung about the personal
turmoil inherent in both sexual desire and sexual assault prior to *Little
Earthquakes* – let alone on the same album. As such Amos can be considered
an ally of such pioneering contemporaries as Courtney Love, Björk, Polly
(P.J.) Harvey, and riot grrrl bands Huggy Bear and Bikini Kill, all of whom
challenged the extreme frontiers of gender and sexuality in the early 1990s.

As Amy Raphael rightly observes in *Never Mind the Bollocks: Women
Rewrite Rock*,

> For young women (and men) in the 1990s who are still striving for
> change and for parity between the sexes, feminism has become a more
> mischievous and slippery concept, part of a wider cultural agenda
> that questions all received notions of gender and politics ... [28]

What I find particularly intriguing about Raphael's statement is that the observable shifts in lyric content that accompany personal politics – the 'fuck and run' of Liz Phair, the 'Lick/lip my legs/lips' of P.J. Harvey – seem to be clustered around the period 1991–4. Clearly, such artists as Madonna helped shape the agenda, but the defiant sexual confrontation of, for example, Courtney Love ('so much clit she don't need balls') and the angry confessional of her fast and furious grunge rock far exceeded the 1980s' call for personal empowerment. In particular her excessive onstage sexuality (the Kinderwhore, 'fucked up Lolita' image of the early 1990s) coupled with her militant 'femmeniste' politics and confrontational lyrics ('Here you come sucking my energy, drill it in my good hole so that I can see, you are so much bigger than me' ('Babydoll') and low-slung guitar (evocative of male rock) are challenging. She is not easy on the ear, and *Pretty on the Inside*, Hole's September 1991 debut album, comes across as loud, brash, fast, furious and, above all, full of frustration.

It is interesting to note that, prior to its release, neither the album, nor the singles had received any radio airplay, nor did it achieve any significant chart success. By the end of 1991, however, it had received critical acclaim from Elizabeth Wurtzel (author of the critically acclaimed novel *Prozac Nation*) – 'probably the most compelling album to have been released in 1991', *New Yorker*, 17 September 1991 – and had been included in *Melody Maker*'s Top Twenty Albums list. Its success was due largely to Love's credibility as a rock singer, the forceful, tinny sound of the strummed guitar and Caroline Rue's pounding snare and tom fills, not least on 'Babydoll'. More specifically, the lyrics, the rough and often messy sound of the guitar, and 'lo-fi' production have a persuasive 'fit'. This is reflected in the construction of the riffs in, for example, 'Teenage Whore', where menacing seconds (E/F), diminished fifths and an open E string are played in unison by the bass and guitar, to highlight the natural rhythm of the words ('When I was a teenage whore') which, in turn, is emphasised by the drums on 'teenage whore'.

It was the band's overall aggressive stance (specifically the heavy guitar riffs and vocal delivery) which distanced it from such contemporary 'chick rock' bands as Babes in Toyland and L7. More specifically the music had attitude, it was 'in yer face' and political ('there is no power like my pretty power') and while Courtney Love refuted Hole's link to the emergent riot grrrl movement there is nevertheless a comparable challenge to representations of femininity in the adoption of babydoll dresses, heavy makeup, challenging lyrics and furious frustration (' … and hey where the fuck were you when my lights went out?'). It is this sense of frustration that, in many ways, drives the gender politics of the early 1990s. Riot grrrl politics, for example, attempted to reclaim and politicise the word girl (with its traditional connotations of passivity and immaturity) and to re-present it as a wholly positive term, grrrl. So, not a girl because of the easy cook rice and late bedtimes, not a woman because of the pre-pubescent dresses, the messy bedrooms and the toys ... But a girl – a grrrl – who is a rebel and where the music she identifies with is identified with rebellion, disturbance, riot. Riot grrrl music then sets out to invite alarm and draw on the concept of disobedience.

(zine *Intimate Wipe* 2)

Although the identification of rebellion and disturbance suggests, initially, another page in the saga of youth cultures, the significance of riot grrrls lay equally in their explicit challenge to popular notions of adolescence, femininity, youth cultures, political identity, and in their celebration of grrrl power. More specifically, the use of 'zines' (e-zines, www) as lines of communication in which grrrls could share information and voice opinions on such issues as incest, abuse, self-abuse, abortion rights, date rape, and lesbian relationships facilitated frank dialogue and helped to overcome problems of isolation and alienation. This sense of 'tell it how it is' was also reflected in the DIY music. 'Use the Force' (Huggy Bear) told of young people who were into heroin, who were bulimic (because they think they will only attract others if they are thin), who are wired up for erotic bleeding, who are into self-mutilation as a means of release of tension – 'the kids who are sick on slow speed and poor education' and who are suicides at sixteen.

Empowering young women and providing a space where they are free to express themselves without being directly compared to, or overshadowed by, boys links the riot grrrl movement to feminism and lesbian separatism. Huggy Bear, for example, problematised and gendered the way in which an audience views a live performance by issuing handouts requesting that girls and women stand near the front of the stage instead of at the back, stressing the importance of female address and identification:

I really wanna look at female faces while I perform. I want HER to know that she is included in this show and that what we are doing is for her to CRITICISE/LAUGH AT/BE INSPIRED BY/HATE/WHAT-EVER.

It is this sense of process and interaction – rather than end product – that is most significant in assessing the significance of riot grrrl. The music is arguably evocative of English punk circa 1978 (Huggy Bear) or American garage circa 1966 (Bikini Kill) and generally marked by an almost fanatical rejection of virtuosity (which arguably relates strongly to the riot grrrls' rejection of 'cool' – the assimilation of male culture via toughness) and which also accounts for the girlish dress codes. The lyrics and style of delivery, however, have maximum impact, not least in such songs as 'Suck My Left

One' where Kathleen Hanna (Bikini Kill) relates a horrific tale about incest 'and a turning of the tables, a reclamation of woman's rights to be sexually ferocious'.[29]

The sense of ferocity is equally present in P.J. Harvey's second album *Rid of Me* (1993). However, unlike the upfront vocals of riot grrrl, Harvey's songs are more often characterised by a sense of ambiguity. Her lyrics, for example, often lie low in the mix and are not provided on the album sleeves, while the sex/gender of the 'you' in her songs is never specified. Combined with her idiosyncratic speech-based singing style and the extremes of her timbral range, individual words and phrases are often hard to pick out. Such ambiguity is further obscured by the extreme deliberation of her guitar style with its hacking riffs. The title song, in particular, 'lurches menacingly between revenge fantasies ('I'll tie your legs together,' ... 'make you' ... 'keep you') and the desperate neediness of the backing chorus, "lick my legs" (sung by drummer Rob Ellis in an excruciating, humiliated falsetto)'.[30]

The horror of the song lies in a refusal to negotiate and the fact that we – as audience – can hear only one side of the exchange. This feeling of entrapment – and hence the desire for resolution/escape – is created musically by the interval of a minor seventh which is played in a relentless, percussive and unchanging two-bar rhythmic figure between guitar and bass. The drums also contribute to the mood of confinement, playing the same quaver pattern throughout almost the whole song, with the snare on the second and fourth beats and a very gradual crescendo with the toms on the first and third. Together with a lack of dynamic movement, there is an overwhelming feeling of suspense, a desire for something to happen, for the tension to resolve. The first harmonic movement occurs with the phrase 'You're not rid of me yet'. But, like the words themselves, no resolution comes. Rather the music becomes even more unsettling as the bass and guitar move from Am7, to Gm7 to Fm7 and back again, the threat of the lyrics combining with a bar of 3/4 and bar of 5/4 over the omnipresent drum pattern to underpin a feeling of growing unease. This intensifies with the words 'Don't you wish ... ' where there is a complete textural change (a rise in volume, distorted guitar, heavy use of snares, cymbals and a rising pattern on the toms that points the lyrics) The speeding up of the harmonic riff (still with the same three chords) finally encodes a mood of desperation/panic, but a return to the original pattern, and a reiteration of the lyrics confirms that there is no way out.[31]

As Reynolds and Press observe,

> The songs of PJ Harvey dramatise the conflicts of possessing a body, of desiring and being desired, in a way that's sexually charged but not exactly sexy. Polly Harvey has perfected a kind of self-exposure, in lyrics and self-presentation, that uniquely combines seduction and threat, intimacy and estrangement[32]

– or, as Elvis Costello once commented 'a lot of her songs seem to be about blood and fucking'. It is possibly this sense of obsession, not least the mantra-like menace which underpins her lyrics, and the swooping percussiveness of her vocal style that provoked such labels as 'the mad bitch woman from hell' in the May 1994 edition of *Q* magazine. Fellow interviewees Tori Amos and Björk disagreed, recognising more a sense of personal cool – 'a bit like Clint Eastwood; her spirit – everything's understated'.[33]

It was this sense of cool and, possibly, camp humour ('I got my girl and she's a wow, mansize, got my leather boots on') that led to her famous duet with Björk who was receiving three major awards at the February 1994 Brit Awards. Björk had already made three LPs with the Sugarcubes before releasing her solo album *Debut* (1993). It was, as she explains, 'really, really easy to make … I just sat down with a lot of diaries and books and I was almost like an editor. I had so much material to choose from.'[34] The result was a coolly innovative record. Produced by Nellee Hooper (who had previously worked with Soul II Soul, Massive Attack and Sinead O'Connor), the album mixed upbeat love ballads underlain by a clubby house feel ('Violently Happy'), with jazzy ballads ('The Anchor Song') and ambient trance grooves.

Unlike *Little Earthquakes* and *Rid of Me*, which reward repeated listenings, *Debut* is immediately accessible. Not only is Björk's vocal delivery clear – each word audible despite the often quirky delivery – but there is an interesting mix of styles which range from the upbeat narrative of 'There's More to Life This' with its four-on-the-floor house groove and quixotic asides ('we could nick a boat and sneak off to the island'), to a sophisticated jazz style which has more than a passing resemblance to the standards she admired in her teens – 'My Funny Valentine', 'Cry Me a River' ('Just so simple, like pure pop, but in a completely cool way, with all the passion and the heat'.)[35] More specifically, her voice is flexible and this adds tonal colour to such upfront phrases as 'His sense of humour suggests exciting sex' ('Venus as a Boy') and a knowingness to the 'something huge is coming up' of 'Big Time Sexuality'. Low throaty growls are followed by soaring highs and a sensitive feel for word-painting – the intimate little girl voice of 'one day … it will all come true' contrasting with an almost yodel-like delivery on 'I can feel it' that comes dangerously close to quarter-tone clashes against an ambient groove.

Above all, the album has a sensual quality which is largely attributable to the imaginative synths, keyboards and programming of Marius de Vries, the unstinting richness and ingenuity of the instrumental arrangements (harp, Hammond organ, brass, tabla and strings), the minimal rhythms, and shuffling backbeats. It was, as Björk acknowledges,

> the perfect thing. The album had been in my head for ten years, it almost had a life of its own … but then I found Marius – the person

who's perfect with synthesisers – and I could say 'Listen, I want a sound like that fluffy bit on top of a coconut.' And he'd respond, 'You mean like that?' Marius was so good at understanding things like that.[36]

On a more cynical note, I could suggest that *Debut* attempted to corner the lucrative corner of club culture while attracting jazz and indie fans, yet there is little doubt that Björk's career to date has shown her to be a woman in charge. Her interest in production has led to a tight control over the quality and direction of albums; her pop promos are professional and intriguing, and she is well marketed. More specifically, she has had to learn to make decisions, 'to learn to decide "now"! If it wasn't the right decision – me to blame.'[37] It is this ability both to manage her career and maintain a strong musical integrity that separates Björk from the merely commercial. Like Tori Amos, Courtney Love and P.J. Harvey she remains, first and foremost, a musician, a woman who expresses truthfulness to personal experience and community. For me, they are the most significant women singer songwriters of the early 1990s.

NOTES AND REFERENCES

1 Middleton, R. (1996) 'Understanding Pop', MA module, Milton Keynes: Open University, p. 19.
2 See, for example, de Beauvoir, S. (1952) *The Second Sex*, New York: Bantam, and Monique Wittig's discussion 'One is Not Born a Woman', in Abelove, H., Barale, M.A. and Helperin, D.M. (eds) (1993) *The Lesbian and Gay Studies Reader*, London: Routledge, pp. 103–9.
3 See Brooks, A. (1997) *Postfeminism, Cultural Theory and Cultural Forms*, London: Routledge, p. 209.
4 Dyer, R. (1993) *The Matter of Images. Essays on Representation*, London/New York: Routledge, p. 2.
5 Middleton, *op. cit.*, p. 73. I would also acknowledge Simon Frith, *Performing Rites. On the Value of Popular Music*, Oxford: Oxford University Press (Chapter 2), which informs my own discussion.
6 Pavletich, A. (1980) *Sirens of Song*, New York: Da Capo Press, p. 239.
7 Frith, *op. cit.*, p. 19.
8 Meyer, L.B. (1956) *Emotion and Meaning in Music*, London: University of Chicago Press, p. 40.
9 The aeolian, or natural minor, is most often found in the death motifs of heavy metal. It is also used by Madonna in her song 'La Isla Bonita' and its associations with death.
10 Tong, R. (1992) *Feminist Thought. A Comprehensive Introduction*, London: Routledge, p. 111.
11 Grant, L. (1994) 'Groopers in the Sex War', *The Guardian*, London. 22 February.
12 Reynolds, S. and Press, J. (1995) *The Sex Revolts. Gender, Rebellion and Rock 'n' Roll*, London: Serpent's Tail, p. 268.
13 Tori Amos donated the proceeds of the concert and the single, 'Silent All These Years' to the Rape, Abuse and Incest National Network.

14 The reference to walls relates to the Great Wall of China, to the video construction of walls as separate fortresses and to china as a synonym for a tea-service and its relationship to the formal of the tea ceremony, and to the commonplace of the kitchen table, with its cracked cups, where conversations so often take place (china as in 'bring out the best china/best tea service').

15 The interval of a fifth has significance within the hierarchy of sound, the harmonic series and the pentatonic scale. It is associated with Gregorian chant and, hence, mysticism. Within a diatonic frame of reference, parallel fifths create a stark feel, and a sense of equivocation. This is due to the absence of the defining major or minor third.

16 Tori Amos, Notes accompanying the music to *Little Earthquakes*, US Amsco Publications, p. 60.

17 Again, Amos's musical background would suggest itself here in that the opening syllable 'Chi' falls on an *appoggiatura*, a non-essential and unprepared harmony note. Other instances occur, for example, in the Beatles' 'Yesterday'. It is a technique that evokes a mood of thoughtful reflection.

18 Greer, G. (1999) *the whole woman*, London: Transworld Publishers, p. 27.

19 *Q* magazine, May 1994.

20 Mary Daly, cited in Tulip, M. (1990) 'Religion' in Gunew, S. (ed.) *Feminist Knowledge, Critique and Construct*, London: Routledge, p. 233.

21 Malins, S. (1994) 'Tori Amos', *Vox*, May, p. 29.

22 Greer, *op. cit.*, p. 94.

23 Female genital mutilation (FGM) has been condemned as a violation of human rights by the International Conference on Population and Development, the Fourth World Conference on Women in Beijing, the World Health Organisation, UNICEF and the United Nations Family Planning Authority. Male genital mutilation is seldom condemned. *Ibid.*, p. 94.

24 Hester, M. (1992) *Lewd Women and Wicked Witches*. London: Routledge, p. 112.

25 Malins, *op. cit.*, p. 31.

26 I am grateful to Crayton Harrison, a fellow subscriber to Rocklist, for his reply to my question 'What was the concert like?'

27 Reynolds and Press, *op. cit.*, pp. 378–80 cite such examples as Van Morrison's scat soul 'inarticulate speech of the heart', Iggy Pop's bestial howl at the climax of the Stooges' 'TV Eye'. Female artists include Liz Fraser (Cocteau Twins) and Lisa Gerrard (Dead Can Dance) as well as *avant-garde* divas Yoko Ono and Diamanda Galas

28 Raphael, A. (1995) *Never Mind The Bollocks. Women Rewrite Rock*, London: Virago Press, p. xx.

29 Reynolds and Press, *op. cit.*, p. 329.

30 *Ibid.*, p. 339.

31 Thanks to my student Tim Davis whose thoughtful insights inform my own analysis.

32 Reynolds and Press, *op. cit.*, p. 338.

33 Raphael, *op. cit.*, p. 75.

34 *Ibid.*, p. 69.

35 *Ibid.*, p. 72.

36 *Ibid.*, p. 70.

37 *Ibid.*, p. 72

13

ARTIFICE AND THE IMPERATIVES OF COMMERCIAL SUCCESS

From Brit Pop to the Spice Girls

Although Tori Amos, Björk and P.J. Harvey have continued to produce significant albums, the crash entry, in 1994, of Brit Pop into the UK charts seemed to sweep aside the passion and rage of the women singer song-writers, replacing it with a more hip pop rock. Designed to appeal to laddishness, Brit Pop coincided with such TV shows as *Men Behaving Badly* and the increasing popularity of football that culminated in Euro 96 and the 1998 World Cup. Bands such as Oasis (Manchester), Blur (London), Pulp (Sheffield) and the Lightning Seeds (Liverpool) seemed to signify a curious sense of both Britishness and regionalism, and a rootedness in the music of such groups as, for example, the Beatles, the Kinks and the Small Faces. As Amy Raphael rightly observes, 'Brit Pop didn't challenge ... it didn't threaten blokes; it catered instead to lad fantasy, to slam dancing, po-going and gobbing.' To paraphrase, it was the return of the familiar older brother.[1]

For the teenage girl, the major attraction was the boy group, Take That. Formed in September 1990, the group – Howard Donaldson, Robbie Williams, Jason Orange, Gary Barlow and Mark Owen – released their first number one single, 'Pray', in July 1993 and achieved eight no.1 singles over their five-year career. Their performance style, especially in their early videos, was characterised by dance routines, staged in specifically constructed studio spaces with an emphasis on choreographed unison timing. In their first video *Do What You Like* (dir. Ro Newton and Angie Smith),

> the boys dance in leather jackets and lycra cycling shorts. At intervals, they also appear naked, as they lie on the studio floor while having their butts wiped by a female model with a mop. Although the scene set by the video has sexual connotations ... the smiling and jumping of the boys during the dancing produces an overall feeling of good clean fun which is more innocently playful than seriously sexual.[2]

Later videos stress a party mode where the group is joined by others (friends) and where there is an emphasis on the boys at leisure in different locations (the beach, the café bar, a garage and a gym – the traditional space for developing a well-honed body). Despite the shift in emphasis, all Take That videos focus on the spectacle of the male body where the viewer is constantly offered 'areas of intimate flesh'[3] in various stages of undress. Although sexually inviting, the group nevertheless had a homosocial laddishness and, as such, it is not too surprising that they became 'acceptable' idols for pre- and early teenage girls[4] as well as attracting a following among young gay males. Followed by Boyzone, East 17, Upside Down and 3T, boy groups continued to flourish and, as such, it is not too surprising that record labels recognised the potential for reinvesting in what was, at the time, a dormant market segment, the all-girl groups. In retrospect, however, there is little doubt that the arrival of the Spice Girls on to the pop scene stimulated more than a run of top singles and a challenge to the dominance of lad culture. Rather, they introduced the language of independence to a willing audience of pre- and teenage girls – girl power.

'Wannabe', their first single, was released in the autumn of 1996 and was significant in toppling Gary Barlow's debut solo single from the no. 1 chart position and in keeping fellow Take That member Robbie Williams' debut single at no. 2. It was to hold the UK no. 1 spot for seven weeks. Clearly the timing of the release was important. The break-up of Take That had been hinted at for some months and their final single 'How Deep is your Love' and, in particular the accompanying video (dir. Nicholas Brandt), provided a sado-masochistic framework for the 'death' of the group. Barlow, in particular, is singled out by a beautiful but deadly killer dressed, symbolically, in a full-length red dress. Drawing on the castration vocabulary of such films as *Basic Instinct* (1992), his face is scored by the prongs of a fork which is then plunged into his throat. More significantly, he is later shown to die, plummeting over the edge of a cliff, pushed by the enigmatic woman in red. The others, it seems, are soon to follow. The shock ending of the video, where the destruction of the individual body provides an obvious analogy for the death of the group, is in stark contrast to the feelgood mood of 'Wannabe' (June, 1996). Where 'How Deep is your Love' juxtaposed the demand for serious commitment with the threat of mutilation and death, 'Wannabe' highlighted eternal friendship and a sussed attitude towards sexual relationships:

> If you wanna be my lover
> You gotta get with my friends

More specifically, the musical mix of break beats and soul (drawing on Michael Jackson, 'Human Nature', 1983) allowed for a riveting dance routine and performance on *Top of the Pops*. Together with clever and catchy lyrics, not least the invention of such catchphrases as 'Zig-a-zig-ah' for sex, the song, like the image of the group itself, came across as vibrant and contemporary. Without doubt, it was a much higher quality act than contemporary band, Boyzone whose *Top of the Pops* performance of Cat Stevens' 'Matthew and Son' had directly drawn on Take That's 'Babe', with the group sitting on stools, swaying out of time, and miming the simple harmonies. Whatever else, the Spice Girls were well-rehearsed, professional and fun, an ideal group for the approaching school summer holidays. The phrases surrounding the Spice brand ('It's a girl's world – she who dares wins', 'Freedom fighters – Future is female – Spice Revolution') tapped directly into a concept which had been largely untouched by the more militant riot grrrls or, indeed, such traditional girl bands as Bananarama – popular feminism.

As discussed previously, the advent of the term postfeminism in the mid-1980s seemed to imply both an ending and, in retrospect, the emergence of a more upbeat feminism that engaged directly with popular culture and the ways in which this impacted upon women. While traditional agendas were retained (equal pay, crèches, abortion rights etc.), postfeminism seemed to posit a more playful and ironic identity, one which was encapsulated by Mary Russo's evocative phrase 'flaunting of the feminine' and the recognition that 'to put on femininity with a vengeance suggests the power of taking it off'.[5] The concept of masquerade[6] and the possibility of using stereotypical aspects of femininity as a political tool had been given a specific focus by the challenging stance taken by such artists as Annie Lennox, Madonna and k.d. lang and their sexual stylising of butch/femme identities. More specifically, both their performances and the ensuing articles in the popular press resonated with the realisation that feminism itself belonged to the field of popular culture and that it had become a potent agent of change, particularly in the field of popular music. Cyndi Lauper, for example, made a strong feminist statement in her video for 'Girls Just Want to Have Fun' (1983) with the album (*She's So Unusual*) reaching no. 4 and selling more than 4.5 million copies. By the 1990s, the issues surrounding feminism had surfaced in such films as *Thelma and Louise*, in Susan Faludi's *Backlash* and Naomi Wolf's *The Beauty Myth*, but it was clear that many of the clichés surrounding feminism since the 1970s (especially the association with separatism and, at tabloid level, the omnipresent connotations of 'burn your bra') were still causing many to distance themselves from the women's movement and its politics. Thus, while such notions as independence and self-confidence were acceptable, discussions of gender-specific roles, identity and representation (not least within popular music) were often perceived as *heavy,* resulting in what appeared at the time, to be a backlash against feminism itself.

The impact of the Spice Girls, then, was to provide a new twist to the feminist discourse of power and subjectivity. By telling their fans that feminism is necessary and fun, that it is part of everydayness, and that girls

216

should challenge rather than accept traditional constraints – 'What you looking at boy? Can you handle a Spice Girl? – they sold the 1990s as 'a girl's world' and presented the 'future as female'. As Catherine Driscoll tellingly asks 'when did any form of feminism become the image of a pop group ... can anything feminist be so prominently popular (even for a short time)'?[7] It is not insignificant here that all five Spice Girls have a different image, a different personality, so giving an impression of independence within a group setting. Postmodernism is, after all, largely concerned with identity, that is, an identity constructed out of a recognition of otherness and difference, 'a politics which embraces a recognition of the multiple, pregnant, and contradictory aspects of both our individual and collective identities'.[8] For the young teenager in a multicultural society this is significant. During a period when belonging, being part of the gang, depends upon conformity to the norm, the emergence of the Spice Girls provided access to five different 'girls' who nevertheless were committed 'friends' and who shared a similar drive to succeed and, significantly, have fun *en route* – sexy, determined Geri, scary Mel B with her frizzed hair and pierced tongue, sporty Mel C with her tracksuit bottoms, sweet pig-tailed Emma and posh Victoria in her designer-label clothes. Moreover, it seemed from the onset, that the identification with a pre- and early teenage girl audience was encapsulated both by the adoption of nicknames and the collective 'gang' name itself. Spice Girls are not Spice Sisters (despite the friendship angle) nor Spice Mothers.

It is, perhaps, stating the obvious to note that sisters/mothers have specific associations for this particular age group. Sisters within the family structure may fight and often do not identify with shared pop star idols. As McRobbie and Garber observed in 1975, 'Teenybopper culture offers girls a chance to define themselves as different from and apart from both their younger and older counterparts. They are no longer little girl and not yet teenage girls.'[9] Hence the need for the mainstream market to provide an unrolling list of potential 'fantasy' figures with whom to identify. While these have most often been boys with a certain degree of effeminacy (from Tab Hunter, Cliff Richard, the early 'mop top' Beatles and, more recently boy groups) young female stars have been less significant – although such figures as Kylie Minogue, Cathy Dennis and Bananarama have proved notable exceptions. Similarly, the challenge to parental authority during puberty would equally situate the term mother as outsider, at best someone who is loving and supportive but nevertheless old. This is tacitly acknowledged in the opening to the Spice Girls' single 'Mama' – 'she used to be my only enemy and never let me free, catching me in places where I know I shouldn't be ... '. It is interesting to note, however, that the negative associations of mother are quickly replaced by a 'but now ... ' which prefixes the more friendly relationship encouraged by the Spice Girls – mother as part of an extended gang which also includes the 'hippy mother' and 'academic big sisters' in feminism, Madonna, and Neneh Cherry (famous for her debut solo LP *Raw Like Sushi* (1989) and for performing on stage while pregnant).[10]

The contribution of the media to the success of the Spice Girls is well documented. In a nutshell, early coverage tended towards the projection of a fun-loving girl band who appeared to take on 'laddish' values. ' "Do the Spice Girls have a message for the good readers of Arena?" They answer as one "Get yer knobs out" ' (*Arena*, January 1997). *Sky* magazine renamed them, according to image – Glam, Raucous, Baby, Sporty and Spice Fatale. Meanwhile, tabloids printed columns on Geri's past as a page three model. The most serious piece of journalism was on the fact that the band had pronounced Margaret Thatcher to be the greatest woman ever and, as such, a true Spice Girl (*The Spectator*, December 1996). Interviews revealed that it was her personal pride in Englishness that they admired, a point which is reflected in their own regionalism and a vow never to live anywhere but England – a dig at supergroups such as the Rolling Stones.

To an extent, then, it would appear that media coverage was identifying and constructing a more tabloid-defined audience with an interest in sexual, rather than musical, performance and, indeed, the cover for their first album shows Geri dressed in a red pvc dress which, in other contexts, might well suggest s/m. It is also apparent that *Sky* magazine's survey on 'who is the nation's favourite Spice Girl' and which yielded such reasons for preference as 'big tits and luscious lips', 'she's a little peach' and 'because she's right filthy looking' added to the impression that the group were situated within the traditional page three bimbo scene.[11] However, it is apparent that the girls' ability to deal with the press, and hence, with men generally, evidenced a brash confidence that was attractive to their teenage fans. They are forthcoming, willing to talk, challenging rather than negotiating the space more frequently given to women within the male-defined world of the music business and humorously debunking such contemporary groups as Oasis who Geri termed 'the Spice Girls in drag'. Of equal significance they are demonstrably wild, overturning tables and streaking through hotel corridors (*Wannabe* video), but sensible, in control, advocating safe sex 'Be a little wiser baby, put it on, put it on' ('Two Becomes One') – good advice when research shows that single mothers are reaching an all-time high in the UK, and that sexually transmitted diseases are on the increase. As a news commentator recently explained, 'This is not due to British girls having more sex at a younger age than others in Europe, but rather that they do not use condoms' (BBC News, May 14 1999). Coupled with 'Say You'll Be There', where the Spice Girls decide 'we should be friends' not lovers, the message comes through clearly that relationships can be channelled and controlled by the girl – that this is 'cool'.

Such points are also demonstrated in fanzine articles in Spice Girl magazines where there is again an emphasis on stating where they come from and what they stand for. For the teenage girl this is significant. The Spice Girls are both streetwise and quick to acknowledge that each member of the group has separate strengths, that these are valued, and that collectively this gives them strength. 'What I think is fan-fucking-tastic about us is that we are not perfect and we have made a big success of ourselves ... ', 'We were all individually beaten down ... Collectively, we've got something going. Individually, I don't think we'd be that great.'[12] There is also a shared recognition that parents' beliefs often hold back a child, 'parents and then the child's reception at school' and that classes in self-esteem, self-motivation might help young people to branch out and adapt more to the 1990s' entrepreneurial society.[13]

Meanwhile for the pre-teen there are hair bands and socks, gloves, scarves, sweatshirts and an opportunity to identify/be their favourite personality – Sporty Mel C, Sexy Geri, Sweet Emma, Scary Mel B or Posh Victoria. To an extent, processes of identification have not significantly changed. As McRobbie and Garber observed in 1975,

> young pre-teen girls have access to less freedom than their brothers. Because they are deemed to be more at risk on the streets from attack, assault, or even abduction, parents tend to be more protective of their daughters ... Teenybopper culture takes these restrictions into account (and can be) ... quite easily accommodated into school-time or leisure-time spent in the home ... .[14]

The situation in the 1990s has, if anything, become more restrictive for the young girl as even the traditional 'freedom' to walk to and from school with friends has now been increasingly superseded by the child being taken to and from school by an older sibling and/or parent. It is also evident that the cost of joining the Spice Girls' commercially based sub-culture can be high. With the Spice Girls Style Guide 'tell(ing) ya just how you can copy the Spicies ultra cool Girl Power image' the pressure was on acquiring an identifiable image. Major stores were quick to capitalise on the desire to wear comparable outfits to the Spice Girls and advice was offered on how you could find less expensive versions of designer wear at high street supermarkets if you wanted your daughter to remain part of the club.[15]

The tendency for young girls to define themselves as part of a fan community is obviously not new. However, the emphasis on forming an active feminine identity which, in the 1970s relied largely on the ability to engage with magazines, radio, TV and the associated fantasies constructed around individual stars, shifted. In particular, the Spice Girls' personal interface with their young audience and their commitment to their fans was evidenced in their major television appearances with mums and daughters and their hit song 'Mama' ('Mama I love you, Mama I care, Mama I love you, my friend, my friend'). On a more informal level, there was also a willingness to be ambushed by fans. As Philip Norman observes,

I can see Mel B's Afro hair nodding as she hugs each of them in turn. Mel C is hemmed in by a further group at the reception desk. 'So long – 'ave a great time tonight,' she finally says, so attentive to them that she heads for the wrong exit.[16]

More specifically, their ability to communicate effectively resulted in, what seems, a commonsense assumption that girls ruled. As a manufactured, vocal pop group, then, it seemed that they were fulfilling the criteria of being 'sussed chicks who not only look cool, but … know how to exercise a bit of Girl Power'.[17] As the cover to *Spice* states, 'this vibe is contagious, feel it, catch it', a sentiment that is hammered home in both the single and the video to 'Wannabe'.

As anyone interested in advertising knows only too well, the impact of a product upon a market depends largely on its unique selling point and the correct identification of a target audience. It is thus interesting to observe that the key words in the vocals – tell, want and really – are accompanied by footage of the Spice Girls which projects both a feeling of untutored individuality and a mood of fun. They are 'everygirl' out on the town looking for some 'zig-a-zig-ah'. More specifically, a feeling of bantering girl-talk is achieved as the words are sung/chanted by the individual members of the group:

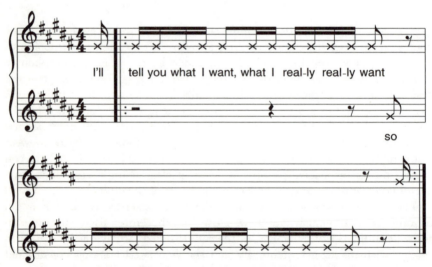

tell me what you want, what you real-ly real-ly want

It is a 'conversation' that the majority of teenage girls recognise and, as such, there is a complicity which is emphasised by the Spice Girls coming across as untrained (in that their voices appear natural), individualistic (a point enhanced by the fact that all five perform equal singing roles, rather than the more traditional lead/backing vocals arrangement), and slightly outrageous (in their teasing lead into 'zig-a-zig- ah'). Visually this is under-pinned by their 'caught in the act' behaviour in the *Wannabe* video – throwing the guestlist in the air and mockingly surrounding the doorman, running through the hotel attempting to provoke the onlookers into having a good time, their actions followed by a lunging portable camera to enhance the sense of 'this is really happening', the seeming 'naturalness' of Mel B joining the first chorus late.

Musically, the song is energised by a highly syncopated synthesised riff:

and, for example, the way in which the repetitive lyrics and rhythm are heightened (in the bridge) by a denial of the onbeat. This is picked up in the video where the camera moves rapidly from singer to singer before the release of tension on the word 'zig-a-zig-ah':

It is, as one of my students observed, a comparable experience to the modern blockbuster 'rollercoaster ride' where pleasure is mainly gained through movement and special effects. In the video this is achieved by the impression of continuous action and changes in frame rate. Special effects and the good-time feel of the music thus combine to produce a video which is well produced with a varied texture. The rap intro ('Tell me want you want, what you really, really want') is also noteworthy in

recalling the interface between (British Prime Minister) John Major's crumbling Conservative government and Tony Blair's enticing new Labour one. Blair's victory, indeed, seemed assured after he proved he knew the names of three Spice Girls whereas poor benighted Major could identify only two.[18]

However, despite the fact that 'Wannabe' sold two million copies and won three awards in the *Smash Hits* poll and that between June 1996 and December 1997 the Girls had no. 1 singles in thirty-seven countries, commentators generally remarked on the fact that the Spice Girls were a manufactured group and hence lacking in talent and doomed to plummet. In particular, it was rumoured that they didn't really sing, that they weren't real performers, that their film *Spiceworld – the Movie* was simply a weak pastiche of the Beatles' *A Hard Day's Night*, that their second album was not achieving mass sales on a par with the first, and that their manager, Simon Fuller, had been having an affair with Emma. It was a rumour that could only cause damage to the 'everygirl' image of the group. Thus, despite having made the Spice Girls a global attraction and creating multimillion pound sponsorship deals with such trademarks as Sony, Benneton, Asda, Pepsi and BT, Fuller was sacked, and the group announced they would be self-managing. Then, on the eve of their appearance on the British national lottery television show Geri (Ginger Spice) walked out, giving rise to further speculation as to the future of the group. In particular, the question was raised as to whether the Spice Girls would prove to be yet another instance of the dubious pleasure associated with building up celebrities 'only for the savage pleasure of tearing them down again'.[19]

In retrospect Geri Halliwell's departure provided a real opportunity for the Spice Girls to prove that they were rather more than a manufactured group with dubious singing abilities. As Emma explained in the *Sunday Times News Review* (21 June 1998) 'It was something we felt like we needed to do as a group ... To go on to the next stage. It was like going on but going back to our roots ... . We wanted to take back that responsibility for ourselves.' The first decision was that Geri would not be replaced. As a group they were too tight. Management roles gradually evolved, with Mel B becoming 'tour monitor', Emma taking on personnel and charity, Victoria merchandising and sponsorship and Mel C liaising with record companies, providing advance notice of new recordings and videos. It seemed yet another example of the group's emphasis on individualism – doing what you're best at – a point that was reflected in their third album which featured both individual and ensemble tracks. More specifically, the tour continued, proving conclusively that they could sing on stage. As Philip Norman observed,

> a teeming vista of excitedly chattering, jumping and wriggling seven and eight year olds ... (saw) an act pulling out all the stops to prove they really are what people said they couldn't possibly be ... .

Sporty Spice's voice in particular has the instant, turbo-charged power of a pigtailed Joe Cocker. The evening's high spot is her duet with Scary of the Annie Lennox/Aretha Franklin number 'Sisters Are Doing It for Themselves ... the finale, the Sister Sledge song 'We Are Family'. And you'd better believe it.[20]

There is little doubt that the Spice Girls have been one of the major musical phenomena of the 1990s. Commercially they have had a massive impact, with hit songs, videos, sell-out tours and an array of merchandising. Scary Spice's bare midriff has now become *de rigeur* for teenage girls, and pierced navels and tattoos are in fashion. Arguably, it is this success that has accounted for both musical derision – not musical, not artistic, 'a cartoon feminist pop group'[21] – and the accusation that they are defined by consumption and hence feeding the insatiable desire for image-related paraphernalia that seems endemic to the 1990s.[22] Two facts in particular proved irksome to purists and academics alike: they were primarily targeted at girls and they incorporated a somewhat sloppy feminist message into their marketing.

It is obvious to those who have followed the Spice Girls' career that any implication of passive mediation (they are a manufactured group, they are marketed as 'for girls') seriously underestimates their own sense of purpose. As such, both the identification with a pre- and teenage girl market and their espousal of feminism are rather more than well-targeted sales gimmicks. Similarly, while the allegation of 'manufactured' can be mitigated by the argument that the five original Spice Girls were all professional by the age of seventeen or eighteen, with Emma starting at the age of three, this does seem a somewhat defensive strategy. Rather, it would seem that the old debates surrounding authenticity and cultural value were being resurrected to pass judgement on the Spice Girls and that popular, commercial success was again being associated with the ideological evils of mass culture.

It is interesting here to refer briefly to the girl groups of the late 1950s/early 1960s who also provided a point of identification for teenage girls. The Chantels, in particular, were significant in being the first young Black female group to emerge in what had previously been a predominantly male arena (the Valentines, Cadillacs, the Moonglows). While there had been other all-female groups in the 1950s (the Miller Sisters, the Three Tons of Joy, the Hamilton Sisters, the Beverley Sisters) these tended to be women rather than teenage girls. The age of the Chantels' (the girls were all in their early teens at the time of their first release) is thus important and their pioneering of 'girl-talk', which in turn influenced such groups as the Shirelles, the Crystals and the Ronettes, was to epitomise the sound of girl group rock which flourished between 1958 and 1965. However, despite or, indeed because of, their success, girl groups were largely castigated as 'producer's music' (many songs having been written by contract songwriters, hired by music publishers Don Kirshner and Al Nevins, and housed in the 'Brill Building' in New York). The main allegation was that women in the girl group era had no creative input, or part in the composition, lyric writing and production of the songs they sang, and that all the girlgroup songs were written by men, so invalidating any sense of girl-talk authenticity. It is important to note then, that almost all of the songs sung by the most popular groups were written by songwriting duos which included women – Carole King with Gerry Goffin, Ellie Greenwich with Jeff Barry, Cynthia Weil with Barry Mann. More specifically, the two songs released on the Chantels' first single 'He's Gone' and 'The Plea' (1957) were composed by fifteen-year-old Arlene Smith, albeit arranged by record producer Richard Barrett.

Like the Spice Girls (whose names appear on their song credits), the majority of the Chantels' songs were concerned with relationships, albeit within the dominant codes of romance (lost love as in 'Goodbye to Love', 'He's Gone', 'Memories') or the hope of finding love ('Every Night I Pray', 'Whatever You Are'). Sadly, due to the extent of racism at the time, Black groups such as the Chantels were given virtually no publicity on radio and it is generally accepted that the Shirelles heralded what is now viewed as the true beginnings of the girl group era, popularising the girl group sound, look and lyrical style and having their first no. 1 hit with 'Will You Still Love Me Tomorrow', a curiously logical follow-up to their previous release 'Tonight's the Night'. Their song was significant in homing in on the problems of 'going the whole way' and in addressing 'the dilemmas of sex and love, of anxiety and elation, of rationality and passion so familiar to all girls growing up and yet usually so carefully glossed over in pop'.[23] In contrast to their opposite numbers, the male teen idols, whose songs seemed to concentrate on such issues as eternal love and devotion, there was a direct engagement with the complexities of teenage emotions and musically the songs were well crafted and vocally engaging.

There are, then, parallels with the Spice Girls, not least in the group's ability to tap directly into the emotions of a young teenage audience, albeit tempered by a romantic vocabulary that generally assumes a 'happy ever after' once the girl has found her own true love. Clearly the Spice Girls' sense of controlling the situation is missing as evidenced in the Shirelles' hit 'Tomorrow' where the big question of whether the relationship will last or 'will my heart be broken when the night meets the morning sun' contrasts with the more pragmatic approach of 'if you want my future, forget my past' ('Wannabe'). This sense of being controlled is equally evidenced in the Shirelles' dependence upon their producer, Luther Dixon, who had almost total artistic control over their output, choosing the songs, the arrangements and controlling the sound produced.[24] In 1962, Dixon decided to leave the Scepter recording label. Not surprisingly, the Shirelles were obliged to continue recording with the label on a new low-budget production policy.

Their popularity and sales declined, largely due to poor quality recordings and arrangements, and although they were arguably the most successful girl group of their time in the US, they had little financial gain. Moreover, the money they had earned (supposedly held in trust by record label owner Florence Greenberg) was nonexistent as all profits had been expended for recording costs, promotion, touring, arrangers' fees and so on.

Again, there are useful points of comparison. The Spice Girls' first managers, Bob and Chris Herbert, who had the original idea of promoting an all-girl group who appealed equally to boys and girls, and who had selected the five originals after an extensive mass audition process, had subjected the five to an intensive course of singing and dancing. The first indication of girl power came 'when the Herberts became so much dust beneath Spicy platform heels'.[25] The sacking of manager Fuller similarly reflected a determination to control their own destinies and, in a society and business which remains dominated by sexism and, in the former instance, class, they proved that they were able to make choices about their lifestyle and work and remain commercially on top, clearly a big step forward from the 1950s. Parallels can also be drawn with Madonna whose early reception by feminist writers was flavoured by such castigating terms as formulaic, trivial, commercial and shallow, but who was later hailed as a heroine of self-actualisation. Certainly, there is a similar musical exuberance and humour which confirms my premise that feminism is not only for the serious and which focuses the issue of what constitutes a feminist agenda in the 1990s.

It is not irrelevant here to reflect briefly on Julie Burchill's observations on why girls have finally overtaken 'complacent, confident boys' (*Guardian Weekend*, 4 April 1998). She attributes this to the impact of lad culture which, 'while purporting to be pro-male has, in fact, acted as feminism's Trojan Horse ... helping boys to remain stuck in an infantile, obsessively anti-cerebral state and still feel cool'.[26] The Spice Girls, then, provided an ideal counterpart and their identification with, and promotion of, girls heralded a streetwise recognition that being empowered does not necessarily have to involve being top in maths exams. Rather it means taking control of your life and, significantly, promoting this as *fun*. And herein lies the rub. Second-wave feminism has had to take itself seriously. Women have had to (and still do) confront inequality, and pop stars are no exception. However, as my book has argued so far, there are many agendas with which to engage and which can loosely be grouped under nice girl/bad girl. Since the advent of punk, for example, girls have increasingly assaulted the 'phallusy' of male supremacy. From Vivienne Westwood, Chrissie Hynde, through to Madonna, Courtney Love and Björk there are countless examples of 'girls behaving badly'. It is arguably a more problematic course than that taken by the Spice Girls and, as Germaine Greer sagely points out 'the career of the individual bad girl is likely to be a brief succession of episodes of chaotic drinking, casual sex, venereal infection and unwanted pregnancy, with consequences she will have to struggle with all her life'.[27] Despite the Spice Girls' claim to be indebted to Madonna and their dubious advice 'be a spice girl not a nice girl', it is clear that their platform heels are planted firmly on the good side of the line and that their politics and mode of communication are shaped by the evils of conspicuous consumption. At the same time their specific commodification, not least on the videos, posits power and action: 'don't' just talk about it, live it'.

Arguably, the most significant point here is the fact that the 'living it' is immersed in pop culture and that the Spice Girls' understanding of feminism is somewhat fragmentary. As Kathy Acker reports in her now famous interview with the Spice Girls, they cite Freud but openly acknowledge their lack of political education and their scepticism towards politicians, the media and 'intellectuals chatting in bathrooms'.[28] 'I didn't really know that much, you know, history, but I knew about the suffragettes. They fought. It wasn't long ago.'[29] Their relationship to feminism, then, is largely informed by their personal experience of life. It thus involves strong views on racism, on the need for motivation and self-esteem and the fact that 'it's wrong to have to fit into a mould or role in order to succeed'.[30] It is not too surprising, then, that as a group who believe strongly in the importance of communication that their feminist agenda is essentially concerned with the everyday life of their young fans. It is equally unsurprising that their views, like the lyrics to their songs, are expressed in the vernacular – 'girl power', 'girls are best'. The argument that the Spice Girls are cartoon feminists is, then, less dismissive than it may at first appear. Thus while the politics surrounding the Spice Girls are arguably characterised by struggle – struggle over value, meaning, importance, ownership – their effect on the emerging culture of girl power as a distinct sphere of everyday activity is undeniably significant. In particular, they have shaped and constructed both an oral culture and a particular image of the 1990s. As Germaine Greer writes in her discussion of girl power: 'Pop is followed by print is followed by video and film, and nothing that a parent generation can do will have any effect than to increase the desirability of the girlpower way of life.'[31]

The link between pop and a way of life is significant. As Richard Middleton points out, pop is central to the construction of identity – 'it helps us to feel who we are ... (it) skirts the traps of realism and determinism, as well as idealism, by insisting that the music's meanings and effects are not only constituted (by socially formed tastes, needs, positions) but also constitutive ... '. He builds his argument with reference to Simon Frith's contention that 'pop constructs our sense of identity through the experiences it offers of the body, time, and sociability, experiences which enable us to place ourselves in imaginative cultural narratives'.[32] Clearly the observation that pop offers membership to imaginary communities is not new. What is more significant to any discussion of the Spice Girls is the point that 'music ... suggests that our social circumstances are not immutable'.[33] Their emphasis on 'being who you wanna' has demonstrably shaped the experience of their young fans and, while girl power has limitations, the fact that the Spice Girls have shown how to take control of their lives is important. More specifically, they have presented a more pragmatic and practical side of feminism, one which has been hailed by working-class young women who were previously alienated by its underlying concepts and middle-class language –

> Next time a bloke feels your arse, patronises you, slags off your body – generally treats you like shit – forget the moral high ground, forget he's been instilled with patriarchy and is a victim too, forget rationale and debate. Just deck the bastard.[34]

The use of the vernacular is important in returning the reader to the politics of pop. The Spice Girls are not profound. Their music, like their videos and live performance, is pure pop essentially concerned with pleasure and fun but tempered by an acute sense of humour and a feisty V-for-Victory sign. As one student observed, part of the reason why they are so popular is because they present the world in inverted commas. Everything is 'nice and happy'. Moreover, they have made a difference, not least in being the first mixed-race all-girl vocal group to front the tensions between individuality and collective identity that are intrinsic to both 1990s' feminism and pop music. As such, they have moved the twin goalposts of equality and difference one step further.

NOTES AND REFERENCES

1 Raphael, A. (1995) *Never Mind the Bollocks. Women Rewrite Rock*, London: Virago Press, p. xxv.
2 P. McDonald (1997) 'Feeling and Fun. Romance, Dance and the Performing Male Body in the Take That videos', in Whiteley, S. (ed.) *Sexing the Groove: Popular Music and Gender*, London: Routledge, p. 287.
3 *Ibid.*, p. 293.
4 As discussed previously, there has traditionally been an acceptance of boy-next-door appeal and an emphasis on codes of romance. It is therefore not too surprising that the solo careers of Gary Barlow and Robbie Williams have stressed this angle, albeit that Williams has also maintained a strong fun angle in his live performances.
5 Russo, M. 'Female Grotesques: Carnival and theory', in Reynolds, S. and Press, J. (1995) *The Sex Revolts. Gender, Rebellion and Rock 'n' Roll*, London: Serpent's Tail, p. 316.
6 See Doane, M. (1982) 'Film and the Masquerade: Theorizing the Female Spectator', *Screen* 23 (3–4): pp. 74–88.
7 Driscoll, C. 'Girl Culture, Revenge and Global Capitalism. Cybergirls, Riot Grrls, Spice Girls', unpublished paper, p. 7.
8 Nicholson, L.J. (ed.) (1990) *Feminism/Postmodernism*, London: Routledge, p. 12.
9 McRobbie, A. and Garber, J. (1997) 'Girls and Subcultures' in Gelder, K. and Thornton, S. (eds) *The Subcultures Reader*, London: Routledge, p. 120.

10 Musically, sister/mother also have strong connotations, Soul Sister being one such example which predicates a particular style of singing. It is interesting to note here that the Spice Girls' choice of 'We Are Family' (West Palm Beach, Coral Sky Amphitheatre, June 1998) came as an affirmation of sisterly closeness after the departure of Geri Halliwell. The Spice Girls also evoke memories of the 1950s' vocal group the Beverley Sisters, whose warning advice 'Lord help the mister, who comes between me and my sister' is resurrected in 'God help the mister that comes between me and my sisters' ('Love Thing'). Although the rap intro to 'Wannabe' is the nearest the Spice Girls come to sounding like Spice Mothers, the feisty image of Geri came closest to the red-hot mama image of vaudeville. While this is containable in a group that also includes the binary, sweet Emma, it is apparent that such connotations have been tempered by a more contemporary identity – a loving wonderwoman who also happens to come across as sexy ('Men are so easily led aren't they? It's nothing to do with me – just a pair of tits that's all' – Geri, Sky TV, 1997) The mother image is also picked up on in Victoria's recent pregnancy and here her live performances reflect the Girls' admiration for Neneh Cherry.

11 In England, the tabloid newspaper *The Sun* prints a daily photograph of a topless model. The derogatory term 'bimbo' has been coined to describe a young woman with a 'good' body but a decided lack of intellect.

12 Acker, K. (1997) 'All Girls Together', *Weekend Guardian*, 3 May, p. 16.

13 *Ibid.*, p. 16.

14 McRobbie and Garber *op. cit.*, p. 119.

15 TV fashion shows were quick to pick up on the desire to 'look like your favourite Spice Girl'. Advice was provided on buying comparable clothes with models showing items of clothing from designer label to such high street stores as C&A. The main point of discussion appeared to centre around how low down the price bracket you could go and still have the right effect. This was picked up in the documentary-style feedback from mothers and daughters.

16 Norman, P. (1998) 'Gone But Not Forgotten', *Sunday Times News Review*, 21 June, p. 1.

17 *The Spice Girls Style Guide* (1997) Dennis Oneshots Ltd, p. 32.

18 Norman, *op. cit.*, p. 1.

19 *Ibid.*, p. 2.

20 *Ibid.*

21 Comment in *Melody Maker,* quoted in Golden, A. (1997) *The Spice Girls. An Uncensored Account*, London: New Books Press, p. xvi.

22 Designer labels and, most recently, the limited number of Manchester United shirts (worn for their triple win – the League and Cup double, followed by their 2:1 win at Barcelona in their match against Bayern Munich in the Champions Cup final) have created a large and expensive market. This includes the majority of Spice Girl fans, significantly drawn from the eight to twelve age range who were quick to buy the associated merchandising, hence drawing criticism about the group's marketing tactics.

23 Greig, C. (1989) *Will You Still Love Me Tomorrow*, London: Virago Press, p. 30.

24 Gaar, *op. cit.*, p. 36.

25 Norman, *op. cit.*, p. 2.

26 Burchill, J. (1998) 'The Age of Reason – I Knew I Was Smart', *Guardian Weekend*, 4 April, p. 7.

27 Greer, G. (1999) *the whole woman*, London: Transworld Publishers, p. 310.

28 Acker, *op. cit.*, p. 19.

29 *Ibid.*, p. 16.

30 *Ibid.*, p. 16.
31 Greer, *op. cit.*, p. 319.
32 Middleton, *op. cit.*, p. 73 and Frith, S. (1996) *Performing Rites*, Oxford: Oxford University Press, Chapter 2.
33 *Ibid.*, p. 74.
34 Greer, *op. cit.*, p. 318.

SELECTED DISCOGRAPHY

10,000 Maniacs
Blind Man's Zoo, Elektra (1989)
Earth Pressed Flat, Barnone (1999)
Hope Chest (The Fredonia Recordings 1982–1983), Elektra
In My Tribe, Elektra (1987)
Love among the Ruins, Geffen (1997)
Our Time in Eden, Elektra (1992)
The Wishing Chair, Elektra (1989)

All Saints
All Saints, London (1999)
All Saints (The Remix Album), London (1999)

Tori Amos
Boys for Pele, East West (1997)
From the Choirgirl Hotel, East West (1998)
Little Earthquakes, East West (1992)
To Venus and Back, Atlantic (1999)
Under the Pink, East West (1994)

Fiona Apple
Tidal, Columbia (1996)

Joan Armatrading
Hearts and Flowers, A&M (1990)
Joan Armatrading, A&M (1992)
The Key, A&M (1986)
Me, Myself, I, Spectrum (1993)
Secret Secrets, A&M (1985)
Shapes and Sizes, RCA (1995)
The Shouting Stage, A&M (1988)
Show Some Emotion, A&M (1992)
Sleight of Hand, A& M (1986)

Square the Circle, A&M (1992)
To the Limit, A&M (1998)
Track Record, A&M (1984)
Walk under Ladders, A&M (1988)
What's Inside, RCA (1995)
Whatever's for Us, Castle (1989)

The Au Pairs
Equal but Different, RPM (1994)
Live in Berlin, Essential (1996)
Playing with a Different Sex, RPM (1992)
Sense and Sensuality, RPM (1993)

Babes In Toyland
Fontanelle, Southern (1992)
Nemesister, Warner Bros. (1995)
Painkillers, Southern (1993)

Joan Baez
Anyday Now, Vanguard (1989)
Baptism, Vanguard (1995)
Blowin' Away, Legacy Records (1990)
Brothers in Arms, Gold Castle (1991)
Carry It On, Vanguard (1996)
Come From The Shadows, A&M (1988)
David's Album, Vanguard (1995)
Diamonds And Rust, A&M (1975)
Farewell Angelina, Vanguard (1990)
From Every Stage, A&M, (1993)
Gone From Danger, Guardian/Angel (1997)
Gracias A La Vida, A&M (1994)
Honest Lullaby, Legacy Records (1990)
Joan, Vanguard (1989)
Play Me Backwards, Guardian/Angel (1996)
Recently, Guardian/Angel (1996)

Ring Them Bells, Guardian/Angel (1995)
Speaking Of Dreams, Guardian/Angel (1996)

Bananarama
Bananarama, London (1984)
Deep Sea Skiving, London (1987)
Please Yourself, London (1992)
Pop Life, London (1991)
True Confessions, London (1982)
Wow, London (1987)

Beverley Sisters
Green Fields, Music For Pleasure (1996)
Sisters,Sisters, Polyphonic (1999)
Sparkle, K-Tel (1985)

Bikini Kill
Pussy Whipped, Wiiija (1993)
Rejects All American, Kill Rock Sisters (1996)
Yeah, Yeah, Yeah, Kill Rock Sisters (1994)

Björk
Debut, One Little Indian (1999)
Gling Glo, One Little Indian (1997)
Homogenic, One Little Indian (1997)
Jalamanta, Man's Ruin (1999)
Post, One Little Indian (1999)
Telegram, OneLittle Indian (1999)

Blondie
Autoamerican, Chrysalis (1994)
The Best of Blondie, Chrysalis (1988)
Blondie, Chrysalis (1994)
Eat to the Beat, Chrysalis (1992)
The Hunter, Chrysalis (1994)
No Exit, Beyond/RCA (1999)
Parallel Lines, Chrysalis (1994)
Plastic Letters, Chrysalis (1994)

Kate Bush
The Dreaming, EMI (1991)
Hounds of Love, EMI (1990)
The Kick Inside, EMI (1994)
Lionheart, EMI (1994)
Never for Ever, EMI (1990)
The Red Shoes, EMI (1993)

The Sensual World, EMI (1989)

B*witched
Awake and Breathe, Gloworm/Epic (1999)
*B*witched*, Gloworm/Epic (1998)

Catatonia
Catatonia, Crai (1993)
Equally Cursed and Blessed, Blanco y Negro (1999)
International Velvet, Blanco y Negro (1998)
Way Beyond Blue, Blanco y Negro (1996)

Tracy Chapman
Crossroads, Elektra (1989) 190
Matters of the Heart, Elektra (1992) 190
New Beginnings, Elektra (1995)
Tracy Chapman, Elektra (1988)

Neneh Cherry
Homebrew, Circa (1992)
Man, Hut (1996)
Raw Like Sushi, Circa (1992)

The Corrs
Forgiven Not Forgotten, Atlantic (1996)
Talk On Corners, Laval/Atlantic (1997)

P.J. Harvey
Dry, Too Pure (1992)
4 Track Demos, Island (1993)
Is This Desire, Island (1998)
Rid of Me, Island (1993)
To Bring You My Love, Island (1995)
To Bring You My Love/The B-Sides Album, Island (1995)

Lauryn Hill
The Miseducation of Lauryn Hill, Ruff House (1998)

Huggy Bear
Taking the Rough with the Smooth, Wiiija (1993)
Weaponry Listens to Love, Wiiija (1994)

231

Natalie Imbruglia
Left of the Middle, RCA (1997)

Janis Joplin
Anthology, Columbia (1997)
Can't Go Home Again, Legend (1998)
Cheap Thrills, CBS (1992)
Cheaper Thrills, Edsel (1990)
Do What You Love, Legend (1998)
Farewell Song, Columbia (1997)
Kozmic Blues, CBS (1989)
Live at the Winterland 1968, Columbia (1998)
Live at Woodstock 1969, Koch (1993)
Magic of Love, ITM (1992)
Pearl, Columbia (1999)

Carole King
City Streets, Capitol (1989)
Fantasy, Epic (1997)
Jazzman, Tring (1992)
Music, Pickwick/Sony Collector's Choice (1994)
Pearls/Time Gone By, Connoisseur Collection (1994)
Really Rosie, Legacy (1999)
Speeding Time, Atlantic (1996)
Sweet Season, Tring (1992)
Tapestry, Epic (1999)
Wrap Around Joy, Thunderbolt (1992)

L7
The Beauty Process, Slash (1998)
From Osaka or Omaha, Man's Ruin (1999)
Hungry for Stink, Slash (1997)
L7, Epitaph (1992)
Smell the Magic, Sub Pop (1995)

k.d. lang
Absolute Torch and Twang, Sire (1994)
All You Can Eat, Sire (1995)
Angel with a Lariat, Sire (1988)
Drag, Sire (1997)
Even Cowgirls Get the Blues, Sire (1993)
Ingenue, Sire (1996)
Shadowland (The Owen Bradley Sessions), Sire (1988)

Cyndi Lauper
A Night to Remember, Epic (1992)
Hat Full of Stars, Epic (1996)
She's So Unusual, Epic (1989)
Sisters of Avalon, Epic (1997)
True Colours, Portrait (1990)

Annie Lennox/Eurythmics
1984, Virgin (1984)
Be Yourself Tonight, RCA (1985)
Diva, RCA (1999)
In The Garden, RCA (1987)
Luminous Basement RCA (1980)
Medusa, RCA (1999)
Peace, RCA (1999)
Reality Effect Logo (1979)
Revenge, RCA (1986)
Savage, RCA (1987)
Sweet Dreams (Are Made Of This), RCA (1999)
Touch, RCA (1999)
Touch Dance, RCA (1999)
We Too Are One, RCA (1989)

Lotte Lenya
Berlin and American Theatre Songs, Masterworks (1989)
Cabaret, Columbia (1999)
Happy End/The Seven Deadly Sins, CBS (1991)
Lenya, Bear Family (1998)
The Threepenny Opera, Masterworks (1994)

Madonna
Bedtime Stories, Maverick (1994)
Erotica, Sire (1992)
The First Album, Sire (1984)
Give It to Me, Receiver (1991)
I'm Breathless, Sire (1990)
Immaculate Collection (The Best of Madonna), Sire (1990)
In the Beginning, Receiver (1999)
Like a Prayer, Sire (1994)
Like a Virgin, Sire (1984)
Ray of Light, Maverick (1998)
The Royal Box, Sire (1991)
Something to Remember, Maverick (1995)
True Blue, Sire (1994)
You Can Dance, Sire (1995)
Wow, BR Music (1996)

Janis Martin
Elvis Presley and Janis Martin, Picture Disc (1988)
The Female Elvis, Bear Family (1997)
The Rockin' Gal Rocks On, Bear Family (1984)
The Rockin' Gal Sings My Boy Elvis, Bear Family (1984)

MC5
Babes in Arms, Shellshock/Pinnacle
Back in the USA, Atlantic (1993)
Do It, Revenge (1998)
Kick out the Jams, Elektra (1993)
Live in Detroit 68/69, New Rose (1994)
Motor City is Burning, Essential (1999)
Thunder Express, Jungle (1999)

Kylie Minogue
Enjoy Yourself, PWL (1989)
Kylie Minogue, De-Construction (1996)
Kylie Minogue, De-Construction (1999)
Kylie – The Album, PWL (1988)
Let's Get to It, PWL (1991)
Rhythm of Love, PWL (1990)

Joni Mitchell
Blue, DCC (1999)
Chalk Mark in a Rainstorm, Geffen (1993)
Clouds, Reprise (1988)
Court and Spark, Asylum (1983)
Dog Eat Dog, Geffen (1996)
Don Juan's Reckless Daughter, Asylum (1988)
For the Roses, Asylum (1987)
Ghosts, Metro Independent (1997)
Hejira, Asylum (1987)
The Hissing of Summer Lawns, Asylum (1987)
Hits, Reprise (1996)
Joni Mitchell, Reprise (1987)
Ladies of the Canyon, Reprise (1999)
Miles of Aisles, Asylum (1976)
Mingus, Asylum (1988)
Misses, Reprise (1996)
Night Ride Home, Geffen (1997)
Shadows and Light, Asylum (1980)
Songs to a Seagull, Reprise (1968)
Taming the Tiger, Reprise (1998)
Turbulent Indigo, Asylum (1994)

Wild Things Run Fast, Geffen (1992)

Alanis Morissette
Jagged Little Pill, Maverick (1995)
Supposed Former Infatuation Junkie, Maverick (1998)
Unplugged, Maverick (1999)

Alison Moyet
Alf, Columbia (1998)
Essex, Columbia (1994)
Hoodoo, Columbia (1993)
Raindancing, Columbia (1990)

New York Dolls
Lipstick Killers, ROIR (1994)
Paris Burning, Skydog (1996)
Red Patent Leather, New Rose (1994)
Rock 'n' Roll, Mercury (1994)
Seven Day Weekend, Receiver (1993)
Teenage News, Red Star (1997)
Too Much Too Soon, Mercury (1994)

Laura Nyro
Classics, Elite (1993)
Eli and the Thirteenth Confession, Columbia (1997)
Gonna Take a Miracle, Beat Goes On (1991)
Live at the Bottom Line, Cypress (1989)
Mother's Spiritual, Line (1994)
New York Tendaberry
Walk the Dog and Light the Light, Columbia (1994)

Sinead O'Connor
Am I Not Your Girl, Ensign (1992)
I Do Not Want What I Haven't Got, Chrysalis (1990)
The Lion and the Cobra, Ensign (1987)
Universal Mother, Ensign (1994)

Liz Phair
Exile in Guyville, Matador (1993)
Juvenilia, Matador (1995)
Whipsmart, Warner Bros. (1994)
Whitechocolatespaceegg, Parlophone (1999)

The Pretenders
The Pretenders (1st Album), WEA (1983)
The Pretenders II, WEA (1993)
Learning To Crawl, Sire Records (1987)
Get Close, Sire Records (1986)
Packed, Sire Records (1990)
Last Of The Independents, Sire Records (1994)
Don't Get Me Wrong, Carlton (1994)
The Isle Of View, Warner Bros. (1995)
Viva El Amor, Warner Bros. (1999)

Suzi Quatro
Daytona Demon, Disky (1998)
If You Knew Suzi, Laselight (1996)
Rock Hard, Connoisseur Collection (1990)
Rock 'til Ya Drop, Biff (1988)
Unreleased Emotion, Connoisseur Collection (1998)
What Goes Around, North Of Watford (1996)

The Raincoats
Looking In The Shadows, Rough Trade (1996)
The Kitchen Tapes, ROIR (1998)
Moving, Rough Trade (1994)
Ody Shape, Rough Trade (1994)
The Raincoats, Rough Trade (1993)

Helen Reddy
Angie Baby, Hallmark (1997)
Centre Stage, Varese Sarabande (1999)

Martha Reeves and the Vandellas
Black Magic, Motown (1972)
Dancing in the Street, Tamla Motown (1969)
Natural Resources, Tamla Motown (1970)
Ridin' High, Motown (1968)
Sugar 'n' Spice, Tamla Motown (1970)

Republica
Republica, De-Construction (1997)
Speed Ballads, De-Construction (1998)

Michelle Shocked
Arkansas Traveler, London (1992)

Captain Swing, London (1989)
Kind Hearted Woman, Private Music (1996)
Mercury Poised, London (1996)
Short Sharp Shocked, Cooking Vinyl (1988)
Texas Campfire Tapes, Mooncrest (1986)

Jane Siberry
Jane Siberry (1st Album), East Side Digital (1991)
No Borders, Duke Street (1997)
The Speckless Sky, WEA (1987)
The Walking, Reprise Records (1987)
Bound By The Beauty, Reprise (1989)
When I Was A Boy, Reprise (1993)
Maria, Reprise (1995)
Teenager, Sheeba Records (1996)
Child, Blackbird Recording Company (1997)

Siouxsie and the Banshees
Hyena, Wonderland (1995)
Join Hands, Wonderland (1995)
Ju Ju, Wonderland (1995)
Kaleidoscope, Wonderland (1995)
A Kiss in the Dreamhouse, Wonderland (1995)
Nocturne, Wonderland (1995)
The Peel Sessions Vol.1, Strange Fruit (1987)
The Peel Sessions Vol.2, Strange Fruit (1989)
Peep Show, Wonderland (1995)
The Rapture, Wonderland (1997)
The Scream, Wonderland (1995)
Superstition, Wonderland (1995)
Tinderbox, Wonderland (1995)
Through the Looking Glass, Wonderland (1995)
Twice upon a Time, Wonderland (1995)

The Slits
The Cut, Island (1990)
In The Beginning (An Anthology), Jungle (1997)
The Peel Sessions, Strange Fruit (1998)

Patti Smith
Dream of Life, Arista (1997)

Easter, Arista (1997)
Gone Again, Arista (1996)
Horses, Arista (1996)
Never Enough, CBS (1987)
Peace and Noise, Arista (1997)
Radio Ethiopia, Arista (1997)
Wave, Arista (1997)

Spice Girls
Spice, Virgin (1996)
Spiceworld, Virgin (1997)

Dusty Springfield
A Girl Called Dusty, Philips (1989)
A Very Fine Love, Columbia (1998)
Am I the Same Girl, Spectrum (1996)
Blue for You, Spectrum (1993)
Dusty...Definitely, Philips (1990)
Dusty in Memphis (Remastered), Mercury (1995)
From Dusty with Love, Philips (1990)
Everything's Coming up Dusty, Beat Goes On (1989)
In Memphis Plus, Philips (1989)
Reputation, Fame (1995)
Reputation and Rarities, EMI GOLD (1997)
Where Am I Going, Philips (1999)

Sweet Honey in the Rock
Feel Something Drawing on Me, Cooking Vinyl (1995)
Good News, Cooking Vinyl (1989)
In this Land, Earthbeat (1993)
The Other Side, Cooking Vinyl (1995)

Sacred Ground, Earthbeat (1996)
Still on the Journey, Earthbeat (1993)
Sweet Honey in the Rock, Cooking Vinyl (1995)
Twenty-Five, Rykodisc (1998)
We All Everyone of Us, Cooking Vinyl (1995)

Throwing Muses
The Curse, 4AD (1992)
Horse Tornado, 4AD (1988)
Hunkpapa, 4AD (1989)
In a Doghouse, 4AD (1998)
Limbo, 4AD (1998)
The Real Ramona, 4AD (1998)
Red Heaven, 4AD (1998)
Throwing Muses, 4AD (1986)
University, 4AD (1998)

The Tourists
The Tourists, RCA (1981)

Suzanne Vega
Days of the Open Road, A&M (1995)
Nine Objects of Desire, A&M (1997)
Solitude Standing, A&M (1993)
99.9F, A&M (1997)
Suzanne Vega, A&M (1993)
Tom's Album, A&M (1991)

With thanks to Mike Dine (Salford University) for preparing this discography

INDEX